MEMORIALS OF EDWARD BURNE-JONES

MEMORIALS OF EDWARD BURNE-JONES

by Georgiana Burne-Jones

With a new Introduction by John Christian

Volume I 1833–1867

Lund Humphries
London

This edition of *Memorials of Edward Burne-Jones*
published 1993 by Lund Humphries Publishers
Park House
1 Russell Gardens
London NW11 9NN

British Library Cataloguing-in-Publication Data
A catalogue record for this book
is available from the British Library

ISBN 0 85331 631 7

Publishing History
Memorials of Edward Burne-Jones was first published in 1904
by Macmillan and Co. Ltd, London. For this edition a new
Introduction by John Christian has been added to Volume 1.

Printed in Great Britain by
Bookcraft Ltd, Bath

CONTENTS

VOLUME I

		PAGE
INTRODUCTION by John Christian		vii
CHAPTER I.	1833-1844	1
II.	1844-1848	14
III.	1849-1851	35
IV.	1851-1852	54
V.	1853	71
VI.	1854	97
VII.	1855	109
VIII.	1856	127
IX.	1857-1858	152
X.	1858-1859	178
XI.	1860	202
XII.	1861-1862	222
XIII.	1862	241
XIV.	1863-1864	259
XV.	1865-1867	286

VOLUME II

CHAPTER XVI.	1868-1871	1
XVII.	1872-1874	28

		PAGE
CHAPTER XVIII.	1875-1878	58
XIX.	1879-1881	90
XX.	1882-1885	118
XXI.	1885-1886	148
XXII.	1887-1889	174
XXIII.	1890-1891	204
XXIV.	1892-1895	226
XXV.	1893-1895	250
XXVI.	1896	277
XXVII.	1897	301
XXVIII.	1898	327
INDEX		351

INTRODUCTION

THE closely-knit circle of successful late-Victorian artists was, by any standards, an extraordinary phenomenon, without any meaningful precedent and certainly unparalleled since. The princely lifestyle which so many of them enjoyed, in Holland Park, St John's Wood and elsewhere, is eloquent testimony to their self-esteem and prosperity, while the honours showered upon them – knighthoods, baronetcies, Orders of Merit, in Leighton's case even a peerage – leave no doubt that society endorsed their status. The substantial biographies, generally in two volumes, which they tended to inspire is further proof of their contemporary reputation, although closer inspection underlines how fragile that reputation was. No member of the fraternity who died between 1882 (Rossetti) and 1915 (Walter Crane) failed to be the subject of a biographical record, but those who lived on, into a world irrevocably changed by the Great War and the advent of Post-Impressionism, fared far less well. Henry Holiday may have forestalled events by publishing his autobiography in 1914, but William Blake Richmond had to share a 'life' with his father (1926), and other survivors – Poynter, Waterhouse, Marcus Stone, Dicksee – went unsung. Oddest of all was the fate of Luke Fildes, who did not receive biographical treatment until 1968 – so late that it coincided with the long-delayed Victorian revival, which of course placed it in a totally different perspective.

The purpose of these biographies was twofold. On the one hand, they were meant to be 'official' records, whatever that may mean. On the other, they were intimate accounts by writers close to their subjects. Indeed Holiday was not the only artist who wrote his autobiography. W. P. Frith, William Bell Scott, Holman Hunt, Crane and Herkomer did likewise, Scott and Hunt for the very good reason that they had an axe to grind. Most, however, busier or less egocentric, were prepared to leave the job to family or friends. Rossetti's biography was written by his brother, Millais' and Fildes' (when it came) by their sons, Madox Brown's by his grandson. Watts's and Burne-Jones's were done by their widows, Spencer Stanhope's by his niece, Mrs Stirling, who was also responsible for a joint life of her sister and brother-in-law, Evelyn and William De Morgan (this being another post-war production). Moving outside family circles, we find Leighton being tackled by his friend Mrs Barrington, Whistler by his admirers the Pennells, Albert Moore by his pupil A. L. Baldry, and William Morris by J. W. Mackail, the son-in-law of his lifelong friend, Burne-Jones.

Perhaps because they were 'in-house' productions, the work of informed amateurs, these books are of varied literary merit. Many are read from duty, as essential historical sources, rather than inspiring examples of the biographer's craft. J. G. Millais' *Life and Letters* of his father (1899) tends to fall into this category; so do Mrs Barrington's *Life, Letters and Work of Frederic Leighton* (1906), and Mary Watts's 'annals' of her husband's life (1912), which today seems embarrassingly hagiographical. Walter Crane's *An Artist's Reminiscences* (1907), a most worthy compilation that never fails to turn up some nugget, is yet another example. Others are more entertaining. Bell Scott's *Autobiographical Notes* (1892) has the fascination of his prickly personality, and Ford Madox Hueffer's 'record' of his grandfather's career (1896) betrays the skill and intelligence to be expected of an early work by the future Ford Madox Ford. Two further contributions can only be described as achievements of crucial significance: the numerous volumes of family papers so scrupulously edited by William Michael Rossetti, and that other bedrock of Pre-Raphaelite studies, Holman Hunt's *Pre-Raphaelitism and the Pre-Raphaelite Brotherhood* (1905). Its relentless self-justification may be tiresome, but its scope, authority and descriptive power are deeply impressive.

But perhaps only two examples can truly be said to transcend their genre and succeed both as sources of information and works of art: Mackail's *Life of William Morris* (1899) and the *Memorials of Edward Burne-Jones* by the artist's wife Georgiana (1904). They are entirely different in approach, one being the polished performance of a brilliant scholar, the other the inspired creation of a woman who had never written a book before; but each is, in its way, a masterpiece. Mackail himself told Sydney Cockerell, William Morris's secretary, that he thought the *Memorials* 'a work of genius'; and Cockerell, to whom Lady Burne-Jones read chapters when the book was in progress, found it 'intensely interesting and moving'.[1] Both might be suspected of bias, but Charles Eliot Norton thought it 'every way remarkable',[2] and recently so disinterested a critic as Kingsley Amis has described it as 'the best book on that whole circle'.[3]

No doubt the success of the two biographies is partly due to the inherent interest of their subjects. Few would deny that Morris and Burne-Jones are more rewarding studies than Leighton and Alma-Tadema, or even Watts and Millais. Neither, by comparison, was an establishment figure. It was typical that both lived in Georgian houses some miles west of Leighton and his satellites in their purpose-built studio-houses in Holland Park; and Burne-Jones's power base was the Grosvenor and New Galleries, not the Royal Academy. None the less, both had many contacts in the wider artistic community; both died, like Leighton and Millais, in the late 1890s, the point at which the Victorian art-boom may truly be said to have ended; and both could well have come down to us in a duller form than they have if they had not had outstanding biographers. The credit for seeing that they were so well served must go to Burne-Jones himself. It was he who commissioned Mackail to write the life of his dearest friend, and he encouraged Georgiana to write his own biography. As she put it at the beginning of the second volume, 'he realised in late years that some memorial of him would certainly be written, and even spoke to me once of the possibility of my doing it. The reason he gave for wishing this was uttered almost parenthetically – "For you *know*".'

Georgiana Burne-Jones's own story has been told more than once, and need only be touched on here.[4] Born in Birmingham in 1840, she was the third surviving child of George Browne Macdonald, a Methodist minister, and his wife Hannah. There were eleven children, of whom four died young; their upbringing was strict, money was scarce, and every three years George would be posted to a new circuit, involving a complete upheaval. But there was nothing depressed or straight-laced about this family; on the contrary, high-mindedness went hand in hand with high intelligence and high spirits. United by strong bonds of affection, the children were all well read, and the girls particularly were noted for their strength of character. This was to take them far, enabling four of them to establish one of those dynasties of talent which played such a crucial part in Victorian cultural life. Georgiana, or Georgie as she was always known, married Burne-Jones in 1860. In 1865 her elder sister Alice married the artist and art administrator John Lockwood Kipling, leaving immediately for India where their first child, Rudyard, was born later that year. In 1866 two of the younger sisters were married. Agnes became the wife of Edward Poynter, one of the leading academic artists of the day and in due course head of the Slade, Director of the National Gallery and President of the Royal Academy; while Louisa, one of the 'babies' of the family and a great pet of Burne-Jones, married the industrialist Alfred Baldwin. Their only child, Stanley, the future Prime Minister, was born in 1867.

All accounts of Georgie stress her physical smallness. George Eliot addressed her as 'Mignon', and Charles Eliot Norton, writing in 1869, thought her 'as slight and small a lady as Stothard ever drew ... There is always a quaint, pretty idyllic look about her as she enters the room, for her dress corresponds with her face and figure in its piquant and not extravagant originality.' Norton was also struck by her 'latent depth of character ... As you come to know her better ... you find more and more that wins not only affection but respect.'[5]

In fact in none of the Macdonalds was the family sense of idealism more pronounced. 'In that little frame', wrote her sister Edith, 'dwelt a noble spirit, ever reverencing the highest and seeking the beautiful. She seemed immune by nature from any small aims or self-conceit.'[6]

Georgie shared other Macdonald characteristics. Like all the sisters she was musical, with a fine soprano voice. Norton's account continues: 'She will sing for an hour delightfully from Haydn, from Cherubini, from Bach, or will turn from these composers to the lighter style of the old Shakespearian and Ben Jonson songs, or the still older English airs and French chansons'.[7] In early life she also showed a talent for drawing. This was to be a casualty of her connection with artists of genius, but the literary gift which she inherited from her mother was, as the *Memorials* show, to prove more durable. She shared with the rest of the family a keen sense of humour, and she could be witty and scathing in criticism. She was never robust in health, again like most of her siblings, although she lived to the age of seventy-nine, dying in 1920.

She herself tells in the *Memorials* how she met Burne-Jones when she was still a twelve-year-old 'child in a pinafore', fell at once for this clever, odd-looking boy with his strange mannerisms, became engaged to him in 1856 at the very outset of his career, and subsequently enjoyed thirty-eight years of marriage. That marriage in retrospect has a fairy-tale quality about it. The unknown youth she had committed herself to was to become one of the most famous artists of the day, bringing her position, comparative wealth, a title. Far more important (as a Ruskinian socialist, she found the baronetcy deeply embarrassing), it gave her the rich mental food for which she had craved from childhood. But there were strains as well. The greatest was undoubtedly caused by Burne-Jones's passionate affair with the Greek beauty Mary Zambaco in the late 1860s.[8] It blew over, and Georgie, who was still only in her late twenties, coped superbly, with the wise advice of George Eliot. But the marriage undoubtedly suffered, nor was Mary the only young woman in Burne-Jones's life, even if his later relationships do seem to have been platonic.

But Georgie herself was not the easiest of people to live with. Graham Robertson, describing his first visit to The Grange as a boy, wrote of her as follows:

> Out through the window I was led, across a lawn to where under a big mulberry-tree sat a tiny lady: as she turned to receive me I met her eyes and became aware of a great personality. The quiet in those wonderful eyes of clearest grey was, I knew, the centre of the strange stillness that lay upon the place, yet beneath and beyond could be sensed an Energy, dominant, flame-like. Eyes like those of Georgiana Burne-Jones I have never seen before or since, and, through all our long friendship, their direct gaze would always cost me little subconscious heart-searchings, not from fear of criticism or censure, but lest those eyes in their grave wisdom, their crystal purity, should rest upon anything unworthy.[9]

For someone of Burne-Jones's temperament – easy-going (for all his neurosis), enjoying the occasional flirtation, appreciative of the rabelaisian aspects of life – day-to-day contact with such unswerving moral rectitude must have caused tension. As Robertson wrote in a later, more unguarded moment, 'E.B.-J.'s surroundings were so extremely correct and "proper" that I think he *had* to break out occasionally'.[10]

In later years, then, the couple to some extent went separate ways. Georgie found consolation in a close friendship with William Morris, who, some have claimed, is the true hero of the *Memorials*; she also put much of her energy into charitable work and committees, causing Burne-Jones to complain of neglect. He for his part turned for emotional support to his beloved daughter and her family, as well as to the aforementioned Egerias. But the marriage was never in danger of collapse. It was not Georgie's way to make scenes (her nephew Rudyard Kipling remembered her being 'sorry. Never, *never* angry'),[11] and in any case, as she told Rosalind Howard at the time of the Zambaco affair, 'there is love enough between Edward and me to last out a long life if it is given us'.[12] That 'love' still shines from the pages of the *Memorials*. As for Burne-Jones, his deep affection for Georgie is evident in his frequent expressions of concern for her health, and in the well-known portrait that he painted of her in the early 1880s.[13] He also knew that she alone provided the peace and stability that were essential for his work. His career has a charmed quality that it is hard not to envy. Morris, the ideal friend, appeared at exactly the right moment; so did Rossetti, the ideal hero. Equally in Georgie he found, almost effortlessly, the near-perfect wife. She 'saved him', wrote Edith, 'from all business cares and worries . . . , thus leaving him free to devote undisturbed time and thought to his life's work'.[14] Lady Frances Balfour described her as 'the guardian of B.-J.'s time, and a very inexorable one', recalling an occasion when she called to see him, only to be told that he was 'secluded from interruptions'. Not surprisingly, she found Georgie 'rather daunting'.[15]

The first of the sisters to marry, Georgie was also the first to be widowed. On Burne-Jones's sudden death in 1898, by now in her late fifties, she gave up The Grange and retired to their holiday retreat at Rottingdean. There during the next six years she raised her monument to his memory, a labour of love which, we are told, she was both relieved and loth to finish.

In fact the book is almost as much of a monument to herself, so vividly does it reflect her personality. Perhaps the first thing that strikes any reader is that it could only be written by a woman of rare sensitivity. She is particularly good on children, and her sympathy is easily aroused, for instance by the tragic figure of Lizzie Siddal. But whatever her theme she paints her canvas with a delicacy and perception that seem peculiarly feminine. 'Only a few years ago (Edward) took up a wall-flower from the centre of the dinner-table one evening, and smelling it, said, "I'm four years old again in Mr Caswell's garden".' How clearly and economically that evokes two images, nearly sixty years apart. The pages glitter with gems of this kind; Ruskin dancing at Winnington ('He looked very thin, scarcely more than a black line, as he moved about amongst the white girls in his evening dress') is another memorable example, but perhaps no better than Mrs Madox Brown recalling her loquacious husband to his 'duties' with the carving-knife, the Carlyles making tea, the Marshall house-hold, the glimpses of Ruskin's parents, or the idyllic picture of weekends at Red House. Who can read the *Earthly Paradise* and not sympathise with Georgie, who confessed to 'stabbing [herself] with pins' to keep awake when Morris read the poems aloud; or look at a Burne-Jones stained-glass cartoon without recalling that he drew them 'downstairs' after dinner, making a 'soft scraping sound' with the charcoal as he traced the long lines of the drapery and uttering a 'momentary exclamation of impatience when the stick snapped off short, as it so often did, and fell to the ground'? Georgie clearly revelled in shaping these brilliant vignettes from memory. 'I do not know a more intimate and frank biography', wrote Norton. 'It is as if his wife had written it for their children and close friends.'[16]

But 'intimacy' does not preclude a strong element of restraint. 'I grieved in the darkness because I was leaving the place where he lived', she writes of the train journey from Birmingham to London when her father was posted there in 1853; it is her way of telling us, subtly but quite unequivocally, that at the age of thirteen she was already in love. Her comment on Burne-Jones's Oxford circle – 'I am confident that the mystery which shrouds men and women from each other in youth was sacred to each one of them' – is another marvel of reticence which leaves no shadow of doubt as to her meaning. The account of Burne-Jones's death in the last paragraphs of the book displays an emotional stringency which is no less moving for being carefully calculated.

But if Georgie is fastidious, she also reveals a mind of extraordinary toughness. Wisdom and shrewdness are hallmarks of her style, whether she is describing Red Lion Mary ('she could be trusted like a good woman to show kindness to another woman whose goodness was in abeyance'), giving an example of 'the true common sense of genius', or explaining her husband's susceptibility to the charms of Little Holland House. Nor is her sense of humour ever far from the surface. Forty years after the event she can still recall with amusement how, as Burne-Jones's prospective bride, she was 'inspected' by bossy Mrs Prinsep. Even such a hero as Ruskin does not escape her critical eye. Brantwood, for all his taste, is even 'duller' than Denmark Hill; and she takes an almost malicious delight in recording his verdict on an oil painting when asked the medium by Cardinal Manning: 'Pure watercolour, my lord'. But her sharpest barbs are reserved for those she dislikes: to them, in true Macdonald fashion, she can be merciless. Here is her caustic description of a 'stimulating hour' with the headmistress of Winnington School:

> Miss Bell was an extremely clever woman of a powerful and masterful turn of mind, evidently understanding that Ruskin was the greatest man she had ever seen, and that she must make the utmost use of the intimacy he accorded her and the interest he took in her school. At dinner the first evening she talked as much as if it were her last opportunity of speech, and as one listened to her it seemed that no subject could be too high and no difficulty too great for her to deal with.

Still more devastating is her treatment of Charles Augustus Howell, whose wilful meddling in the Zambaco affair had caused her and Burne-Jones intense, unforgivable pain. He makes only one brief appearance in the book but it could hardly be more telling. 'And on this day of the union and reunion of friends there was one who had come amongst us in friend's clothing, but inwardly he was a stranger to all that our life meant. This was Mr Howell.'

As her picture of Miss Bell shows, Georgie was keenly aware that true strength of character does not involve self-assertion, and she herself was careful to avoid this trap. On the title page her name is modestly reduced to her initials. Describing a visit to S. Ambrogio, Milan, with her husband and Ruskin, she writes: 'two of the little company knew and felt and understood all they saw, but the third looked chiefly at them'. More important, whenever possible she lets her characters speak for themselves, quoting extensively from letters, conversations and reminiscences. This is particularly so in the second volume, which is often little more than a skilfully constructed patchwork of quotations. She was lucky in that the circle she was describing were, almost without exception, highly articulate, Burne-Jones himself being the most articulate of all. He was not one of those artists whose creative energies are entirely absorbed in their work. Before he decided to become a painter he had been a brilliant pupil at King Edward's School,

Birmingham, and then gone on to Oxford intending to enter the Church. This intellectual equipment remained with him for life. He was a formidable scholar and antiquarian, took a lively interest in current events, and had enormous charm and a genius for self-expression. His epistolary skill developed early and, despite his insistence to the contrary, was clearly indulged with pleasure. The youthful mock-medieval missives written in the persona of 'Edouard, Cardinal de Byrmyng-hame', the moving letters to his son at Marlborough, and those written to William Kenrick in the 1880s about setting up and equipping art institutions in Birmingham, are random examples which give some idea of his range. He was equally remarkable as a conversationist. Many recorded his speech and none more assiduously than his assistant T. M. Rooke, who took detailed notes of talk in the studio during the last three years of his master's life.[17]

C. E. Norton, whose evidence is so often relevant in this context, wrote of Burne-Jones in 1904: 'I have never known anyone in whom there was a finer mingling of the poetic imagination and the artistic temperament with the traits of a large, generous, deep nature. He was in this akin to Shakespeare. He had a noble and perennial gift of humour, and the tenderness of heart of a woman.'[18] Occasionally this 'gift of humour' and 'tenderness' find expression in a whimsicality which grates; Rossetti put it rather cruelly in 1881 when he wrote that his follower's 'style of conversation [was] getting beyond the pussy-cat and attaining the dicky-bird'.[19] But this was partly a matter of 'period' and does not seriously obscure the depth of his mind, or mar the effect of his endlessly inventive skill as a spinner of words.

This skill, the acute, wide-ranging intelligence behind it, and Georgie's editorial discretion, result in a portrait which has few real parallels in the history of British art. Indeed so rich is the presentation of Burne-Jones's personality that it sometimes has the paradoxical effect of making us forget that we are dealing with an artist at all. Whistler, if he had read the book (he died the year before it was published), might have been tempted to make the same jibe that he made about the multi-talented Leighton: 'Paints a little too, I believe'. The emphasis on the extra-artistic dimension is exaggerated by Georgie's refusal, once again out of modesty, to discuss what she calls 'the technicalities of art'. This is unfortunate since, even without specialist knowledge, she could have told us much of value. What fruitless speculation about 'studio' intervention in Burne-Jones's work she might have saved us if she had said more about his use of assistants and the way his studio was organised. How much ill-informed guesswork about models she could have forestalled if she had identified these more frequently; and how interesting it would have been if, like Hueffer in his life of Madox Brown, she had said more about payment and prices, a subject with which, as we have seen, she was fully conversant. There are personalities, too, that one wishes she had mentioned: Albert Moore, for example, who seems so relevant to Burne-Jones's development in that melting-pot period, the 1860s; or Walter Pater, no less significant in relation to his Italianate phase in the 1870s. He must have met them both, but neither makes the briefest appearance. Nor, for that matter, does Oscar Wilde,[20] although his friendship with Burne-Jones is well documented. This may be for obvious reasons, but Georgie was no prude; she mentions Simeon Solomon, going out of her way to stress that he was 'a friend of mine as well as Edward's'.

Whatever the reason for Wilde's absence, there can be little doubt that, for all her regard for the truth, Georgie did edit the record where she deemed it necessary. Burne-Jones's former assistant Charles Fairfax Murray described the *Memorials* as 'nothing but a collection of facts that may be useful to a future biographer, but [giving] an incomplete impression of him from much being omitted, purposely of course'.[21] We also know that she persuaded Rooke to destroy many of his notes of studio conversation, which must have been one of the few discreditable acts of her life.[22] Her reluctance to discuss money may have been due to a feeling that the subject was vulgar, just as she may have feared that revelations about assistants would reflect unfavourably on Burne-Jones's reputation. But her chief piece of editing is her failure to make any mention of

Mary Zambaco, who was, after all, an important model for Burne-Jones quite apart from his mistress. As has often been observed, the only reference to her is in fact an omission. The year 1869, when the affair reached its dramatic climax, is simply dropped from the narrative, and is missing from the dates given at the top of every left-hand page.[23]

There was of course nothing unusual about such editing; nearly every Victorian biographer was at pains to shield his subject from the prying eyes of posterity. The great exception was Froude's life of Carlyle (1882-4), and Norton was certainly thinking of this when, assessing the *Memorials*, he wrote: 'Intimate as the book is, there are no revelations in it of the sort which have made so many biographies an offence not less against good breeding and good morals than against good letters'.[24] Since Burne-Jones was a lifelong admirer of Carlyle, there can be little doubt that he too read Froude's life and discussed it with Georgie. Indeed it may be that the *Letters and Memorials of Jane Welsh Carlyle*, Carlyle's tribute to his dead wife which Froude edited and published concurrently with the life, suggested to Georgie the title of her own biography.

Whatever the conventions of Victorian biography, Georgie could hardly be expected to write about her husband's affair with another woman. Nor should she be blamed for failing to anticipate the preoccupations of modern art-historians. Her perspective was entirely different and must be accepted on its own terms. In fact the book is invaluable as a historical source. Georgie's habit of quoting extensively from Burne-Jones's letters and conversation results in many vital statements of principle. 'I love to work in that fettered way', a confession he makes in connection with his designs for mosaic in the early 1880s, says much not only about his decorative art in general but his whole aesthetic approach. Equally significant is his explanation of why his faces have no 'expression' in the conventional sense ('they are not portraits of people in paroxysms ... [but] types, symbols, suggestions'); or the reason he gives for designing his own studio properties: 'so that what eventually gets onto the canvas is a reflection of a reflection of something purely imaginary'. As for his assertion that 'I don't want to pretend that this isn't a picture', and his rebuttal of the claim that it was a drawback if an artist appeared to be painting 'out of his head' ('The place where I think pictures ought to come from'), these encapsulate the rejection of naturalism which now makes him seem so much more 'modern' than the British impressionists, who at the time represented the avant-garde reaction to Pre-Raphaelitism. Experience also shows that Georgie's own narrative is often more evidential than it might appear. To take one example among many: in her account of the year 1858 she describes how she and Burne-Jones visited Ruskin in the basement of the National Gallery where he was sorting the drawings in the Turner bequest. 'He received us very kindly', she writes, 'setting us to amuse ourselves as we liked with the drawings that lay about while he worked and then talked, or pointed out any special thing. He showed us, too, some old pictures lately brought back from Italy by Sir Charles Eastlake, but not yet hung.' It is only when we have read round the subject, and made an attempt to identify those 'old pictures', that we realise that this rather chatty little passage provides a fascinating insight into Ruskin's assiduous attempt to direct Burne-Jones's early development.[25]

But none of this data would 'tell' as it does without a brilliant context. Georgie's greatest achievement was to evoke an atmosphere, to reveal, in the most vivid and convincing terms, what it was like to live through the heady events she describes. The rise of the second wave of the Pre-Raphaelite movement was one of those epiphanies which occur from time to time in the English romantic tradition, one which had wider repercussions than most; and the book is the record of a vision, seen by Burne-Jones in youth, fading, as visions must, but requiring him, like all true romantics who have enjoyed such experiences, to devote his life to its recovery. If it gives, as Murray claimed, an 'incomplete impression', this is perhaps partly the reason; things extraneous to the main purpose are omitted, not so much from a wilful desire to distort the picture as from a sense that they are irrelevant. Although the second volume has a distinct character and value of its own, the first is inevitably more compelling. A series of preliminary climaxes – the dream of the Middle Ages in Port Meadow, the commitment on the quayside at Le Havre, the discovery of the *Morte d'Arthur* – build up to the revelation of Rossetti and the *annus mirabilis* of 1856. From then on the story is a long diminuendo. Four times the vision seems to be renewed by Italy, albeit under different forms. In the 1890s, like many artists at the end of their lives, Burne-Jones returns to first principles; this involves a revived feeling for the Grail legend, so closely associated with his aspirations from the time when, at Oxford, he and Morris had planned their Order of Sir Galahad. It is a story, too, of great outward success, resulting from an unremitting struggle to give the vision tangible form. But the piercing intensity of the original experience could never, in the nature of things, be regained.

To talk of visions and epiphanies is not a mere figure of speech. Burne-Jones and Morris were originally destined for the priesthood, and Ruskin's insistence on the sacerdotal nature of art did much to ease their transition from one vocation to another. Georgie tells her story with such conviction and authority because she too, present at the time and watching events through the eyes of love, believed implicitely in the new dispensation. 'I felt in the presence of a new religion', she writes, and describes being taken to 'the shrine of Rossetti at Blackfriars'. Her life, no less than Burne-Jones's, was to be permanently transformed. 'I sat at the feet of those "great ones"', she told Sydney Cockerell in 1915, 'and do so still'.[26] For her the vision was expressed partly in her 'inexorable guardianship' of Burne-Jones, partly in a rather naïve form of socialism inspired by Ruskin and Morris.[27] It emerges again in her few surviving drawings, which clearly reflect values current in her circle.[28] But its most enduring monument is the *Memorials*, which not only recount the experience but often do so in a form – a series of images of startling intensity and in bright, prismatic colours – that can only be described as 'Pre-Raphaelite'.

The exhibition of his collected works held at the New

Gallery in 1892-3 left Burne-Jones 'deeply disheartened', but he consoled himself with the hope that it might help 'some such fantastical creature as I was at twenty'. About the same time he wrote that he liked young artists to seek his advice since 'it is for them I paint. If ever they would look at me as I have looked at Mantegna, what a well-rewarded ghost mine would be.' Georgie quotes both remarks and clearly hoped that her book too would prove inspirational. In 1916 it was read by Vanessa Bell, who could only complain of Burne-Jones's 'incredibly sentimental ... view of himself and his holy mission'.[29] But that was at the height of the inevitable reaction to Pre-Raphaelitism and all its works; today a more sympathetic attitude prevails, and the reader may well be a 'fantastical creature' at the outset of his or her career who will respond not only to the story itself but to the dimension of personal example that is built into it so firmly. It is a book that 'keeps' well too, bears re-reading and seldom fails to come up with some profound idea. If we begin by being thrilled by its picture of youthful idealism, we may end by finding comfort in the knowledge that Burne-Jones in later life suffered deep depression and bitter disillusion. But 'comfort' is never a feeling which the book allows us to indulge too long; staunch and trustworthy friend as it is, it can also be challenging and disturbing. Georgie's formidable personality still breathes from its pages, and we are sometimes uneasily aware that those 'eyes of clearest grey' are turned on us, silently enquiring, 'in their grave wisdom', if we ourselves have kept faith with the dreams of youth.

NOTES

1. Both comments occur in Cockerell's unpublished diaries, now in the British Library; see the entry for 16 November 1902 and the summary for 1903.
2. Sara Norton and M. A. DeWolfe Howe (eds), *Letters of Charles Eliot Norton*, 1913, II, p.351.
3. Kingsley Amis, *Memoirs*, 1992 (Penguin) edition, p.105.

4. There are two modern sources: A. W. Baldwin, *The Macdonald Sisters*, 1960, and Ina Taylor, *Victorian Sisters*, 1987. Information can also be gleaned from two volumes of reminiscences by members of the Macdonald family: Frederic W. Macdonald, *As a Tale that is Told*, 1919, and Edith Macdonald, *Annals of the Macdonald Family*, 1928.
5. Norton and DeWolfe Howe, op.cit. 1, p.344.
6. Edith Macdonald, op.cit. p.36.
7. Norton and DeWolfe Howe, op.cit. 1, p.348.
8. For an account of this, see Penelope Fitzgerald, *Edward Burne-Jones. A Biography*, 1975, chs 9-10.
9. W. Graham Robertson, *Time Was*, 1931, pp.74-5. Georgie's grand-daughter Angela Thirkell had very similar memories; see her book *Three Houses*, 1953 edition, p.50.
10. Kerrison Preston (ed.), *Letters from Graham Robertson*, 1953, p.491.
11. Rudyard Kipling, *Something of Myself*, 1992 (Penguin) edition, p.40.
12. Quoted in Fitzgerald, op.cit. p.121. Some revealing comments on marriage, clearly based on personal experience, occur in a letter that Georgie wrote to Sydney Cockerell at the time of his engagement in 1907; see Viola Meynell (ed.), *Friends of a Lifetime. Letters to Sydney Carlyle Cockerell*, 1940, p.122.
13. Private collection, on loan to Leighton House, Kensington. The portrait is reproduced in Fitzgerald, op.cit. between pp.144 and 145, and in the catalogue of the Arts Council's Burne-Jones Exhibition, 1975-6, p.77.

    Although this is Burne-Jones's most important portrait of Georgie, she appears in the family group reproduced here (*Family Group*, plates to Volume II) and in several of his more imaginative works. There is also a portrait drawing by Rossetti, *c.*1860 (private collection; Virginia Surtees, *Dante Gabriel Rossetti. A Catalogue Raisonné*, 1971, no.276 and pl.402) and a watercolour by Poynter, 1870 (private collection; repr. Baldwin, op.cit. frontispiece, and Fitzgerald, op.cit. between pp.48 and 49). As for photographs, Georgie herself reproduces a childhood likeness (*Memorials*, plates to Volume I), Fitzgerald a group of the Burne-Jones and Morris families, 1874, and Meynell a *carte de visite* showing her in old age (Meynell, op.cit. facing p.122).

14. Edith Macdonald, op.cit. p.56.
15. Lady Frances Balfour, *Ne Obliviscaris*, 1930, I, pp.229, 237.
16. Norton and DeWolfe Howe, op.cit. II, p.351.
17. A selection of Rooke's notes was published in Mary Lago (ed.), *Burne-Jones Talking*, 1981.
18. Norton and DeWolfe Howe, op.cit. II, p.351.
19. John Bryson (ed.), *Dante Gabriel Rossetti and Jane Morris. Their Correspondence*, 1976, p.173.
20. Unless he is referred to in the sentence beginning 'Of one whose life had wandered ...' in the penultimate paragraph of Chapter XXVI.
21. Meynell, op.cit. p.91.
22. The evidence occurs in Sydney Cockerell's diary entries for December 1904 and January 1905.
23. Penelope Fitzgerald (op.cit. p.122) also suggests that the slightly misquoted line from a sonnet by Keats ('Heart, thou and I are here, sad and alone') which heads Chapter XVI (1868-1871) is an oblique reference to the traumatic events of 1869.
24. Norton and DeWolfe Howe, op.cit. II, p.351.
25. See John Christian, '"A serious talk"; Ruskin's place in Burne-Jones's artistic development', in Leslie Parris (ed.), *Pre-Raphaelite Papers*, 1984, p.193.
26. Meynell, op.cit. p.123.
27. For an amusing description of this in action, see Angela Thirkell, op.cit. pp. 78-80.
28. A study in watercolour of a dead bird, dated 1857 (Tate Gallery, no.4941), is obviously inspired by Ruskin. Two pen-and-ink sketches of women in Renaissance costume preening themselves in front of mirrors while skeletons look on, both dating from *c.*1861, betray the prevailing

interest in Dürer, Rethel and other German masters (see John Christian, 'Early German sources for Pre-Raphaelite designs', *Art Quarterly*, Detroit, XXXVI, 1/2, 1973, p.68 and fig.24).

29. Frances Spalding, *Vanessa Bell*, 1983, p.152.

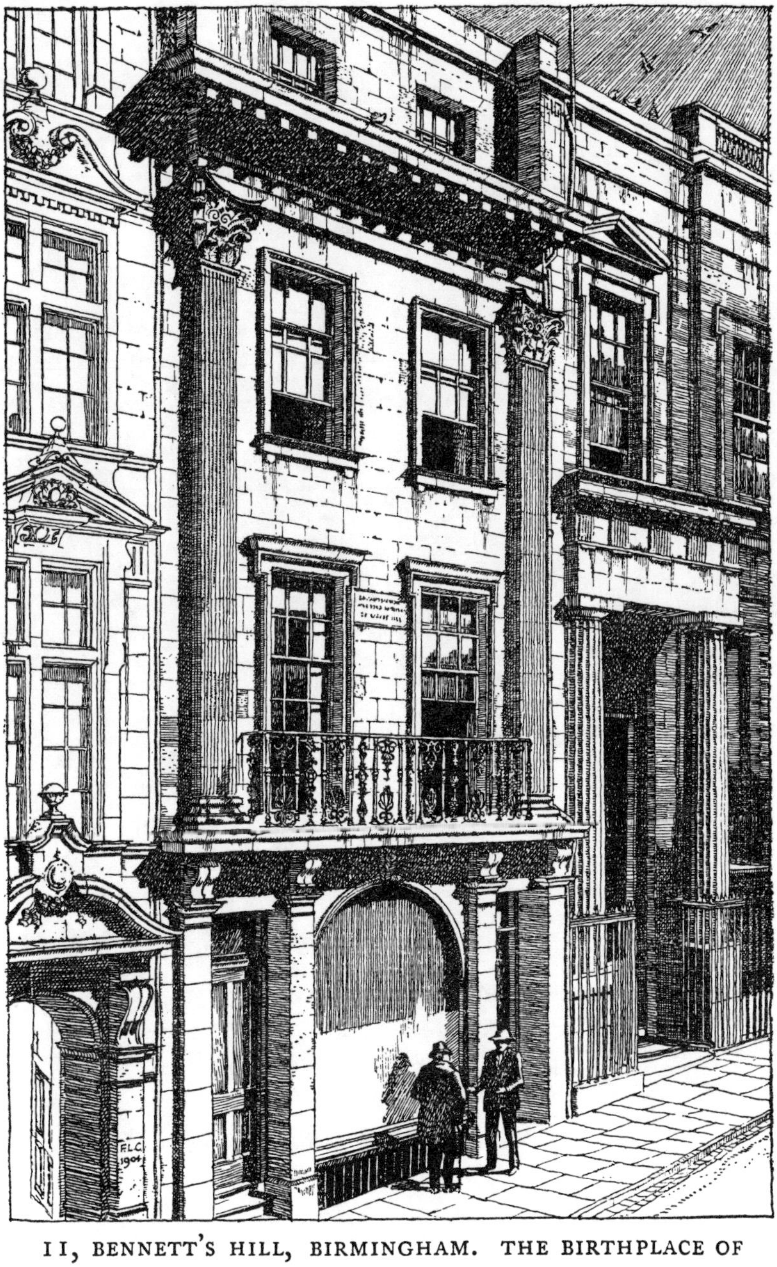

II, BENNETT'S HILL, BIRMINGHAM. THE BIRTHPLACE OF EDWARD BURNE-JONES

MEMORIALS OF

EDWARD BURNE-JONES

CHAPTER I

1833—1844

My mother groaned, my father wept,
Into the dangerous world I leapt.

THE mother who bore her little son on the 28th of August, 1833, did not live long enough to know anything about him, for within a week she died. He was the second child of his parents; but the first, a girl, had not survived her infancy, so that his birth was expected in a special way to bring with it comfort and fresh hope. Before it happened, they removed into a new house, built for themselves, and life was to begin again.

The marriage of Edward Richard Jones and Elizabeth Coley was one of great affection, and when, in his thirty-second year, the young husband found himself suddenly a widower, with a baby of six days old left to him in exchange for the wife of his heart, he could feel no joy in the innocent cause of such sorrow. Of this the child himself was never conscious, but the father spoke of it long afterwards with regret and self-reproach, saying that until his boy was four years old he could scarcely bear to take him into his arms. Not even a portrait of the mother exists: the only one known to have been made was an ivory miniature, which, in an unlucky moment, was given into the hands of her child when he was so young that he himself destroyed it. Thus there remained only the name of mother to a man who, more than most, would seem to have needed one.

Nobody was able at first to come and take permanent care of the infant, who, after passing through the hands of one incompetent nurse after another, fell before long into such poor case that a friend of the dead mother bestirred herself actively to find some one more fitting for the charge of both house and baby. This person was a Miss Sampson, who had never known the mother, and to whom the melancholy, unworldly young father who could not rejoice in his own son was incomprehensible; but the child she fostered tenderly.

The street in which they lived, Bennett's Hill, Birmingham, was a new one in the heart of the town—a short, wide street connecting two busier thoroughfares, not much used by vehicles, because of its steepness, but with a good deal of bustle afoot when it was completed. The houses in it were then chiefly banks and offices, as indeed they are to this day. No. 11 was an exception, however, for it was built with a "show-room" in front, a quiet room, carpeted with a red floor-cloth and filled with mirrors, picture-frames, and sometimes a few paintings. A side-entrance admitted to the house, and at the back was a yard, with a workshop in it where Mr. Jones himself worked. What caused him to be a carver and gilder we never knew, for he was not brought up as one, but it was understood that Mr. Benjamin Coley, his wife's father, who did not much like the marriage because he thought his daughter "might have done better," made a condition of his consent to it, that her husband should have some settled business: and possibly this one was to be had.

Before meeting Miss Coley Mr. Jones had always lived in London with his widowed mother; but she had lately died, and he was alone in the world when he first saw his wife. This was at Stourbridge, where they both happened to be staying at the same time; and, as nothing tied the young man now to one place more than another, he obeyed the impulse to follow her when she returned to her native town of Birmingham. His marriage to her in 1830 decided where he was to spend the rest of his life.

They had about three years together of what he called perfect happiness, before her death; and then everything changed. His simple heart, however, followed the straight path, and turned its baffled feeling into laborious work for his child's sake, little as he cared himself for the world out of which his "Betsy" had been taken.

Whatever his business may have been at first, it certainly was never very flourishing, and as the child grew older, the father worked harder. He has told me that for years he often rose at four in the morning and did not get to rest until midnight. When he did go, however, he found his young son hours deep in sleep on a little bed in a corner of the room.

So far as is known there was no foreshadowing of the gifts of this child in the family of either parent. On the mother's side we have not any record beyond the grandparents, and on the father's, of only one generation more, whilst the Christian name of the great-grandfather is forgotten. In Edward's own handwriting is this brief genealogy:

Don't know his name, but he was
a schoolmaster at Hanbury.

EDWARD BIVEN JONES, m. EDITH ALVIN.

KETURAH. EDWARD RICHARD JONES, m. ELIZABETH COLEY.

EDITH. EDWARD BURNE-JONES.

Biven was the maiden name of the great-grandmother at Hanbury, but all we know of her family is that a brother of hers, named Edward Biven, who was a wine merchant in Lambeth, adopted her son—his nephew and namesake—and brought him up to London. This Edward Biven Jones married a Mary Edith Alvin (called "Edith" only in Edward's note) and died early, a few months after the birth of his second child, who was Edward Richard, the father of Edward Burne-Jones. The other child was a girl, Keturah, whom her great-uncle, Edward Biven, adopted in succession to her father, and who married a Mr. Thomas Burne. She and her husband were god-parents by proxy to Edward when he was baptized at St. Philip's Church, Birmingham, on the 1st of January, 1834. The names then given to the child, Edward Coley Burne, explain themselves as being those of his father, mother, and aunt.

Next door to No. 11, Bennett's Hill, at the time of Edward's birth, was already living a family to whose friendship he owed much of the pleasure of his first years. The household was a Jewish one, and almost patriarchal in character; for the two partners of a firm of merchants established in Birmingham, Messrs. Neustadt and Barnett, had married two sisters, and both families, including children, a widowed mother, and a maiden aunt, lived together under the same roof. These children were coming into the world about the same time that Edward was born, and one of his earliest memories was that of the happy life on the other side of the wall, and the kind welcome always given to him there. A member of the family now living says that he took his place among them "as a cousin," and in that house the word "cousin" meant much. They shared all their pleasures and amusements with him, nor was he excluded even from their holy days and festivals. At the Feast of Purim he dressed up with the other children, and was so eager for the merry-making that when the day came round he was always the first guest to arrive.

Miss Sampson was passionately devoted to Edward, and it is pathetic to think how slight a clue she ever had to his nature. He loved her in the way that children often love parents from whom they greatly differ, seeming never to criticize her and never to confide in her. She was uneducated, with strong feelings and instincts, and she must have suffered much in seeing him, as he grew up, for ever slipping away from her, gently though he treated her, and tightly as she clutched him to her heart. The little body, however, which his soul inhabited lay peacefully and happily at first within her arms.

It always seemed as if nature had intended him for a strong man, for his chest was broad and his limbs straight: but perhaps those early motherless months left their mark upon him, preventing fulfilment of the promise. Miss Sampson was never weary of telling how frail she found her nurseling when first he was given into her charge: often repeating, with the fond insistence of mother and nurse in one, how when the great day arrived for him to be put into "short sleeves," they had to cut off the sleeves of his little dresses an inch at a time lest a sudden chill might undo all her care.

From the first Mr. Jones realized that so delicate a child must have as much country life as possible, and in the summer time he used regularly to send his little boy with Miss Sampson to lodge a few miles away, for the sake of purer air. These yearly visits to villages and farms were a happy thing for Edward and often mentioned in later days. He remembered going when very young to a place, then on the outskirts of Birmingham and now swallowed up in it, the name of which was "Nineveh," and heaven only knows the background of imagination that this one word made for the child, who thought that of course it was "Nineveh in the Bible." Miss Sampson could throw no light on the fact of its being within three or four miles of their own front door. She had strange friends, he said, to whom she used to take him—for her fidelity would not allow her to leave the child when she went out: and long before she dreamed of it, his watchful soul was awake and listening. One of the errands on which he remembered they went together was to an old gentleman who kept a cloth-shop: "Miss Sampson used to go there and buy cloth to be made up into clothes for my father and me, in the funny old-fashioned careful way we used to live. He wore gaiters and a little old, low-crowned hat, and spectacles, of course, and after a time he gave up his shop—I forget why—and grew older and older and littler, but still had some cloth left to sell where he lived, and Miss Sampson and I used to go there and buy it."

With all these friends she talked ceaselessly. He never forgot how one of them blamed him for profanity when he was building a small city of stones that he called "Jerusalem." "You mustn't say 'Jerusalem,' Edward," sank deeply into his mind. As he grew older, Miss Sampson used to be puzzled sometimes by his silence, and would ask suddenly, "What are you thinking of, Edward?" To this demand he told us that he early invented an answer in one word: "Camels."

Two friends of his father, a Mr. and Mrs. Caswell, contributed much to the happiness of his childhood, for they loved him and thought him gifted. They were childless, and used to invite him to their house for days at a time. Mrs. Caswell, a silvery little old lady when I first saw her, told me how when he was staying with them, they would delight to watch him in his bath, as real parents might have done, and of a game equally enjoyed by all three, when he would escape from the tub and from her hands, and spin round and round the room with laughter, and sing "Jim Crow" as he danced, while she and her husband joined in the fun and admired all he did. It was

> Motherless baby and babyless mother,
> Bring them together to love one another.

Later on, Mr. Caswell was the first person who seriously noticed Edward's drawing and tried to direct it, by giving him engravings to copy. One of these copies, done when he was seven years old, still exists; the subject is a group of deer, and Mr. Caswell's remarks are written literally *upon* it. The child never forgot this, and as long as he lived spoke of the irritation he had felt on seeing words written across the sky. Mr. Caswell himself, after he had retired from business, took great delight in buying old pictures of a moderate size at sales, and touching them up according to his fancy, and Edward was very happy watching him squeeze the paint he used out of little bladders.

Then there was the bliss of the garden with Mrs. Caswell (they lived a short distance out of Birmingham); going with her to smell the flowers and pick currants and gooseberries, and the delicious pies that came of it. Only a few years ago he took up a wall-flower from the centre of the dinner-table one evening, and smelling it, said, "I'm four years old again in Mr. Caswell's garden. How kind they were to me, Mr. and Mrs. Caswell, and I never thought about it." Another of his memories was of being on a visit to them when a friend came in bringing the news of the massacre in the Khyber Pass. He says, "I was a very little chap, and was terrified at the idea of all the men shut in by the rocks, and being shot down and killed from above without being able to do anything."

When he was between four and five years old, one of his mother's younger sisters—Amelia—became the third wife of a Mr. Choyce, a farmer then living in the depths of the country at Wootton in Warwickshire, where her kind heart made her soon invite her pale little town nephew to come and see them. This was the first of many visits. Here he found some cousins-in-law, the children of Mr. Choyce's former marriages, but was so soon adopted by them as a real relation that they will henceforth be spoken of as such without qualification. The change of going from a street in town and a house where he was the only child, into the midst of family life, the freedom of the fields and the delightful bustle of a working farm, must have been a true shock of pleasure, and he often spoke of the life at Wootton as if he recalled it day by day. The eldest of the young people there was a clever girl, Maria, who is still living, and her sister Kitty was a pretty and charming creature both then and all the days of her life. These two made a great impression on Edward, and as, when a boy, he generally preferred the company of his elders to that of his juniors, he finally chose them for his especial friends. One of them says, "When he first came to Wootton, before he was six years old, I remember his attempts at drawing which we thought so clever for a small boy." He used to draw them all with their distinguishing peculiarities, if they had any. The curls which the young ladies wore were unmistakeable, but he was baffled by what he called the "big heads" of the maid-servants, namely their caps. About this early habit of drawing we have his own words recorded by a friend, an artist, who, talking to him of David Copperfield and his neglected childhood, remarked in passing that he himself never remembered feeling unhappy when he was left alone. "Ah," said Edward, "that was because you could draw. It was the same with me. I was always drawing. Unmothered, with a sad papa, without sister or brother, always alone, I was never unhappy, because I was always drawing. And when I think of what made the essence of a picture to me in those days it's wonderful how little I have stirred. I couldn't draw people, of course, but I never failed to draw mountains at the back of everything just as I do now, though I'd never seen one."

Miss Maria Choyce, who was some ten years older than himself, was as kind to him as a sister, and to her, a few years later, he revealed much of his inner life.

Before this, however, came the building up of his physical health, and his careful father, not content with pure inland air, sent him also to the sea. Blackpool, on the Lancashire coast, was the place chosen, probably because the children next door, the little Neustadts and Barnetts, were going to it, and the whole joyous troop lodged together in one house during their stay. Edward used to declare that when they were all together Miss Sampson, out of complaisance to their friends, made him keep the Jewish Sabbath as well as the Christian one, and that he felt the ordinance to be extremely tedious; but no doubt in their own way the children softened the dispensation. He also complained with much comical exaggeration that she was in the habit of adopting for his benefit, on the spur of the moment, various rules for the education of children which she might hear of or notice in practice among her acquaintance. For instance, her admiration, he said, was aroused by the method of a lady, who, when fruit was on the table, thought it good to say to her children, "Now, you may take your choice, my dears, but you may only have one. You see, there are apples and pears and nuts and currants, so you may choose any one of these." But if under this new law Edward ever chose a currant, I am sure Miss Sampson gave him "one" several times over.

His memory went back very far, both consecutively and in the way of detached pictures of scenes. Writing in 1873 to a friend, he says that he recollected quite well the Queen's Coronation, which took place when he was four years old, and being carried to the Town Hall, "to see where the poor folk were going to be feasted, and a general sound of happiness in the air, and the ringing of bells." Also, "being allowed to wave a banner in the air in front of the house, and that gave me more happiness, I think, than anything that has happened to me ever since."

To his daughter, when she was travelling in the Midland counties in 1884, he wrote, "Give my love to Warwick, where I once lived a while, and saw a lady paint bronze colour on a butterfly for an album. I was about four—it looked very beautiful. I don't remember why I was at Warwick. In all those regions I went about as a 'little'—to school when I was five, at Henley-in-Arden, so give it my love."

The "living" at Warwick is probably a mistake, as there is no record of his having been in that neighbourhood except when at Wootton, from which place, however, he might easily have been taken over for a visit to Warwick. But a child reckons not by days nor years in the world he makes for himself, and the joy of seeing the lady paint the butterfly would wipe out time.

The school at Henley-in-Arden that he mentions was one to which, when staying with his Aunt Choyce, he sometimes accompanied an elder cousin, and it was on the Henley Road, not at Henley itself, which was too far from Wootton for the boys to walk.

The Chartist riots in 1839, during which his father was

sworn in as a special constable, made a great impression upon him, and he suffered many things in imagination because a maid-servant, while putting him to bed, used to fan his terrors by grisly stories of what was happening, or might happen, in the streets. In his childhood he had many restless nights with bad dreams, and would often wake up with a cry, when he said he always found his father or Miss Sampson standing by his bed, looking at him with "large, anxious faces," that terrified him afresh; and he warned us not to stand looking closely at children in their sleep lest they should awake suddenly and be startled. All through his life he was a dreamer of dreams by night as well as by day.

As soon as he was old enough to walk out alone with his father, they used to go together on the day of his mother's death and visit her grave. He said that his father used to grip his hand very tightly and to cry, which frightened him. Sixty years after it happened, he writes, "Sunday was Sep. 3rd. I always keep it with what piety I can. That was the day my mammy died—the sixth day after my birth." Some one who personally knew this mother is reported to have said that a distinguishing quality in her was good sense, "good practical common sense more than ordinary," and a sister of hers writes that "she was very much beloved, recited poetry well, and was pretty." Fair in complexion she must have been, for Edward's father and all his family were dark, but her child was extremely fair in hair and skin, with eyes of a light colour. There is a bad portrait of him as a child of seven, which when he grew older he would gladly have cut into ribbons, but forbore because it would have grieved his father. In it he is represented with curling hair, which he never had. The reason of this, he told me, was that Miss Sampson, jealous of that charm in his little friends next door and determined he should not be outdone by them, curled it herself for that occasion if never again. The only thing of interest in the picture is that he is represented holding a slate, upon which a church is drawn, so that drawing was evidently already considered his characteristic occupation. He remembered asking the artist to put in the church. A prettier picture is produced in the mind by the words of an old friend: " My first recollection of Edward is of a little boy in a red frock shelling peas."

There is no record preserved of how and when he learned to read and write: possibly Miss Sampson taught him, but it is plain, from some fragments of letters to his father, that before he was nine years old he wrote with ease and was fond of reading. The handwriting, even of the first of these notes, is clear and careful, with a sense of pleasure in the use of the pen shewn by flourishes after the signature; whilst for further ornament he has added two elementary birds. It is dated Blackpool, June 20th, 1842, and begins:

" My dear Papa, I should be very happy to see you at Blackpool, if you could come. I like the town very much indeed, but I think it should not be called Blackpool as there is more white houses than red ones."

Another scrap of the same time begins with the word " Bridge," and then goes on, " you see what a deal I think of the Bridge by the ornaments at the bottom." But the drawing to which this refers is lost. There is also a sentence which must have been written or spoken by millions of children since time at seaside places began, *nomine mutando.* " If I am a good boy Miss Sampson says we shall have a donkey ride to-morrow." And " to-morrow " is recorded, when it had become yesterday, in the next letter. At the top of the page, above the date, is written, " This is more like a hermitage," which is explained as one reads further.

" Blackpool, June 23rd.

" My dear Papa,

" I have just done the drawing my uncle wished me and hope he will be pleased with it. Yesterday I had a donkey ride and liked it very much, but coming back a little boy put a string round the donkey's leg which Miss Sampson was on and threw her off and caused a pain in her head and soon went away. You said in Miss Sampson's letter at the top Hermitage, but I don't think you live like a Hermit if you have such a many friends coming in as you say. I only wish you could send me Æsop's Fables, but that I suppose you cannot. I have a great variety of very pretty stones and the shells are not very pretty.

"June 24th. This morning I bathed for the 3 time and liked it so much that I had twice as much as before. I am in want of books very badly. I expect a letter from you every day, please to send me a very long letter. We are all a great deal better, I might have said quite well and stout. Please to tell the children next door I am very sorry not to have wrote to them before, but I am so buisy running about the sands and fields.

"P.S. Please to give my kind love to Grandpapa and Mr. Caswell."

There is a postscript added by Miss Sampson for the comfort of the father: "You would be delighted to see Edward, he looks so well and I think gets stronger every day." The uncle of whom he speaks in this letter was a half-brother of his mother's, a Mr. Samuel Perry, who was always kind to him.

What with country air, sea air, and the attention of Miss Sampson, the child's bodily health was now established at a fair level; and certainly also the foundations had been laid of that citadel of the soul in which through life he entrenched himself. Miss Sampson's "I know you better than you know yourself, Edward," which he used to quote, was but a vain effort to reassure herself.

In the year 1843 the Choyces left Wootton, removing to a farm called Harris Bridge in Leicestershire, which had been tenanted before by another member of their family. Here Edward continued to visit them every year, and though he was considered rather delicate in the chest, he led the same outdoor life as other boys in summer, and is remembered as having been "full of fun and spirit." Whilst he was quite little, his chief playmate was a girl cousin rather younger than himself, because the boys' games were thought too rough for him, but later on he joined in their cricket and bathing. The name of the stream in which they bathed, the Sense, afforded many a jest to the elder girls, who used to urge them to drink whilst in its waters, and to drink deeply. There is a letter to his father from Harris Bridge, undated, but, to judge by the writing, some three or four years after the Blackpool ones, and in it he speaks of walking to Twycross and back (three miles) to ask for letters, and of "sitting up till Sunday on Saturday night," so that his health evidently no longer needed any special care.

These glimpses are mostly of life in the country and in holiday time, but I can find no account of his doing any lessons at home or of his going to any preparatory school in Birmingham before he entered the Free Grammar School.

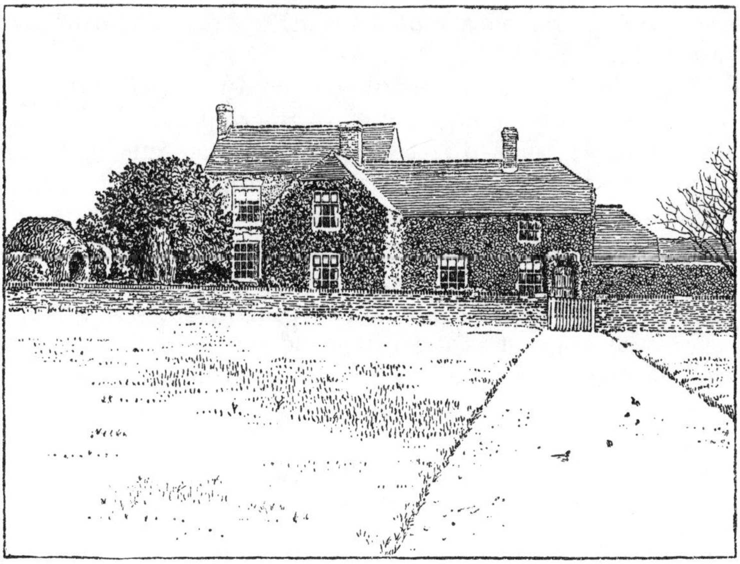

HARRIS BRIDGE.

CHAPTER II

CHILDHOOD
1844-1848

KING Edward's School, Birmingham, as it now stands, was rebuilt in 1834 by Sir Charles Barry, in a style much like that afterwards employed by him for the Houses of Parliament. Through its wide, dark entrance the king's young namesake passed and took his place as a scholar on the 3rd of September, 1844. This day was the anniversary of his mother's death, and he was just eleven years old.

The whole building probably looked brighter then than it does now after sixty years of weathering and smoke, but the gateway leading directly into a dark vestibule, and then on to a dim hall and corridor, can never have seemed cheerful. From the street the appearance of the school is still unchanged, except that it is now somewhat crowded in and dwarfed by the height of the buildings right and left which have replaced its earlier and less pretentious neighbours. Sixty years ago it stood out handsomely, and its depth could be seen as well as its breadth of frontage.

The school was divided, then as now, into Departments, Classical and English, or "Commercial," as the latter was familiarly called. The fact of Mr. Jones' placing his son in this Department proves that his intention at the time was to give him merely such an education as would fit him for business. Boys on this side of the school usually left at about sixteen. Latin was taught in both schools, but Greek in the Classical only. No fees were paid by the scholars, the endowment being one of the richest in the kingdom, and, except for the cost of books, education was absolutely free.

There were at this time some 450 scholars altogether, and it was essentially a day school, though the head and second masters each took about twenty boarders in their own houses. The Classical Department had a slight majority in numbers over the English. There were no separate class-rooms, the whole tuition being carried on in two large and lofty stone-floored rooms in the upper story of the building, and, on the English side at all events, the lower classes were so large that it was impossible for the masters to handle them properly. "The Babel was awful," says an old pupil, "but it taught us to shout and was probably good for the lungs. The din was increased by the outside street traffic. We never sat down to say our lessons, and the younger boys would be half-dead with fatigue and quite incapable of attention before the hour was up. There was no break in the work from 8.30 to 12, and from 2 to 5." Small wonder that it is added, "Only boys of exceptional ambition or wits could make decent progress. A boy never dreamt of asking explanations of his difficulties: the free use of the cane alone could drive us forward until we reached the higher classes, which were less crowded." That the art of teaching was not studied then as it is now, Edward's own words bear witness:

"At school we were plunged into Caesar without a word of explanation. The master never told the boys that the Commentaries were the Diary of the man we had learned of in history, written in the form of letters to the Senate of Rome, or any least thing about it. We began not even at the beginning, but right in the middle of all the technicalities of bridge-building—as good as learning a trade in Latin, for the Romans were splendid bridge-builders. Of course before long I found my feet, but for a dullish boy it was hopeless."

In spite of these defects, however, King Edward's School won for itself a fame for scholarship second to none, as is proved by its supplying four Senior Classics to Cambridge within the four years of 1845 to 1848.

The first Head Master appointed after the rebuilding of

the school was Dr. Jeune, in later years Master of Pembroke College, Oxford, and Bishop of Peterborough. His successor in 1838 was Prince Lee (afterwards Bishop of Manchester), and it was during the last years of his time that the fruit of their joint labours became visible. Though Edward literally entered the school during Prince Lee's time, the two seldom came into personal contact, for the Head Master left Birmingham in 1847, a year before the boy passed into the Classical Department. Three distinguished scholars also left and went up to Cambridge whilst Edward was still on the English side: Westcott, Lightfoot, and Benson.

The house in Bennett's Hill being only a few hundred yards from the school, there was no exercise to be had in the daily walks to and fro, nor were there at that time any organized games arranged for the boys. A playing-field at some distance off was rented for the boarders, who occasionally invited other boys in the upper part of the school to join in their games. But Edward never did this, and as he cared little for walking for its own sake, his amusements in term time were found chiefly within doors. Open-air life at Harris Bridge was, however, enjoyed during the holidays, and intimacy continued with "the children next door."

At home, although he could have no actual assistance in his studies, the atmosphere of the house was helpful because his work was regarded seriously, and he had a room given to him for a study where he could make his own world, without the irksome necessity of having to "put his books away" at any moment. From his father, too, he never met with any of the rough handling or worldly maxims that some men think good for their boys. He says of this himself:

"My father was a very poetical little fellow, tender-hearted and touching, quite unfit for the world into which he was pitched. We had very, very few books, but they were poets all of them, and I remember when I was about 12 or so, he used to read me little poems he had made himself, but as time went on he grew shy of reading them to me.

He used to read in a very touching voice, melodious and pathetic, believing everything he read. I have never heard such sympathetic reading. And he believed all good things that were ever said of anyone, and was altogether unworldly and pious. Like his countrymen he knew nothing at all of art, and couldn't understand what it was about or why it should be; but for nature he had a passion, and would seldom miss a sunrise if it could be seen, and would walk tired miles to see a cornfield."

Another time, talking to a friend about his childhood, he said that his father did not wish him to read novels, and so he did not. One book, however, he possessed from the first, a treasure-house richer than anything withheld from him—Aesop's Fables—and, as we saw from one of his early letters, even the seaside and young companions and a donkey-ride did not make up to him for its absence when it had unfortunately been left at home. How he came to miss the Pilgrim's Progress I do not know, but so it was, until by the time he first saw it, the names in the story jarred upon him so much that he would not read it. Such names as "Mr. Envy" and "Mr. Despondency" he said he could not tolerate. Nevertheless, in the mysterious way that works of genius exhale into the air, the poetry of this one reached him and made its due impression, for there is a design of his which represents the Shining Ones in the Land of Beulah.

The first three or four years at school passed without his seeming to find any very special companions, but there was a boy amongst that lively community who gradually became his chosen chum, and finally a beloved friend. This was Cormell Price, afterwards Master of the Modern School at Haileybury, and for twenty years Head of the United Services College, Westward Ho! For some time the two boys only knew each other by sight and name—and on one side, it may be added, by sound—for when Mr. Price was asked what was the first thing he could remember about Burne-Jones at school, he said at once, "His laugh—I knew him by that before I knew him any other way. I used to hear it and know that Jones was coming out of school, and there he would be, springing from the large front entrance, ready for any fun." As time went on they drew more closely together. The parents for their sake began an acquaintance which deepened into friendship, and Cormell's sisters received Edward amongst them as a brother. He never regretted having had no real brother. His little sister, dead before his birth, was his regret.

On his first entering school, in September, 1844, he was placed in the eighth class, the lowest but one. I am told that this was rather a low place for a boy of his age to take, and proves that his stock of school-learning must have been slender. By the end of the next half-year, however, he had had two removes, and the school lists afterwards tell a story of unchecked progress. By June, 1847, he was in the first class, where he remained for eighteen months, and during the last half-year was "Caput" of the English school.

Abundant traces remain, in the shape of manuscripts of incredible carefulness, that during this time he worked hard, not only by compulsion but of his own free will. His whole intellectual powers converged upon the one outlet then provided for them: books, books, and always books were the gates of the new world into which he was entering, and his imagination was largely engaged in realizing history and romance both in prose and verse. Many a fine holiday afternoon he and Cormell Price spent with favourite books in the old Birmingham cemetery in Icknield Street, which was the only public space within easy distance that was quiet and planted with trees. There was a part of it then, now levelled, which rose high above the rest of the ground, a steep slope of soft red sandstone, with a winding path up it that led to a seat at the top; and there the two boys would read and talk and recite to each other by the hour. Macpherson's Ossian was brought by Price as a contribution to their common store of heroic literature. They used to repeat it aloud as they walked about, taking parts as far as possible. In a volume of ballads and translations which they had was

Taylor's version of Bürger's Lenore, and Edward, when he first learned it, was never weary of reciting the fine stanza:

> Tramp, tramp across the land they speed,
> Splash, splash across the sea;
> Hurra! the dead can ride apace—
> Dost fear to ride with me?

whilst Cormell would answer with another ballad beginning:

> Hark, the storm-fiend of the deep
> Wakes on old Heimdalla's steep,
> Yelling out his mountain glee
> Like a soul in agony!

which was his especial favourite.

But also it was with Edward then, as it continued to be throughout his life, that between work and work he felt as actual a necessity for "fun" as he did for food and air. I can find no other word to describe a characteristic of his which will be recognized by every one who knew him. Gentle and lambent at times, wild enough and noisy at others, whimsical in words, ominous in silence whilst some swiftly-conceived Puck-like scheme of mischief took shape, carrying all things before it, compelling the least likely to join in it, always ending in the laugh that we remember, the cloud-scattering laugh! And whilst I use the word "fun" instinctively, it pleases me to learn that it is thought to be of Celtic origin, akin to one that means "delight, pleasure, desire, longing, a tune, a song," and so may take rank amongst the immortal beguilers of care. Certainly the melancholy that he inherited from his Celtic forefathers would, without this good gift, have overweighted his nature.

Practical jokes too he loved, and boldly defended. The memory of some of those that he had played as a boy never palled upon him: he used to recall them and tell us about them till we almost felt we had been there. Here is one of them. Outside the windows of the top story of his father's house ran a parapet, with just space enough behind it for him to entrench himself and look out, unseen, upon the world below. The story of the officer whom he saw from the watch-tower was as if it had happened yesterday. It was a gallant officer who rode up up and drew rein at a house opposite, and lightly vaulting from his horse, left a beautiful new saddle exposed to the eyes of mischief. A cherished squirt hastily filled with water did the deed, and all its contents besprinkled the fair brown leather. This done, the officer appeared again and suffered a sudden check on discovering it to be wet. He looked up to the sky and down on the pavement; he even held out his hand to feel if rain was still falling! No, the showers in Birmingham were very local, and he must make the best of it and ride away. Another tale he never tired of telling was of a fatal day when, after some prank played in the street, a policeman's hand was suddenly upon his shoulder and he felt that his last hour had come; how he slipped his shoulder from beneath that hand before it could close upon him and fled for dear life with the policeman after him, and the chase so hot that he rushed breathless past his own father's door without daring to stop and enter it.

There are letters written by him in the summers of 1847 and 1848 from Harris Bridge, while on his usual visits there, but they are chiefly duty-letters with no individuality. "I do not know any news to tell you, my occupations are various, of which cricket and bathing are the favourites." Or, "You must please to excuse my very short letters as I am quite at a loss what to talk about." In July, 1848, however, he dates from "The land flowing with milk and cheese" (Harris Bridge was a cheese farm), and says, "Uncle has kindly promised to shew John and me how to survey a field when haymaking is over." There is mention of cricket again, too, of going to see a cricket match at Atherstone; but his interest in the game must have been chiefly reflected from that of others, for he had entirely lost it in a few years.

In this letter are some slight drawings, noticeable only

because one of them is of devils playing cricket, and he had a special reputation at school later on for drawing devils. These are little black silhouettes, and I think no one could augur anything remarkable from them. An inner impulse made him try to represent things he thought of, but it was like a deaf man trying to talk: he had no standard by which to measure what he did.

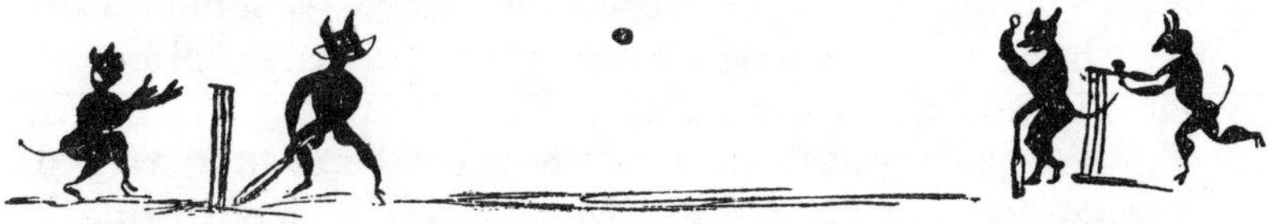

Whilst, however, thus stammering in a yet unlearnt language, he was rapidly developing in other directions. It might seem incredible, but for the mysterious ways of the human soul, that the same boy should have written and illustrated the letter to which I refer, and have also at nearly the same time written two others that have been preserved. They were sent to his cousin, Maria Choyce, after his return to Birmingham, and are upon a subject which they had discussed while he was at Harris Bridge. Her account of their origin is, that a Nonconformist friend, a Calvinistic Methodist, who was "very fond of airing his own opinions," had been staying at the farm during Edward's visit, and that the boy had been immensely interested in him. "We considered ourselves orthodox," she writes, "but found we were very ignorant. He said he would look the subject up when he got home and write me full particulars." The way in which he kept this promise may be seen from two letters which are here given in full. They shew how early developed was his power of independent study and his instinct for finding out authorities and sources of information on a given subject, whilst the eagerness with which he turns to this first theological quest prepares us to understand how fervidly a few years later he entered into and shared all the throes of the English Church. The few mistakes in spelling are left, as having their own significance.

Letter I

"Urbs fumi. Nonae Septembres.
"Anno Edwardi Ioni. 15.

"Dear Y.

"According to my promise I have written to you, but as it is now rather late, having only just finished my studies you will excuse my very short note. At some future time I hope to be able to give you a full description of what will now form my note.

"I have not yet been able thoroughly to understand the tenets of the Calvanistic Methodists. I have made a few extracts from some books on the different sects of Christians.

"First, the sects who differ as to the objects of divine worship are:—Trinitarians, Athanasians, Sabellians, Arians and Socinians or Unitarians.

"Second, Those who differ as to the blessings derivable from the Gospel are:—Calvanists, Arminians and Antinomians.

"1st, The Trinitarians profess the doctrine of Trinity in opposition to the Arians and Unitarians.

"2. The Athanasians are those Trinitarians who receive the creed called Athanasian.

"3. Sabellians taught that the Father, Son and Holy Ghost were one person with three names, that in the Old Testament the Deity delivered the law as Father, descended among men as Son, and descended upon the Apostles as Holy Ghost.

"4. The Arians maintained that the Son (or Logos, sig. Word) is a creature of a nature inferior to the Father, created by him in the beginning out of nothing, and made his instrument in the creation of men and angels, and that [to] this person is delegated the administration of Providence.

"5. Unitarians or Socinians deny the divinity of Christ, whom they affirm to have been only man, who in conformity with an ancient prophecy was chosen by God to introduce a moral doctrine into the world and to reveal the doctrine of a future state.

"6. The difference between the Socinians and Unitarians is this: The Units reject the following articles in the Socinian creed: The Incarnation, the addressing of prayers and praises to Christ, the existence and agency of the Devil, the eternity of future punishment and some also reject baptism. Thus these, viz. the Units and Trinitarians, can never be united. For if the Units are right, then the Trinitarians are gross idolaters, or if the Trinitarians are right the Unitarians are heretics.

"II. Of those who differ as to the extent of the blessings of the Gospel.

"Calvin was contemporary with Luther. His tenets were the same as those of Saint Austin and many others of the primitive church. Most of them were professed by Huss, Jerome of Prague, Bede, Wickliffe, &c. Calvinism was first introduced into Britain in the reign of Elizabeth by those divines who fled to the continent to avoid the persecutions of Mary. It was brought into disrepute by the political and fanatical conduct of the Puritans or rigid Calvinists, which ended in the overthrow of the Church and the death of Charles I.

"The doctrine of Calvanism has been reduced to five points, viz.

1. Particular Election.
2. „ Redemption.
3. Moral Inability.
4. Irresistable Grace.
5. Perseverance of the Saints.

which will I hope occupy part of my next letter in about a fortnight or a month.

"I have been searching a great deal for this scanty supply of information. I have no doubt that the greater part of this was previously known to you, but I have done my best. The subject before completed will occupy two or three letters more.

"With love to all in which Papa and Miss Sampson join,

"Believe me to be,

"Your affectionate friend,

"E. C. B. Jones."

Letter II

"Bennett's Hill,

"October 8th, 1848.

"Dear Maria,

"I received your long letter this morning and have taken the first opportunity to answer it, and as my time is limited you will excuse my commencing the Subject without entering in the passing events.

"I think I concluded my first with enumerating the five principal tenets of Calvin:—

1. Particular Election.
2. ,, Redemption.
3. Moral Inability.
4. Irresistable Grace.
5. Perseverance of the Saints.

They thus explain the first of these. That God thro' Christ has chosen a certain number to everlasting Glory before the foundation of the world, without any conditions whatever to be performed by the creature, and that the rest of mankind he was pleased to pass by, and to ordain to wrath and dishonour for their sin to satiate his rigid justice.

"A more blasphemous tenet one can hardly imagine—it seems to imply in the latter part that some are to be punished both for their own sins and for those elected to glory.

"And then as necessarily follows, they explain 'Particular Redemption' as that our Lord died only for the Elect.

"3. By Moral Inability, that the guilt of Adam's sin is

conveyed down to posterity, whereby we commit sin and are thence subject to death and to all temporal and eternal miseries.

"I think there seems to be a contradiction here, if all are subject to eternal misery: in their 1st Article it is said that the Elect cannot go to Hell, whatever their sins may be, and therefore they cannot be subject to Eternal Wrath. And then returning to their old adage again, they go on to explain Irresistable Grace as 'All whom God has elected to glory he will at his appointed time call from a state of sin to a state of salvation.'

"The Perseverance of the Saints means that the Saints or Elect (being called from a state of death and sin) can never fall into sin.

"You must not take the little additions I have made at the end of each tenet in any other light than a passing remark of my own, but this grand feature in Calvanism seems totally repugnant to the alledged attributes of God.

"There are two sects in Calvanism: those who maintain that God permitted but did not decree the fate of Adam, they are called Sublapsarians, and those who maintain that God decreed his fate, to display his mercy and justice. They are called Super-lapsarians. Calvanism is the established church of Scotland. In England it is taught in the Chapels of Mr. Whitefield and Lady Huntingdon; those of the Independants, many of the Baptists and all Presbyterian chapels connected with Scotland.

"The difference between the Arminians and Calvanists is this. The Arminians maintain that God predetermined to bestow salvation on those only who he foresaw would persevere in the faith of Christ, and to inflict punishment on those who he foresaw would continue in unbelief, so that according to Arminius, election was conditional and reprobation the effect of foreseen wickedness. I like the idea of Arminius; it is decidedly superior I think to that of Calvin. So that his system maintains the doctrine of human depravity, salvation by Christ, justification by faith, and sanctification by the Holy Ghost.

"I think I mentioned the Antinomians in my last. This was a heresy took rise from a perversion of some of Saint Paul's epistles—to the Romans, I think. They maintained that no part of the Old Testament was intended as a rule of faith or practice; that good works do not promote salvation, or evil works hinder it. They were properly speaking the most rigid Calvinists. They also maintained that the Elect could not possibly commit sin. One of their advocates, Crisp, thus writes: 'An elect person (mark every word)—an elect person, in the height of iniquity, and in the excess of riot committing all sorts of abomination that can be committed, God hath no more to lay to his charge than to the charge of a saint triumphant in his glory.' The elect of God are heirs of God and therefore cannot be dispossessed of their right of inheritance.

"I think you asked me in your letter whether or no Trinitarians must be classed with Athanasians. Their tenets are the same—they are in fact the same—but though all Athanasians are Trinitarians all Trinitarians are not Athanasians, that is do not hold the creed of Athanasius. In all other idioms they are precisely the same.

"Having now finished my little series called a treatise on those who differ as to the subject of divine worship, I will commence my next with one entitled 'Distinction as to Church Government.'

"I am now composing an Ancient History in my leisure hours, which are few, as I go to the School of Design 3 evenings pr. wk.

"Hoping you are all quite well, Papa and Miss Sampson join me in love to you all,

"Believe me to remain,

"Your colleague in argument,

"E. C. B. JONES.

"10 o'clock Tuesday Eveg—got Milton to learn, must be up early, look over lessons, hurry over work, get to school, hard work, very!"

I shewed these letters to Canon Dixon, Edward's old

school-fellow and friend, and with his permission will quote what he said after reading them:

"I had no knowledge that he pursued such enquiries. They reveal a good deal to me. They shew the inherent seriousness of his nature. I also admire the distinctness of statement. For a boy of fifteen the range of information is great, especially as there were much fewer books of the sort that would give it directly on such subjects than there are now —and he was so busy with other things. The classification seems to me his own, and is deliciously original: certainly the passing remarks are; and they are keen in judgment, and very decided. The charm of the classification is that it is somewhat quaint. And the striking thing is that in his main divisions, 'Objects of Divine Worship' and 'Blessings derivable from the Gospel,' he should have touched the two first great successive tendencies of theology, the one being Christology (in the early Fathers), the other the nature of grace (in Augustine and after)."

"I have been searching a great deal for this scanty supply of information," says Edward at the end of the first letter. This habit of "searching" for information about anything that interested him was never abandoned. To the last he would steadily read the dullest books through in order to find in them the one fact he wanted, or to make sure that it was not there; he would buy a long series of a magazine for the sake of one special article in a few numbers, and nothing that bore even the name of the subject he was studying was despised beforehand. He read slowly when a man: I do not know whether it was the same with him as a boy.

The fragments that remain of the "Ancient History" mentioned in the second letter are even more elaborate in research and classification than the "treatise" quoted above, besides being specimens of fine penmanship and illustrated with small coloured maps. By this time, the autumn of 1848, he and Cormell Price had become inseparable companions, and the scheme was a joint one, intended as the beginning of a "Universal History for the use of students."

The introduction took them four or five months, and the composition of it was entirely Edward's. After this had been completed, "We decided," Mr. Price says, "to proceed separately in order to get through the work more speedily. Edward chose Egypt, and I was to try my hand on some third-rate kingdom. He took very few weeks to cover the interval from the Deluge to Cambyses, while I was struggling with a solitary page on Lydia or Bithynia."

A sketch for the article on Egypt is extant, as well as the beginning of several elaborate Chronologies of History. In connection with his "three evenings a week at the School of Design" may be mentioned a neat little home-made note-book of this time, containing carefully copied out lessons and exercises upon the principles of light and shade, together with diagrams of primary, secondary and tertiary colours. "Notes &c. on Water Colouring" it is called. This is another instance of his voluntary work, and it is curious to compare with our knowledge of it the report of his drawing-master at school, who was also his master at the School of Design:

"DRAWING. *Might do better if he exhibited more industry.* Thomas Clark. Master."

He always had an "infinite capacity for taking pains," but experience taught him also the secret of rejection, and in some cases that of refusing to take any pains at all. There is no proof that his masters, generally speaking, noticed especial power in him; he himself, looking back on his boyhood, and speaking of it in the impersonal way which lapse of time makes possible, said once, "They never saw anything in me." Yet there is a pleasant record of a day when the Head Master came into the English School and held an examination in general knowledge, having the boys of three classes round him in a big circle in order to test them with unexpected questions; and the answers to many of these no one could give except a boy in the lowest class who knew about the Fortunate Isles and the religions of the Lebanon, and the names of rivers and places which shewed that he realized where things had happened, until at last he was rewarded by words delightful for a boy to hear and never to be forgotten, "How on earth did you come to know that?"

It is certain that on his side he took most particular note of his masters, and from them all singled out one for lasting gratitude. Often in talking of such matters he would say how much he owed to this gentleman, and in one of the letters of reminiscence with which in later years he sometimes gave the key of his past life to new friends he dwelt long on the feeling.

"At Bideford," he writes, "died the only master I ever had who had any brains. When I was fourteen or fifteen he taught me to place my knowledge as it came, to have its proportion. He so kept me to the drawing of maps that the earth has ever since lain beneath me, as if I could see it all from a great height, and he so taught me history that I see it now as a panorama, from the first days. In his time I could draw the coasts of all the world in very fair proportion, without looking at a map, and I think I could do it now, though not so well as then perhaps; and always afterwards, if ever I heard or saw or read up a thing, I knew in what little pocket of the mind to put it. Right up to the end of Oxford days no one could compare with him. His name was Abraham Thompson, a doctor of divinity he was; black hair grew on the back of his hands which I used to marvel at, he was very handsome and dark. Funny little boys are—how they watch. He could be very angry and caned furiously; at times I caught it. I think he grew poor in his last years and had the school at Bideford. I never heard about him at the end. I worshipped him when I was little, and we used to look at each other in class. I wonder what he thought when he looked; I used to think Abraham of Ur of the Chaldees was like him, and I am sure if he had bought a piece of land to bury his Sarah in, he would have been just as courteous as the first Abraham. I was always sorry that he was called Thompson, for I like lovely names,—should have liked one myself and a handsome form—yes I should. So that was Thompson. I have thought how far more needful with a lad is one year with a man of intellect than ten years of useless teaching. He taught us few facts, but spent all the time drilling us that we might know what to do with them when they came. Abraham Kerr Thompson, that was his name, I wonder if any one remembers him. A strange thing he would do, unlike any other I ever heard of; he would call up the class, and open any book and make the head boy read out a chance sentence, and then he would set to work with every word—how it grew and came to mean this or that. With the flattest sentence in the world he would take us to ocean waters and the marshes of Babylon and hills of Caucasus and wilds of Tartary and the constellations and abysses of space. Yes, no one ever taught me anything but he only—I hope he made a good end. But how long ago it all was! It is forty-five years since I saw him."

In this letter allowance must be made for the fact that the writer was focussing his memory upon one figure only; but though at another time he would have willingly recalled the names of other masters for whom he felt regard and respect, I do not think he would ever have withdrawn a word of the affectionate tribute it contains. There were some masters, too, whom he held in deliberate contempt, both when a boy and in his mature age. Broadly speaking, I should say that he disliked school, and suffered a good deal during his time there, but probably not more than any sensitive boy might have done. There was no self-pity in his recollections of it so far as he shared them with us, but a kind of disgust at the little tyrannies exercised both by masters and boys of a low type, and some impatience with the masters as a rule. He used to mention one who would look over an exercise, mark a mistake in it, and then fall into a rage when he met it again a few lines further on, saying, "There is that mistake again! Didn't I tell you?" The School Lists of the names and positions of boys, which at first sight are scarcely more interesting than columns of figures, contain much history to any one who has a key to them, and in looking over the lists of these years I have found silent confirmation of a tale of injustice that I knew. One of the masters, under whom Edward was for a short time, either really disliked him or the boy thought he did, and shewed great favour to another pupil, so that between the two he did not hold the balance even. After a certain examination, when marks were counted, the whole class was surprised to find that Edward came out below the favourite, and fifth instead of first, which they had expected of him. Apparently some one else was surprised too, for an unprecedented thing happened, namely a visit from the Head Master himself, who held a special examination amongst the same boys, with the strange result that though number five remained number five he took the two class prizes and another, and next term was promoted over the heads of the boys above him into a higher class.

Chiefly by the advice of Mr. Thompson, when the time came at which Edward would otherwise have left school, Mr. Jones decided that he should remain there. He was then fifteen years old and for six months had been head of the English Department. No doubt the master returned some of the sympathy with which his pupil regarded him, and the last good office it was in his power to do for the boy was successfully rendered, as before he left Birmingham at the end of 1848 it had been decided that Edward should pass on into the Classical School with a view to entering one of the Universities.

It must have been in the summer of this same year, I think, that he first went to London, on the invitation of his aunt and godmother, who lived in Camberwell, but of whom, although she was his father's only sister, he had hitherto seen little.

This lady had been twice re-married since she and her first husband, Mr. Burne, stood sponsors for Edward at his baptism, and her name now was Mrs. Catherwood. Within narrow bounds her story was an interesting one, and her personality certainly appealed to Edward when he made her acquaintance afresh after her third marriage.

She and her brother had been brought up separately, for when, after their father's early death, she was adopted by her great-uncle, Mr. Biven, she went to live with him in Lambeth, whilst the boy remained with his widowed mother. Somewhere in South London these two lived, I do not know where, and all I ever heard of Mrs. Mary Edith Jones was that she suffered much from rheumatic gout and that her son stayed with her till her death, which took place when he was twenty-six. Meanwhile little Keturah had a sombre time with her great-uncle, and at the age of thirteen found herself without even this semblance of a father. He left her a small fortune when she should come of age, but named no executor; so a friend and contemporary of his, Mr. Burne, undertook the duty of administering the estate combined with the guardianship of the child, "his dear little K. Jones," as she was called by her uncle in his will.

Mr. Burne was forty years older than his ward; he had lately lost a wife some fifteen years his own senior, and had no children. When Keturah was about nineteen, a suitor whose pretensions did not satisfy her guardian made love to her: she liked him, and this gave trouble; the time of her majority drew near; in short, the simplest plan seemed to Mr. Burne that he should say "Marry *me*," and she obeyed him. She must have had a peculiar power of reconciling herself to circumstances, for she went through fifteen years of this marriage with perfect composure. She used to call him Papa, and sit by his knee on a footstool.

But there were two young men, friends of Mr. Burne—Robert Young and James Catherwood by name—who both fell in love with her; yet so steadily, so tenderly and faithfully that one loves the memory of them all. For the old man trusted them both, and saw which of them she would have liked if she might, and was kind to him, and left her sole executrix of his will and free to do as she chose; and when he had been dead a year she married Mr. Young.

Eleven years afterwards she was alone again in the world, and then Mr. Catherwood returned like the needle to the pole, and pleading his long devotion received the reward of fidelity in the shape of six years with his dear Keturah. These three marriages, in which no child had ever disputed her sovereignty, left her young for her age and with an innocent fascination still about her. The carver-and-gilder's shop had always a little troubled her, and she had allowed the bond between herself and her brother to slacken, though keeping up some correspondence with him and remembering the birthdays of her godson; but when she saw Edward as a youth of fifteen she felt the tie of relationship and claimed him as belonging to her, while he in return loved his little aunt with her dark, glancing eyes.

Compared with Bennett's Hill the modest home in Camberwell was brilliant, and the new uncle that Edward found there soon became a friend. Mr. Catherwood was a clever man himself and a brother of Frederick Catherwood, the traveller and explorer in Central America.

Half a page of a letter written home during this visit still exists:

". . . and Uncle have been very kind to me and taken me to St. Paul's and a great many more places. To-day Uncle took me over the Bank of England and gave into my hands banknotes to the amount of one million pounds, which I threw . . ." and on the other side of the fragment ". . . Whitehall, opposite to which palace Charles I was beheaded, and the Economic Museum of Minerals, &c. Aunt will have some company on Tuesday, so I shall be her running footman."

All truly characteristic, the busy going about to see and learn what he could, and the vision of the little aunt claiming the services of her big schoolboy nephew, upon whom she could already count for willing attention and courtesy.

Amongst the pleasures provided for him by his uncle should be named a first introduction to a London theatre. It was the Lyceum, then under the management of Charles

Matthews. Speaking of this in later life, Edward said: "I went to the pit, and stood up and saw a play called the Golden Branch. And there was a beautiful fairy came down the golden branch and held out something, and I thought it was too beautiful ever to be, and I wondered, if I waited till I was grown up, whether she would be too old for me to marry her, which I should think would be more than probable, as she was very likely over forty and I wasn't above fourteen."

With this year, however, I feel that his boyhood came to an end, and now we must enter with him upon the period of youth which leads on to manhood.

CHAPTER III

DOMUS SAPIENTIAE
1849-1851

CANON DIXON says: "I first saw E. B.-J. when he came into the Classical from the Commercial School. He would then be about fifteen. He was a tall, strong boy, and I remember noticing his appearance as he sat proud and erect at his desk among the somewhat younger boys of that class. I soon made him out and found him a great joker among them, with a peculiar catch of a laugh, which had in it disdain tempered with good nature and amusement. I noticed that at once: how often was I to hear it afterwards!"

It was in consequence of his want of Greek that Edward was placed at first among his juniors, where the general work of the class was below his capacity. This, however, proved no disadvantage, as it gave him leisure during preparation time, which he devoted to reading history and to "the placing of his knowledge." The necessary Greek came easily enough to a boy who had already acquired a fair amount of Latin and knew the routine of learning a language, so that his steady passage up the school was not interrupted.

With regard to the instruction in drawing which he received at school, I am bound to say that he never counted it as of any use to him. The master was not incompetent, but, according to the memory of old pupils, was so engrossed with work of his own that he seemed to forget the boys, and seldom descended more than once an hour from his high dais to give any attention to what they had done. A natural consequence of this was that much reading "under the desk" went on, and it became a regular custom to take a book downstairs to the room where the drawing-class was held. During his whole school-course, Edward took only one prize for drawing.

It may have been the influence of Mr. Thompson, in some wide-circling lesson such as Edward describes, that first aroused his enthusiasm for Babylon, Nineveh, Persia and Egypt; certainly he felt it long before he was touched by either Greece or Rome. Quite possibly in the hands of less gifted teachers Greece and Rome were spoiled for him at school, as they have been for many a boy; at all events it was not until some time afterwards that he excavated for himself that more modern world.

A contemporary and fellow-townsman has a sad enough memory of the appearance of Birmingham streets at this time, when he writes that "the whole town reeked with oil and smoke and sweat and drunkenness," but I fear it was true, little as the generation that knows the city now may be inclined to believe it. In the room at his father's house that was given up to him as a study, however, Edward and Cormell Price spent many happy hours in a world of their own creation. This room was at the top of the house and dull enough in itself, very cold also in winter, but boys adapt themselves to circumstances, and they rarely descended into the sitting-room, or "parlour," for greater warmth and light.

Mr. Price says: "I remember what seemed to me well-stocked book-shelves, and our pride in rising to take down particular volumes for reference." Indeed, during his school life, Edward gathered together a considerable library; some of these books were gifts, but more were bought with pocket-money scrupulously saved up for the purpose.

The difference of rather more than two years in the age of these boys, who spent their time together with so much satisfaction, might make one think that at this stage of their lives intimate companionship would have been impossible; yet it was not so, and fifteen and thirteen found common ground both in work and amusement. But Cormell Price was an unusual boy of thirteen, and Edward all through his life made little account of dates or ages: a friend was a friend, whether in the nursery or on crutches. The voice of the younger boy, however, may be distinctly recognized in the following account, given to a sister, of some of the simple treasures which formed a "Museum" that the two friends had made.

"We have quite a Museum at his house, containing a choice collection of Fossils, Coins, Minerals, Shells, and other curiosities. We have 3 very valuable Fossils. Our shells also are good and Papa has promised those two large conchs of his, which you perhaps can remember. Our coins are fair—we have 2 copper ones of William and Mary, 3 or four of Charles II &c &c &c. Amongst the curiosities and relics are a sheet of paper made from the fibres of wood, a stone which was worn round the neck of one of the sailors at the memorable battle of Trafalgar, and a piece of the stone which was erected on Bosworth Field on the spot where Richard the 3rd was slain. The minerals are very numerous. In fine it is a capital concern and is increasing every week, although we are the only two members."

The friendships that Edward made in his new surroundings must be recorded, but always with a note that the feeling between him and his first friend remained unaltered.

Of Richard Watson Dixon we know. Then there was Wilfred Heeley, who was rather older than either Dixon or Edward, and who, though he went to Cambridge, always kept in touch with the men who became the "Oxford Set." And there was William Fulford, senior to any of them, who during school days was chiefly Heeley's friend. A year and a half later came Macdonald, a contemporary of Price's: these two went up to Oxford last of all, in 1854 Faulkner, an important member of the Set, was unknown to the others until they met him at the University. He was not a King Edward's School boy, but had been educated at the Proprietary School, Birmingham.

Beside those mentioned there were others whom Edward

remembered through life, for reasons that always influenced him in friendship. Of one, whom he had scarcely seen since the Birmingham days, he said, so lately as 1897, "He was a very dear schoolfellow. He was not clever. Yet in the midst of a great deal that was going on in the school, in the midst of all sorts of ability and ambition, he blotted out the memory of many a clever boy by his amiability and sweetness of disposition."

Edward was now always drawing in spare time at school, for his own amusement and the entertainment of those about him. "Figure after figure, group after group would cover a sheet of foolscap almost as quickly as one could have written," says a schoolfellow, "always without faltering or pausing, and with a look as if he saw them before him. I have seen him look straight before him into space, as if his copy were there. All the time he would be joyfully talking, and saying what he was doing or going to do."

This habit continued as long as he lived; he must have covered reams of paper with drawings that came as easily to him as his breath. At every friend's house there are some of them. They filled up moments of waiting, moments of silence, or uncomfortable moments, bringing every one together again in wonder at the swiftness of their creation, and laughter at their endless fun. Many of his school scribbles were still of "Devils," which found great acceptance among his companions.

Though the Church came gradually to be considered both by himself and others as his natural destination, yet, since nothing escaped his sense of humour, some of his caricatures were of clergymen. Others of the clerical figures that he drew were serious, and one often repeated was of a young priest standing robed before an altar. A version of this was shewn to Dixon, with the comment: "That is what I hope to be one day."

It is impossible to decide what first drew him towards the High Church movement. Probably he was both drawn and driven, for the barren ugliness of the Evangelical churches and their services at that time cannot be denied. Mr. Jones used to have a pew in St. Mary's Church, where the incumbent, the Rev. J. Casebow Barrett, a leading clergyman of the Evangelical party in the town, made so great an impression upon Edward—not perhaps the one intended, but indelible—that all Edward's friends had to make his acquaintance. Mr. Barrett has been described by a member of his congregation as a man of some eloquence with a theatrical delivery, and given to rhapsodizing upon the pleasures of heaven and the pains of hell; but Edward dwelt especially upon the pomposity of his style.

And while his growing thoughtfulness made these things repellent to him, he was also brought into contact for the first time with an ancient church and its beautiful services. This was at Hereford, where the Cathedral was still unspoilt by restoration. A brother of Mrs. Caswell's lived there, a Mr. Spozzi, who, together with his wife, shewed Edward great kindness and affection. Until far on in the Oxford days he used to go and stay with them in vacations, and was probably happier in his surroundings there than anywhere else.

The house where they lived was near the Cathedral in whose services he delighted; he loved his clever, warm-hearted and cheerful hosts, and amongst their friends found people to like and to admire. One of these was the Rev. John Goss, then just ordained, afterwards Custos of the Vicars Choral and Minor Canon of Hereford. He had a fine tenor voice, and an attractive personality that made him socially very popular, though at that time he must have been almost alone in the High Church views which he held. These views, however, attracted Edward, and Mr. Goss returned his regard. He was an Oxford man who had been there during the soul-searching time of Newman's secession from the Anglican Church, and it was to him, I believe, that Edward owed his introduction to Newman's writings.

To Mr. Goss, also, was due the choice of the college to which Edward afterwards went, for he was an Exeter man himself, and advised the boy to put his name down on its books.

Mr. Townsend Smith, another friend of the Spozzis, was already well known as Cathedral organist and conductor of the "Three Choirs," into whose Triennial Festivals at Hereford he had put fresh life: Mr. and Mrs. Spozzi were musical themselves, she singing and he playing the violoncello, and good music was often to be heard at their house. That they were wide-minded people is proved by their friendly circle including the parish priest of the Hereford Catholic church, who was fond of singing, and often dined with them. Mr. Spozzi possessed some sketches by David Cox given to him by the artist, and rather prided himself upon what he used to say was a Romney—the subject "Lear and Cordelia."

The contrast of a return from the Cathedral city to the Birmingham of those days must have been great, and perhaps one result of this was that, when he was about sixteen, Edward and his father left St. Mary's and the ministry of Mr. Barrett for St. Paul's Church, where the service and doctrine were "high." Incidentally, this uprooting of the "family pew" and its transference elsewhere shews how great his influence with his father must have been.

The importance of ecclesiastical matters henceforth grew rapidly in his mind, and he began to make friends in Birmingham who held the same views as himself. Amongst them were a Mrs. Compton and her daughters, who attended St. Paul's Church, and whose sympathy with him was helpful and pleasant. Probably they strengthened his first inclination towards taking orders, as I have heard that Mrs. Compton was eager in her persuasions with Mr. Jones that he should send his son to the University.

In spite of his action with regard to the church that he regularly attended in Birmingham, Edward when in London always accompanied his aunt to the Evangelical services at Beresford Chapel, Walworth Road, where, strangely enough, his yet unknown hero, Ruskin, had been taken by his father and mother before Edward was born.

When, in 1885, Edward saw this fact mentioned in the fourth number of Praeterita, he hastened to claim the ghostly relationship with his friend:

"Do you know I wrote you a letter weeks ago fully illustrated with finely finished pictures, and when it was done it looked so ugly that I ripped it into bits—it was my remembrance of Beresford Chapel where I too made a semblance of worship. And I remembered the fat cushions into which the preacher pressed his face when he prayed, and wanted to make you laugh with my drawing, and lo! it came out so like that my spirits fell and such gloomy darkness set in that I couldn't send it.

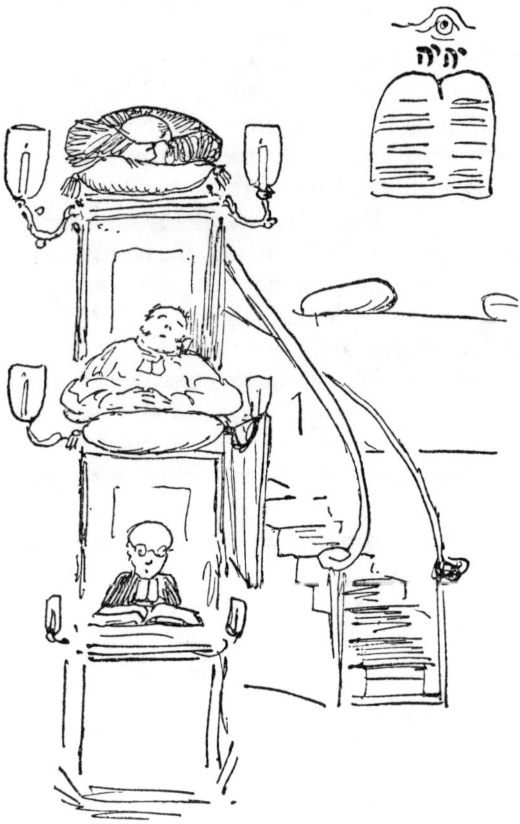

"There were two red fat cushions on a piece of upholstery called a Communion table, and a big fat cushion for the preacher, and a less fat one for the curate, and a hard, dry, mean one for the clerk.

"And I think there was an oil painting of the ten commandments. And when I read, in that most heavenly book called Praeterita, that you had prayed in that dreary

Bethel, I liked the ways of Providence very much. Your parson had been translated by the time I went. And I sat under another who was highly connected, but greatly needed translating."

And Mr. Ruskin wrote in answer, "How ineffably wonderful that you and I both sate—and—behaved properly in Beresford Chapel!"

It is certain that this year of 1849 was one of ardent intellectual activity and exaltation of feeling. Mr. Price recalls it as the time in which he saw most of his friend; for though they were separated in school by Edward's removal into the Classical Department, they met daily at Bennett's Hill and did all their work there together. Edward's class preparation being only Greek, his voluntary study outside the regular school routine went on steadily. His letters to Miss Choyce which have been quoted give evidence of wide and careful research in a direction towards which even his intimate chum did not realize that his mind was turned so strongly. The "Ancient History" was continued, and at the same time he was writing "An Epitome of Ancient Chronology, from the creation of the world to the birth of our Lord." On the first page of this manuscript is written, in a very small, fine hand, "Diligentia vincit omnia. E. J." There remains also part of an elaborate "Table of the Kings of Israel and Judah" and of a "Glossary of the British Poets, explaining the antiquated and abbreviated expressions contained in them." By the end of the year Cormell, who had meanwhile stood at the head of the Commercial School, joined Edward in the Classical Department.

The following note, written at the beginning of 1850, to one of the young friends next door, who was now married and living in London, shews through its fantastic signature the continued bent of his thoughts. The object of the note was to announce the safe return to Birmingham of an aunt who had been visiting the bride in London, but who scrupled to write the message with her own hand because it was after sunset on Friday and the Jewish Sabbath had begun. The illustration shews Edward, preceded by his faithful cat, "Tom," running in to join the family welcome to Miss Lyon.

"11 Bennetts Hill,
"Jany 25.

"DEAR MRS. BEDDINGTON,

"Being authorized by Miss Lyon I take the liberty of writing to you to inform you of her arrival, and cordial reception here.

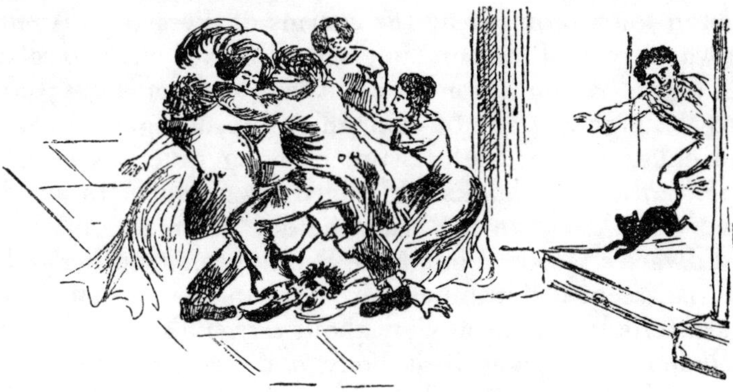

"Your Mama was here a few evenings since, and we thought her in much better spirits than usual—all I believe are also enjoying good health.

"Having only just returned (and that late) from business, that is to say from the public and prominent situation I hold in state affairs, you will excuse the shortness of my note, &c.

"The love and respects of the household divided according to your own judgment.

"With all due respect I presume to subscribe myself
"Your most attached servant,
"EDW. C. B. JONES
"Archp of Canterbury (elect)."

The drawing in this letter is the first we have in which a sense of composition is visible. Hitherto his illustrations had been merely figures brought together without any appearance of design in their relation, but here the design is ingenious and tells its tale. It must be remembered that he had as yet seen no beautiful drawing, and though the grotesque vigour of Cruikshank had evidently affected him, that was not the language for which he was seeking.

"Tom," the cat, an important member of the family at Bennett's Hill, should perhaps have been mentioned before now. He was a fine tabby, of a type that set the standard in his master's mind for all other cats, though sometimes shaken for a moment by the charms of Persians. At first he was a playfellow only, but when Edward went to school and began having lessons to do in the evenings, Tom passed into the higher grade of companionship, and gave up walls and housetops for the pleasure of lying quietly curled up near him and his books. He lived for many years, and indeed was older than the bride the day his master married.

Edward's words about Mrs. Beddington's mother—that she had seemed "in much better spirits than usual"—are characteristic, for his anxiety about a friend's health always included mind as well as body, and his sensitiveness to tones of voice as an index to it was great. "That girl is in trouble," he once said of a bright young friend who to most others seemed just as usual; "there is a little forlorn tone in her voice that I've learned to recognize in women when they are unhappy, ever since she came back from ——. I am sure something has happened."

Canon Dixon's recollection confirms this where he says: "One of his usual salutations to his friends at school was, 'Are you happy?' which was peculiar for a boy. He once varied it by adding, 'or miserable?'"

In the summer of 1850, he either went for the first time to the British Museum or else it was the first time that he realized its value. He was again staying in Camberwell, with the Catherwoods, but now going about London without the necessity for a guide. He wrote to his father of what he saw, and the letter is dated "Camberwell, July 34, 1850." There is also a note dated June 44: perhaps he had been begged to date his letters and so did it without stint.

In any case, this of July 34th says:

"MY DEAR FATHER,

"With very great pleasure we received your letters this morning. I was quite glad to find you writing in such good spirits—it gives me double pleasure.

"To-day I went over the British Museum and spent a considerable time in the Nimroud or Assyrian room; they are preparing a splendid apartment for the reception of them. I was quite surprised at the clearness and beauty of the Sculpture. The bas-reliefs seem to be as perfect as when they emerged from the workman's shop, tho' not quite so clean. They seem to have had a very good idea of anatomy, in which they far outstrip the Egyptians; the feet and hands seem to have been their chief study and the muscles of the arms and legs are finely portrayed. A new light upon Ancient History will soon be elicited when the inscriptions with which all the monuments abound, can be read. One black granite monument contains 210 lines of cuneiform writing. In most of the bas-reliefs the king forms the most prominent object. He is in some hunting the wild bull, in others pursuing his enemies, to whom he bears the most gigantic proportions, always accompanied by the 'feronher' or sacred bird, a kind of talisman.

"The sieges are very amusing. A large battering-ram holding two warriors, one of which is discharging arrows and another shielding both, is the most prominent object. Several persons are swimming upon inflated skins. The besieged are hurling down large stones. The women are tearing their hair, a priest on the walls is offering incense. As the sea or some large expanse of water is to be seen in the distance it seems probable that the sculpture commemorates the conquest of some maritime city, most probably on the coast of Phoenicia, perhaps Tyre or Sidon, which latter town if I remember rightly was captured by

Assarhaddon, Sennacherib's third son and successor. As far as I can recollect it was something like this

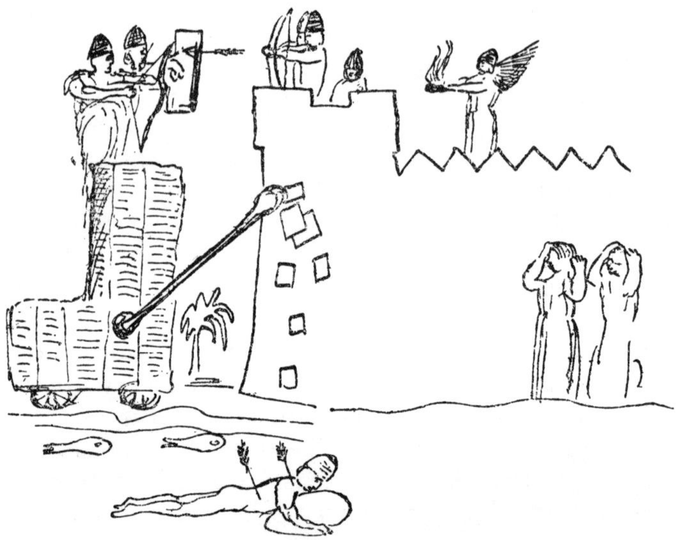

"The Ethnographical rooms delighted me, the Central Saloon pleased me. The Zoological gallery gratified me, the Mammalia saloon delighted me, the Lycian, Nimroud, Phigalian, Elgin, Egyptian, Etruscan, and above all the Fossil rooms put me into ecstasies. I spent a considerable time in the Egyptian Rooms, which in point of Antiquity perhaps excel even the Assyrian. The Egyptians seem to have delighted in the colossal-enormous. Fists nearly 4 feet high must once have belonged to

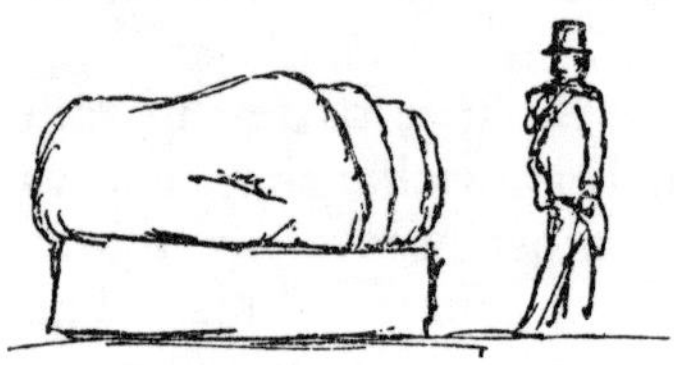

gigantic figures, whereas the Assyrian antiquities for the most part are diminutive, some scarce exceeding 4 feet altogether and the greatest only 7 or 8. The Egyptian antiquities again are chiefly sculpture either in granite or other hard marble, but the Assyrians excelled chiefly in bas-reliefs, there having been but one piece of sculpture as yet discovered, viz., one from Kalah Sherquat, and this has lost its head and is much mutilated. The Elgin marbles taken or imitated from the Parthenon are very interesting. The Etruscan Room chiefly abounds in vases which are in extraordinary preservation. The Lycian room has just been added and is on a very gigantic scale. Price should have been with me to have seen the fossils—Marsilaceae, Equisetaceae, Lycopodaceae, Asphodeleae, Euphorbiacae, Ichthiosauri, Plesiosauri, &c. &c. &c. &c., would have afforded him immense gratification. But I am confining myself to one sight whereas I see a dozen per diem, but I know antiquities are more pleasing to you than the relation of Jullien's music or the fireworks at the Surrey Zoological Gardens. Oh! I've been to the Regent's Zoological Society and seen the Hipp-hip-hip-(hurrah) opotamus,—a great, fat, huge, unwieldy, ugly, grovelling pig, with eyes duller than lead, a huge mouth, enormous jaws, monstrous head, puny legs, preposterous proportions. The stuffed one in the British Museum is 5 times the size and no crushing to see it.

"Oh dear, I've been everywhere.—Going to Gravesend on the water to-morrow, wish you were as jolly, never mind it's your turn next. Hope Essey will write—she shall have the next letter, but now I must conclude. You never can read this, but it must be finished. Give my love to everybody indiscriminately. I never know how to conclude, so excuse all that, and put loves and respects and compliments and regards in their right order,—and believe me

"Your affect son
"EDW. C. B. JONES."

For the rest of his life the British Museum was a place that he turned to with devotion. After his death, a note of instructions to his son was found, directing that his most intimate book of designs should be given to the place where we may believe he first tasted the food for which his soul hungered.

It may seem strange that his enthusiasm had not been aroused by the pictures in the National Gallery, but the very name of painting meant dreariness to him in his boyhood, associated as it was with the dark little pictures which Mr. Caswell used to bring home from sales, or with those that might happen to be sent to his father for framing in a way that would make them worthy to form part of the furniture of somebody's dining-room. "I quite hated painting when I was little," he once said; and again, "Until I saw Rossetti's work and Fra Angelico's, I never supposed that I liked painting. I hated the kind of stuff that was going on then." Words which might be used to explain the whole Pre-Raphaelite revolution, and that make it clear why, from the first moment he saw it, he understood the work of the Brotherhood.

His own drawing, though it had always been a necessity to him as a means of expression, still remained conventional in style, and with no look of enjoyment in its execution. The maps that he drew and coloured were different; he had a reputation for them at school, and freedom and enjoyment were visible in every part of them.

Again we have the help of Canon Dixon in recalling a time when he and Edward were constantly meeting.

"When we came together in the Second Class," he says, "I began to know E. B.-J. more intimately. The Second Class and the First were the two that were immediately under the Head Master himself. Much of their work was in common—that is, there were certain books which both classes took together, and on these occasions (perhaps three mornings out of the six) we used to hear the beautifully modulated voice of Dr. Gifford call 'First and Second Classes': whereupon we all sprang up and crowded round the desk of Sapientia." This was a kind of canopied throne at one end of the room where the Head Master sat. It was of dark oak, and above it was the word Sapientia, carved in old English letters. In front of it a tall standing-desk, with upper and lower ledges for books and ink, formed three sides of a long square, every part of which was fully exposed to the eye of the master, and round this desk both classes stood during a lesson, in two rows, the boys of the Second Class diving between the elbows of those of the First in order to dip their pens into the inkstands that were sunk in the lower ledge. How many distinguished men imagination brings again as boys to take their places at that awful desk, and wonders whether any sign of the future rested on their young heads.

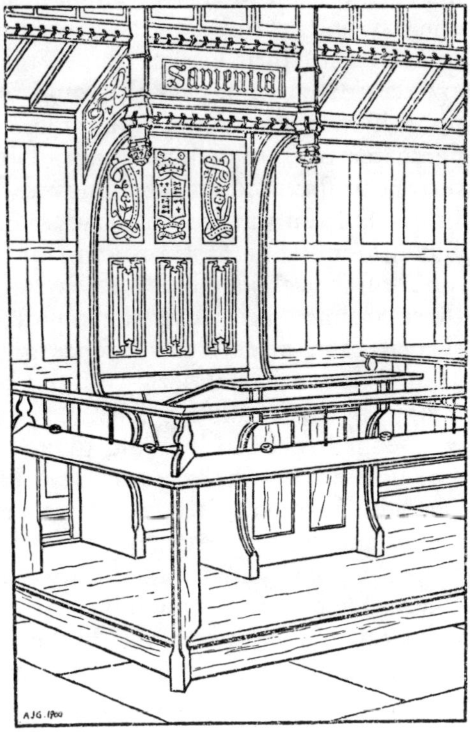

"The First and Second Classes," Canon Dixon goes on, "were under Dr. Gifford himself: it was far easier to go through the whole school without stop or pause than to go from the Second Class into the First. One reason for this was that there was a great difference in scholarship between the Second and the First, though some of the work was the same. We were a long time together in the Second Class."

The following is in answer to a question that I asked:

"He did not leave on me the impression that he was happy in his youth. At school he was high-spirited, boisterous or humorous: but with melancholy beneath. His temper was hot and rather fierce. He would give place to none. But with his friends he was extremely gentle. He was a hard worker and won many prizes. I remember a story that he once, in the Commercial School, carried off an armful of prizes home, rolled them in the door-mat, and then fainted upon them."

His capacity for exhaustion was great; every muscle would relax and his pulse would fail, but again he responded so quickly to restoratives that we always likened his constitution to that of an infant, who is at death's door one day and in full activity the next. The intimate union of body and spirit was in him so marked, that pleasurable excitement when he was ill would produce the same effect upon him as stimulants and tonics. The "hot and rather fierce temper" of which Canon Dixon speaks was a subterranean fire, and as far removed from irritability as the North is from the South. It was not lightly roused either, and seldom at a first provocation. One outburst in the quiet of the school library is remembered which astonished those around and drove the object of it to a distance in surprise and alarm: the offence given, however, was unknown to the bystanders. "But playing with E. B.-J., if I may say so," adds his friend, "was rather like playing with edged tools. He could give terrible looks of anger." The note ends with these words: "His affection was strong when he bestowed it. He was a very affectionate nature, loving and seeking love."

Dixon knew something of Edward also in his own home, where, he says, "I remember envying his position, as he was evidently lord, and did as he liked, asking whom he would to visit him: which was out of the question with me" (as one of a large family). "He always used to have money and nice things about him, to schoolboy extent."

Speaking of the work done in the Second Class, Canon Dixon says further: "My incapacity for mathematics troubled me, and would have stood in my way against being admitted into the First Class, but for the leniency of Mr. Yates, the mathematical master. I think that E. B.-J. had the same incapacity, or something like (we could both do Euclid, but little besides): at any rate, he had a distaste. Now we both fell into the practice (unknown to each at first) of absenting ourselves from school on Monday mornings. By this we avoided giving in a copy of verses and taking out another, two hours of Demosthenes along with the First Class, and two hours of mathematics at the 'mathematical desk' of Mr. Yates. In two or three weeks this became notorious, and we dropped it. But in a little time we made a compact to be absent alternately on those mornings. This went on till it in turn became notorious: so notorious that one morning Mr. Yates said, *sans lever la tête*, 'Is Dixon here?' 'No, sir,' from a dozen voices. 'Then, Jones, come up, and let me see your work.' Thenceforth we were as other boys." The wise "leniency" of the mathematical master to the two boys was justified, as we know, and his pleasant relations with them, in spite of his knowledge that they would do him as their tutor but little credit, are proved by the tone of Canon Dixon's reminiscence, and by the fact that Mr. Yates long preserved, and shewed to his friends, an elaborately drawn and painted map which Edward had made and given to him.

It was in the second "half" of 1851 that Edward followed Dixon, who had been promoted earlier in the year, into the First Class. Heeley had just left with an exhibition to Trinity College, Cambridge. At no time during their school life was there much personal intercourse between him and Edward, but quite enough sympathy and liking to prepare them for a friendly meeting in the future. Fulford, too, whom Edward scarcely knew at all, had gone up to Oxford with an exhibition a term earlier, and no one could have foreseen how closely these men would draw together within the next few years.

In both the two upper classes there was a different and a wider atmosphere than that which surrounded the lower ones: the boys were beginning to look out upon real life, religion and politics were openly discussed, and individuality came into play. Looking back upon this period of Edward's life, it seems as if the thing which had become of surpassing interest to him was religion as associated with the history of the Christian Church and with its actual position in modern times. His imagination had been repelled by almost every visible thing around him, his power of veneration was enormous, and in the Church of which he was a member a movement was going on, having for its object the restoration of beautiful ceremonial and dignity of office. This movement naturally commanded his deepest sympathy, and the collision which it led to between ecclesiastical and state authority excited him so much that he threw himself eagerly into the strife.

Amongst the upper boys of the school great interest was felt in following the struggle as typified by the well-known "Gorham Controversy," which incidentally aroused a fury of debate through the whole country. Many of the elder boys felt seriously about the question, and ranging themselves on one side or the other—by far the greater number being with the Evangelicals—argued the subject with conviction and vehemence. Edward's strengthening religious fervour, joined perhaps to his inborn love for what seemed a losing cause, brought him forward as the leader of the minority. At the time of which we are speaking, Canon Dixon must have been on the opposite side, as he was then a Methodist. Heeley and Macdonald were also of Methodist families and attended the chapels of the sect. But Dixon and Edward both used to go together to Dr. Gifford's Sunday afternoon Greek Testament classes, where attendance was voluntary, and often, when the class was over, they prolonged the time together by walking up and down New Street, talking and arguing as they went. Edward seems to have been particularly anxious to win over his friend to his own point of view, as some of those who thought with him were boys with whom he had no other link, and whom he was reluctantly obliged to consider, as he said, "rather foolish."

There is a story of his asking Dixon to go with him to the theatre one evening, unconscious or thoughtless of the fact that Methodists did not go there. The engagement was made, and Dixon's mother, who was a woman of character and determination, and, I believe, considerable learning, regarded it as an evil thing. She was unhappy about it, and carried her anxiety for her son so far as to urge that if he went she should go also. "My dear mother wished to go with me, but did not persist," Canon Dixon gently writes. From another source I learnt that she walked with her boy to the place of meeting, in order to see what the tempter was like, and after looking at him left the two together.

The regular yearly stay at Harris Bridge ceased when his Aunt and Uncle Catherwood began to claim Edward in London for the summer holidays. But before this change came about he had one day, while staying at the farm, gone over to see the Cistercian Monastery in Charnwood Forest, some eight miles away, and nothing can exaggerate the impression that the visit made upon his mind. Though it is doubtful whether he ever saw the place again with his bodily eyes, the thought of it accompanied him through his whole life. Friends, wife, and children all knew the under-current of longing in his soul for the rest and peace which he thought he had seen there that day; he did not disguise it from them, and in his later years often spoke of the dream which had walked step by step with him ever since, of some day leaving every one and everything and entering its doors and closing them behind him.

On the subject of religious "experience" or of his religious faith, he was silent, and even shocked by what he thought to be any opinion too rigidly or confidently expressed by others. Once I heard him quote with approval the saying of a Samoan chief to a missionary who was pressing him hard as to his conceptions of a Deity: "We know that at night Some One goes by amongst the trees, but we never speak of it." This, however, was in his maturity; as a young man we have proof that he was ready to submit to the formulae of the wisdom of the Church which he venerated, and at one time almost to lay both flesh and spirit in the hands of its priests.

CHAPTER IV

PREPARATION
1851-1852

IN the autumn of 1850, at the Annual Conference of the Wesleyan Methodists, one of their ministers named George Browne Macdonald was appointed to a "Circuit" in Birmingham. He had been for the last three years at Huddersfield, and by the constitution of the Society no minister may stay longer than that time with the same congregation. This rule weighs heavily upon the families of ministers, if not upon themselves, and the list of appointments made by the Conference Stationing Committee is waited for with excitement in the households which, according to its decision, must go North, South, East, or West, whether they like it or not. In this instance the verdict of "Birmingham" gave satisfaction, because in the chances of the itinerancy the Macdonalds had once lived there before, and even though after nine years they might not return to the same circuit, still they would find old friends in the town. During their first stay in Birmingham they had lived not far from Bennett's Hill—for part of the time in a street so near as to be a continuation of it—but nothing ever brought the church-going family and the Methodist one together, and the girl-baby whom they carried away with them when they left was not more ignorant of any meeting to come in the future than the wisest of them all. This time their house was in quite another part of Birmingham, and, so far as one can see, the two families would never have known anything of each other, but that my father removed his eldest son from Wesley College, Sheffield, and brought him home in order to attend

King Edward's School. Harry was admitted there at once, and took his place in the same class with Cormell Price. This change of plan, which seemed at first sight to concern our brother only, proved to be of great importance to his sisters.

The name of Wilfred Heeley has already been mentioned as one of Edward's new acquaintance in the Classical School. His parents were amongst the old friends in Birmingham whom our father and mother had most looked forward to seeing again, and the children of both families felt an inherited liking for each other. Wilfred was often at our house, soon becoming a special friend of my brother Harry, taking also much notice of us younger children. He was a tall youth of about eighteen, and according to the fashion of the time, still in jackets: his talk was always witty and always kind, but a certain shyness and big-boy clumsiness made him occasionally the victim of the little girls to whom he was so indulgent. He could at all times express himself best in writing, and, as he found we enjoyed it, used to amuse himself and please us with writing notes at school and sending them by our brother as postman to one or other of the sisters. These notes have never been destroyed, and are still fresh and charming as when the ink was wet upon them. What he said and wrote lit up a new world for us who, as girls, in those days had small chances of education. It is true we were sent to the usual "Young Ladies' School," or a daily governess came to us, but few fresh ideas reached us in that way, whilst Wilfred's talk was different from anything we had known before, and our intelligence was stimulated by his taking it for granted that we should understand him. Our father, a born lover and student of books, and an efficient help to the studies of his sons, had not time also to direct those of his daughters, for preaching engagements carried him from home most of the week, and Sundays were occupied by services in his own chapel. His library of more than a thousand volumes travelled about with us, each book packed every three years by our mother's careful hands;

but the bulk of it, works on Divinity, was not for us. Upon early numbers of the Arminian and Methodist Magazines and of the Edinburgh Review we browsed freely; Shakespeare was forbidden; Quarles' Emblems and the Pilgrim's Progress were put into our hands; the Robin Hood Ballads we ferretted out from a bottom shelf; and a copy of Grimm's Household Stories, sent to us from outside, made us free of fairyland: but of systematic reading we knew nothing. The Bible was read aloud every day at morning prayers and we heard our father preach from the pulpit; religious instruction at home he left to our mother. Nevertheless he made us feel that he loved us, and by example deeply impressed on us the love of truth and the duty of charitable speech and judgment about others. When our sharp young tongues erred in this respect he would be uneasy, and sometimes make us aware of his disapproval by interrupting the conversation with a sudden question asked across it, such as, "What is the price of potatoes?" which we understood clearly enough. His unworldliness was great. Our mother, though always delicate in health, ruled her large family firmly and gently in his frequent absence, which left her almost as lonely as a widow in the struggles of daily life; but her difficulties were not mentioned to us, and it never occurred to me as a child to think whether we were rich or poor.

Three months after my brother entered King Edward's School, Fulford left it for Oxford. I have said that he was Heeley's friend, but as yet we had heard nothing about him, nor do I think that at this time Harry knew anything of Edward. The next year, however, found them within two places of each other in the same class.

During Edward's last years at school, and whilst he was feeling his way so eagerly in every direction, he made a new acquaintance (I think through his friends the Comptons) whose influence upon him was for a time very marked. This was Mr. J. W. Caldicott, an old Birmingham School boy, who had matriculated in 1846 at Pembroke College, Oxford. Later on he was many years Head Master of Bristol

Grammar School. At the time he and Edward first met he was an ardent Tractarian, a pleasant and able man, clear-headed, and gifted with remarkable keenness and subtlety in argument. Edward liked him very much, and for a time was quite fascinated by his skill as a disputant. It was under Mr. Caldicott's influence that even before leaving school he devoted himself heart and soul to the study of logic, whilst during the time between his matriculation and his going into residence at Oxford, Mr. Price says that he had "a perfect rage for logic and metaphysics." Philosophy and religious polemics were largely read at the same time, indeed, I have often heard him say that he did all the reading on these subjects necessary for Oxford before he went there.

Canon Dixon says that at school "his books seemed neater than others, and superior altogether. He had a way of filling them with finely written notes. He used to bring up to class a copy of the Corpus Poetarum Latinorum, and another of the Poetae Scenici Graeci, which often made me envious, for it shewed his comprehensive spirit. He had, I know, the notion of reading them all through. I had the same notion myself—that of reading all that there was to read. He had a book of English Ballads"—of which we have heard before—"with engravings which fascinated me. I rather think he made a design for one himself, the terrible demon ride, 'Tramp, tramp, across the land they speed,' etc. I asked him once if he believed in witches. He answered, 'I should like very much to do so.' That seems a characteristic saying. He once read aloud a comic or burlesque ballad called Sir Eppo (I think) in a way that I shall never forget."

The school library, says Mr. Price, was a blessed institution to the upper boys, who could not only take out volumes for home reading, but were tacitly allowed to prepare their work there too to some extent. "We used to pass into it through a door to the right of the Head Master as he sat. He never checked our withdrawal during preparation time, and I have no doubt he winked or connived at the liberty we took, for we found quietude there (and genial warmth in winter) and books of reference. We often abused his concession by indulging in the lighter literature of the shelves as soon as we fancied we could pass muster in the lesson in hand." Canon Dixon also writes: "We spent many blissful hours there, the lessons not the only occupation." It was from this seclusion that Wilfred Heeley wrote to us children.

Amongst the books in a catalogue of the library for 1851 are many that Edward always liked. Layard's Nineveh, Catlin's Indians, Curzon's Monasteries of the Levant, and Lockhart's Scott are of the number. It is certain that he read much English poetry, and Shakespeare, Coleridge, Byron and Scott he knew early; it was from Dixon that he first heard of Keats, possibly in one of the "blissful hours." Tennyson's Poems and his In Memoriam are catalogued, and were probably read in the school copy, as I do not think Edward had them himself until Morris gave them to him at Oxford. Lane's Arabian Nights, which he did not possess, much as he loved it, till many years afterwards, is entered, and could not have been missed by him. His passion was at all times for a tale that was told rather than for the drama in any form, and in middle life I have heard him say that it was almost an impossibility for him to read a play.

Amongst novelists Scott and Dickens were his first heroes. Thackeray came later, but for stories generally Mr. Price says he was "omnivorous." Humboldt's Cosmos and Views of Nature he read, and followed with imaginative interest the vast schemes with which they deal. Astronomy had a great fascination for him—almost a terrible one. It was not at school that he met with Newman's Sermons, but, as we have seen, very probably at Hereford, where, after his own way, he had quietly absorbed them—eating and passing on in the strength of the food. How deeply they affected him may be seen from the following words written to an intimate friend at least thirty years afterwards.

"When I was fifteen or sixteen he [Newman] taught me so much I do mind—things that will never be out of me. In an age of sofas and cushions he taught me to be indifferent to comfort, and in an age of materialism he taught me to venture all on the unseen, and this so early that it was well in me when life began, and I was equipped before I went to Oxford with a real good panoply and it has never failed me. So if this world cannot tempt me with money or luxury—and it can't—or anything it has in its trumpery treasure-house, it is most of all because he said it in a way that touched me, not scolding nor forbidding, nor much leading—walking with me a step in front. So he stands to me as a great image or symbol of a man who never stooped, and who put all this world's life in one splendid venture, which he knew as well as you or I might fail, but with a glorious scorn of every thing that was not his dream."

The summer visits to London continued regularly, and with ever increasing affection between Edward and his aunt. Towards her he stood more nearly in the position of a son than any one else did in her life.

Once when staying with her he met her brother-in-law, Mr. Frederick Catherwood, who chanced to be in England at the time. Antiquary, geographer and draughtsman, he touched Edward closely on three sides at once. He had roamed much in his youth, had visited Karnak and Baalbec, and risked his life when at Jerusalem by entering the Mosque of Omar in disguise. His explorations also, in Central America, with the drawings he had made there of the ruined remains of a dead civilization, interested Edward deeply. A letter from the traveller to his sister-in-law, Mrs. James Catherwood, dated San Francisco, April, 1853, says: "Give my regards to Edward when you write to him. I felt very much obliged to him for his attention in coming to meet me at the railway station at Birmingham. I have no doubt he will distinguish himself at Oxford if he can but keep in health. If he were here he would have abundance of employment for pencil and pen with our motley population, representing, I believe, every nation under the sun." But this promising friendship was ended on a day next year when the American steamship "Arctic" went down off Newfoundland in collision with the French "Vesta," and more than three hundred lives were lost.

Mr. Catherwood left three children, and his eldest daughter, whom Edward always regarded as a cousin, has told me of the unusual impression made upon herself and her sister by the nephew of her new aunt, Mrs. James Catherwood. "We saw very little of him," she says, "as he only came to town in the summer and we never stayed in the house together, but we were always wonderfully interested in him. We were shewn all his letters, so unlike any others we had ever seen; and how Lizzie and I looked forward to reading them every six months when we came to spend a rather awe-inspiring week in that childless home. Auntie revelled in our undisguised admiration. In one thing she was perfect, and that was her love for him." Miss Catherwood has also given me a letter that Edward wrote to her during his visit to London in 1850, addressed to the boarding school at Hornsey where she lived when her father was abroad. She had been staying with Mrs. Catherwood at North Addington Place just before he came up, and had left behind her "foure articles of luxurie"—after the fashion of visitors. In January of that year, he had signed a note "Archbishop of Canterbury elect"; now he has become "Cardinal." The letter is addressed "To her most Celestial Highness, ye Ladye Annie Catherwood," and rattles away gaily with—

"May it please your ladyshippe, having been deputed by ye Ladye Catherwood, Countesse of Addingtoune, to advise you concerning sundrie articles of wearinge apparelle, appertaining to Hornsie Universitie, your humble servante hath presumed to address this epistle, beinge dulie impressed with the responsibilitie of the tasque, the michtie honor done thereby to your humble servant, and his own insufficiencie, whereof I do most humblie crave your ladyshippe's favor and mercie, inasmuch as your servante hath hitherto confined himself to less honorable persuits than that of beinge a ladye's scribe.

"The following epistle is by the commande of our ladye addressed to you.

"Keturah, To oure loyalle and liege subject, Annie, greetynge.

"Forasmuch as after diligent search made throughout our domains, and all thereunto appertaininge, onlie two of the foure articles of luxurie (whereof we were by you advised) have been discovered, it hath seemed good to our royalle person, at the instance of our secretarie Edouard, Cardinal de Byrmynghame, to send you timelie warnynge thereof to the ende that summarie measures be forthwith taken by you for the reclaiming of them. Given under our hand, at our palace of Addington this 8th day of June. A. S. H. 1850."

Then follows a postscript by the Cardinal himself:

"Your highnesse seeth by this letter that no opportunitie hath beene lost by your devoted servants at this Castle in obeyinge your behests, and that our labours have but partiallie beene rewarded. The two articles of luxurie afore alluded to are

"1st. a curiouslie wrought piece of mechanism, the worke of some craftie sorcerer or other artist—the use whereof is to us unknowe. Some indeed have idlie saide it to be a trinket, brooch or other article of wearynge apparel, but it seemyth rather to be Camel-hair pencil or other implement wherewith painters do exercise theire mysteriouse arte. Its form is somewhat thus

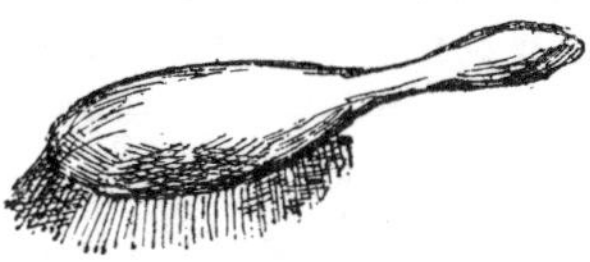

"2ndlie a still more ingenious craftworke, if indeed it be the worke of man, howbeit some here do suppose it to be the upper jaw and teeth of ye Sea-Serpent or other monstre—but concernynge this we knowe nothynge.

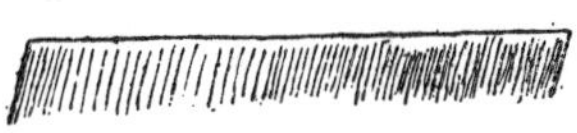

"These articles shall without fail be forwarded in whatever manner shall seem most expediente by oure Ladye, perchance our trustie and right beloved friend Count Frederick [her brother] may transport them. Praying pardon for my audacitie in addressynge you,

"Your faithful, right-trustie and liege servante
"EDOUARD CARDINAL DE BYRMYNGHAM."

The extreme ease with which he wrote is evident from this long spinning of much out of little, but he himself would never allow that he had any turn for writing. In later life he disliked the mechanical act. "I naturally draw," he said, "when I've a pen in my hand," but at first it must have been different, for during the Oxford time Fulford mentions a letter of his said to have been eighteen sheets long.

There is little record left of his home life in these years. He always spoke of it with the tenderness that comes after a time is over, but not as if he would have recalled a day. Both he and his father must have been infinitely lonely at heart in spite of the love that was between them, and as he grew up, though Miss Sampson's devotion never flagged, she was puzzled by him, and jealous of his new friendships. If he brought any one home she was delighted, but if he went out to see any one she was miserable. The very simple way in which they lived prevented the possibility of set entertainments, but so far as it could go the hospitality of the house was perfect. His health remained always just short of strength, and fatigue followed every exertion: I have heard him say that he hardly knew what it was not to be tired. In spite of this, however, his spirits were often high, and his endless sense of humour blessed both him and his companions. His temper was heaven's gift of daily sweetness, though, as Canon Dixon says, he was evidently lord of the home domain.

Somewhere about the end of 1851 Mr. Jones took a house in the Bristol Road, a wide thoroughfare leading quickly into the country, and went to live there for the sake of better air and daily exercise in walking to and from business. The upper part of the Bennett's Hill house was now let for offices, whilst he retained only his own workshop and showroom on the ground floor. No. 1, Poplar Place, Bristol Road, was a small house with a good-sized garden, and this was a great pleasure to Miss Sampson, who was by birth a country woman. But it was not really country life, only suburban, and even in order for them to have that, a portion of the little house had to be let to a "Single Gentleman," and there was no study left for Edward. He still continued to sleep in a narrow bed in his father's room. Christmas Day they always spent together, not necessarily alone, or in their own house, but together, wherever it was. A custom grew up of their joining the Prices, or being joined by them, and on Edward's birthday, also, when it was possible, the two families met.

After Christmas of this year he went to spend part of the holidays at Hereford, and a letter to Mr. Price with the date of January 24th, 1852, shews how happy he found himself there:

"Land of Caradoc,
"Banks of the Wye.

"Dear old Crom,

"You scamp not to write before; here I've been expecting a long, brilliant effusion of your scribbling powers, with a fine poetic description of your peregrinations, and you favour me with the 'skinny' affair lying before me—and now I'll be revenged. If you have enjoyed yourself $\frac{1}{10,000,000}$ part as much as I have you have been in Elysium.

"The morning sun is just up as I emerge from the blankets, the hills of Wales mantled in snow lie beyond, and the meandering Wye flows between us. So soon as bound in cloth I wander by the banks of the lovely river, or round the Castle Green, get into a romantic fit, think how happy we should be together learning Welch, then bolt indoors and bolt my breakfast. This is about the third hour of the day; the next two hours are spent in sweet converse or reading (not Thucydides) and by this time it is Cathedral time, and for an hour I am in Paradise. Oh that you could be with me then! From 12—3, I wander about the country, in the most romantic holes you can imagine, from 3—4 Cathedral, 4—8 occupied, I am sorry to say, in eating and talking, dinner and tea. Then my reading hours commence, and I never think of going to bed before 1—2 or 3, or even later. Parties are horrible things, but I have endured two—Bacchus preserve me from them: girls are such—hm—hang 'em, they do quiz so, and I make such a capital subject.

"By the bye, how have you got on with the Fasti? I haven't done a line yet, and am not going home at present.

"Perhaps on Tuesday I shall leave; passing through Malvern I shall get to Worcester by one o'clock. I have some idea of seeing the Cathedral. I would have sent you a long interesting letter if you had behaved like a gentleman to me—but as it is, goodbye.

"Yours + CANTUAR."

The name he gives to the place from which he writes, "Land of Caradoc," shows how alive the world was to him with legend. He may already have been touched by a foreshadowing of the San Graal story in that of the saint who, shortly before his death, saw two men in glittering stoles enter the church bearing a golden altar between them, on which was written, "Follow us, we have meat to eat thou knowest not of."

There is another letter from Hereford, but undated, which gives the same impression of contentment.

During the first "half" of 1852 some prizes were offered by old pupils upon the occasion of the tercentenary of the foundation of the school. One of these was for essays on the State of Literature in England in the time of Edward the Sixth, and for it Edward and Dixon, together with others, competed. The first prize was taken by Dixon, and for the second Edward was equal with a boy named Valentine. Canon Dixon's reverent mind recalls the time with undimmed interest after many years, in these words: "That Tercentenary was a great day with us all: a great day for Birmingham." Dixon himself took this year, not for the first time, the annual prize for English verse. Between Edward and Valentine there was another "tie," where an exhibition was in question, and the decision was so long delayed—the examiners referring it to Oxford, and Oxford sending it back again to Birmingham—that when it was finally given in Valentine's favour, Edward had already matriculated, his father having determined to send him to Oxford at his own expense.

It was in the early part of this same year that Edward first came to our house, aptly situated in "Nursery" Terrace, Handsworth. The visit was to my brother, and, naturally enough, Cormell Price came also. The exact day on which this happened is forgotten, but not the visit. Edward was then in his nineteenth year, and of his full height; to me he looked a grown man because he wore a coat, but I believe there was in fact an early maturity about him. His aspect made the deepest impression upon me. Rather tall and very thin, though not especially slender, straightly built and with wide shoulders. Extremely pale he was, with the paleness that belongs to fair-haired people, and looked delicate, but not ill. His hair was perfectly straight, and of a colourless kind. His eyes were light grey (if their colour could be defined in words), and the space that their setting took up under his brow was extraordinary: the nose quite right in proportion, but very individual in outline, and a mouth large and well moulded, the lips meeting with absolute sweetness and repose. The shape of his head was domed, and noticeable for its even balance; his forehead, wide and rather high, was smooth and calm, and the line of the brow over the eyes was a fine one. From the eyes themselves power simply radiated, and as he talked and listened, if anything moved him, not only his eyes but his whole face seemed lit up from within. I learned afterwards that he had an immoveable conviction that he was hopelessly plain. His ordinary manner was shy, but not self-conscious, for it gave the impression that he noticed everything. At that time he sat as many men do who are not very strong, sunk down rather low in his chair with an appearance of the whole spine seeking for rest.

At once his power of words struck me and his vehemence. He was easily stirred, and then his speech was as swift and clear as possible, yet well ordered and going straight to the mark. He had a beautiful voice. He seldom came to our house, and I can only clearly remember his doing so three times. The first time I have mentioned, and I think it was then that he astonished me by his demeanour to my youngest sister, a child about three years old, whom he took between his knees and looked at intently, pulling strange faces to amuse her. Evidently he was unaccustomed to children and did not know how to deal with them, for when she was frightened he was surprised.

The second time I remember his coming, my brother was not at home, nor any of the elders, and I, a child in a pinafore, received the message that he left. The last time was when he came to say good-bye to us when our three years in Birmingham were over, and we were going to London. Again I noticed his eloquence when excited. Epithets he always used wonderfully. It was at this last visit, I think, that some one mentioned the name of a certain girl and said of her that she was a "flirt." At the word his face lit up suddenly, and without raising his voice at all he said with the utmost distinctness and volubility: "A flirt's a beast, a bad beast, a vile beast, a wicked beast, a repulsive beast, an owl, a ghoul, a bat, a vampire." And as we sat amazed at the rush of words the usual placid expression returned to his mouth. To him my brother once applied in my hearing the dreadful-sounding name "Misogynist," which, when translated, filled me with admiration and awe. The "chatter" of women had evidently struck him very much, for he denounced it in one of the visits mentioned, muttering to himself under his breath:

Hear the ladies when they talk; tittle tattle, tittle tattle,
Like their pattens when they walk; pittle pattle, pittle pattle.

By this time we had come, through Wilfred Heeley, to know Fulford. We little girls liked and admired him very much, and he was very kind to us. He was the first person we had ever heard read poetry aloud, and admirably he did it, with his fine voice and fervent love of what he read. He had an endless interest in expounding the poets, and naturally found his readiest disciples amongst the girls whom he knew. Towards us he shewed a judgment for which I can never be thankful enough, for he fed us with Longfellow first of all, as the food suitable for our years, and so brought us gradually into a condition more or less fit for the revelation before introducing us to the works of his prime hero Tennyson. It seemed quite natural to us that he should write poetry himself. He loved music, also, and taught us the names and some of the works of Beethoven and Mendelssohn. He was a small man, well and strongly made, and very careful about his dress; not handsome, but when he was happy delightful expressions would pass over his face; his laugh was very taking when it came. There was, for a time, an engagement between him and one of my sisters, and we all especially appreciated the fact that it did not make him neglect the rest of us, but that he still fetched the little ones for walks, or to take tea with him in a comforting way.

He had a personal hero of his own who was not one of the Set, a man named Whitehouse, whom we had never seen. He went up to Pembroke as Senior Exhibitioner from King Edward's School the year before Fulford himself, who expected great things from him. His enthusiasm for this friend was distilled through his mind into ours, and I remember feeling sad that nothing came to justify it before the world.

There was a tradition in King Edward's School, which had distinguished itself so brilliantly at Cambridge, that the few men who chose Oxford for their University should go to Pembroke, because of its Master, Dr. Jeune, having been head of the Birmingham School; but Edward's name was already down for Exeter, and on June 1st, 1852, he presented himself there for matriculation. His friend, Mr. Caldicott, welcomed him to Oxford, and that took away some of the strangeness of the place.

At the end of the first day's examination Edward wrote a note to his father—the image of the lonely, anxious little figure at home could not be laid without it—but the handwriting is scarcely recognizable and excitement is visible in every word. It is dated from Mr. Caldicott's rooms.

"Jesus Col: Tuesday evn.

"Dr father,

"I have not time to say much now—I have passed, but [undecipherable words] were plucked. Mr. Caldicott has been excessive[ly] kind to me. We have just been on the Isis—it is so jolly. But I hardly think I can come down to-morrow—think it must be Thursday first, because to-morrow I have to matriculate. This morning I was in the Schools from 9—4 and shall have to return to-morrow but don't know what time.

"Oxford is glorious!!! And the weather has been magnificent. You must excuse me writing more now, as I am keeping a party from whist.

"Your affect: son

"Edward Jones.

"Love to Sam."

It is all clear—the kind elder host, the fulfilled dream of the place, the summer evening and the whist table, the outsider's name, too, of "Isis" for the upper Thames, marking the novice as clearly as his eager face and manner must have done. A second day in the schools and all was well over: the certificate of his matriculation, dated June 2nd, 1852, lies before me.

He had hoped to go into residence in October, but the College was so full that he was obliged to wait for the Hilary term of 1853. Thus the time between the end of his school life and the following January became his own.

We have seen what Mr. Price says of his course of reading in these months—logic, metaphysics, philosophy, and religious polemics—but *durum et durum non facit murum*, and books of poetry, romance, and devotion were the mortar between the bricks in the rising walls of the house of his life.

Other things also occupied him, the friendships and the mirth of youth, and anxiety about ways and means. And there was a serious illness, the most acute one he ever had, which lasted some weeks.

A pleasant arrangement for the two friends was made that year, when Cormell Price, whose parents had removed to West Bromwich, came to live within a few minutes' walk of Poplar Place. He also was to enter the Church, but in order that he should be able to compete for an exhibition which would send him to college, he was obliged to remain in Birmingham, so a small house was taken for him in Upper Sun Street, and two of his sisters came there to make him a home. The evenings at their house soon became a centre of simple enjoyment. Mrs. Grove, one of the sisters, has told me about them. Fulford, Dixon, Macdonald and others used to meet there. Edward, she says, was the brightest of companions, full of fun, a wonderful imitator, and his laughter always ready. Sometimes he would laugh till he slid down from his chair to the floor and rolled there, holding himself together. He used to preach sermons exactly like various clergymen they knew (Mr. Casebow Barrett amongst the number) and destroy them with amusement. Or he and Cormell would do Grisi and Mario, Cormell being Mario, and playing the accompaniment, while Edward was Grisi, and the two would work each other up into wild fun.

Long years afterwards the same spirit came upon him occasionally as he sat painting in his studio, when he would burst into sudden recitative, and address most commonplace remarks to his daughter in a florid Italian *bravura* style, which she, as a matter of course, would answer in an impassioned flight of song with equally dull words—and so they would go on together till both broke down with laughter. The earlier operas of Gilbert and Sullivan were naturally delightful to him when they came out, being exactly on these lines.

He recovered completely from his illness, and regained his usual health, the state of which always depended greatly upon that of his spirits. His expectations about Oxford were high, and he breathed freely in the atmosphere of enthusiasm. When the New Year came he was ready, and by the middle of January, 1853, he found himself in the city of his hopes.

CHAPTER V

1853

As in water face answereth to face, so the heart of man to man.

IN Oxford Edward found much that he had never expected, but not the thing for which he looked. He had believed that help and strength for the life he had chosen must await him in the University which had so lately been the centre of a great religious movement. Newman's simple and lofty exhortations had sunk into his heart, and created there such belief in the writer as to make even the secession to Rome seem an act upon which it was impossible to pass judgment, and which time alone could shew whether he himself might not feel bound to follow. He had thought to find the place still warm from the fervour of the learned and pious men who had shaken the whole land by their cry of danger within and without the Church. To him it was like a room from which some one he loved had just gone out, and where at every turn he would find traces of his friend. But when he got there the whole life seemed to him languid and indifferent, with scarcely anything left to shew the fiery time so lately past. In his disappointment he turned around, seeking his way in unlooked for loneliness of spirit, and there, shoulder to shoulder, stood his life's companion.

They had met the year before, when they were both up for matriculation, and even sat side by side in the hall of Exeter, but had not spoken to each other. Edward recognized him now, because at that time he had been struck by the appearance of his neighbour, and had noticed also that he finished a Horace paper early in the morning, and folded it and wrote upon it the name of "William Morris."

Then they drifted apart again until the College should have room to receive them. It was still overfull, however, when they were called, so that for the first two terms they had to lodge out by day, and could only sleep in College by using the third room of men upon whom they were quartered.

There was no one at Exeter to begin with whom Edward knew, even by sight, except Morris, so that a large field for possible friendships lay before him; but in some notes made by him after his friend's death, Edward says: "One by one, for one cause or another, I dropped apart from my contemporaries there, and by a fortnight's end it seemed settled that Morris and I only would be companions. We went almost daily walks together, but gloomy and angry disappointment and disillusion were settling down upon me in this first term's experience of Oxford. It was clear we had lighted on a distasteful land in our choice of College. So at Exeter we were very isolated, and before many weeks were past there were but three or four men in the whole College whom we visited or spoke to."

There is a short paragraph before the notes from which I quote, in which Edward explains that some dates given in them may need to be corrected, for they were made without any written help to memory, and that as almost all letters had been destroyed and no kind of diary ever kept, the first years of Oxford life flowed together in his mind. Some of his own letters, however, have been preserved, which mark facts or states of feeling during that time, and these I shall use in addition to the notes, in their proper order so far as possible. The first letter I find this year is one written on the 29th January, just before going in for "Smalls."

To face the worse of two possibilities was always his instinct, as is here seen at the end of a letter of which the greater part was evidently meant only to cheer and amuse his father.

"I am compelled," he begins, "to write sooner and more briefly than I intended, for I find that I must have left the testamur of my matriculation at home, and on Tuesday Mor[ng] it will be required. The key of my writing desk is enclosed; if anywhere you will find it in the top division, a very small insignificant piece of paper, but of the greatest importance. If you hear but a very short account of me for a fortnight you must not notice it—I am in the schools, and it will be a case of Oxford or Van Dieman's Land. Tell me all you know of home affairs, about Sam, and everyone: don't give me any advice above all things: and send me a paper now and then. In return for all these I may graciously inform you of my health and estate, the former is increasing rapidly, the latter decreasing alarmingly, for Oxford is beginning to unfold *his* charms, and I to appreciate them, so you must not be surprised at some heavy calls upon your bank presently: such as the following.

E. Jones, Esq.	£	*s.*	*d.*
Horse too hours a day for six days . . .	3	4	0
Tandem an pair to Woodstock an back with leader's kney broke and trappins likeways	5	10	6
Dogcart to Abbingdon with sharves all broke reglarly to shatters	2	19	0
	11	13	6
Discount allowed for ready money			2
	11	13	4

E. C. Jones, Esqr.		
12 doz. Madeira £2 2 per doz.	25	4
3 doz. Claret £3 per doz.	9	
2 doz. Champagne £3 10	7	
(*sic*)	31	4

Tailors' bills and boating I've not put down, they would take up too much room.

"Oxford is a glorious place; godlike! at night I have walked round the colleges under the full moon, and thought it would be heaven to live and die here. The Dons are so terribly majestic, and the men are men, in spirit as well as name—they seem overflowing with generosity and good-nature; and their pride seldom ascends to haughtiness, or descends to vanity. I wonder how the examiners ever have the heart to pluck such men. Nevertheless I should like to see home and all there, and before this term is over, I shall long to see them. My purgatory will last three weeks or a month, if I am plucked you will see me directly, preparatory to leaving England. I assure you this is no joking, the chances are at most but equal, and if the catastrophe comes I couldn't honourably pursue my course here."

The purgatory did not last quite three weeks, as his certificate is dated February 17th.

Cormell wrote to congratulate him upon this, and received a letter in reply that must have astonished him. It is written with a half-comic assumption of age and experience, and almost all that Cormell had said is commented upon point by point, as if the writer were glad to treat of any subject rather than his own feelings; but towards the end a forecast upon which his friend had ventured, that Sewell and Gresley would one day be made bishops, produces a few stinging words that shew something of what was at work in his mind.

"Sewell and Gresley will never be made bishops," he says; "you entirely mistake the nature of an English bishop if you think that good or clever or progress men stand the least chance before the state ideal of episcopacy. I get touchy on these points since I have seen a little more of the world—a *very* little more, you will say, but enough to disenchant a good deal of my quondam notions. Ask Fulford, we talk of nothing else night and day. He slangs and I growl, and Faulkner demonstrates, and Dixon translates himself into the seventh heaven of poetry—but stay, these are University secrets.

"I shall see you in a fortnight and shall be better able

to tell you what I think of matters than by letter. I am not reading a scrap, being almost always at Pembroke, for my mind is made up to go in for a pass and leave the first hour I can. How beautifully these lines scan—Moore's metre. Ah, well, I'm wretched, Crom, miserable: stop down if you can till 1860.

"Remember me very kindly to your sisters, and old chums at school. Don't say a word to any one about my growling here—the morals of the place must be respected."

Being "almost always at Pembroke" is important. Edward speaks in his notes of a little Birmingham colony already formed at that College when he went up, which Morris and he used to join when they sought for more company than their own. The nucleus of the colony consisted of Fulford, Dixon, and Faulkner, the last hitherto unknown to Edward. His rooms on the ground floor, in a corner of the old quadrangle of Pembroke, stood invitingly ready for men to turn into, and there, about nine o'clock most evenings of the week, the friends met. In the daytime Edward and Morris generally walked together into the country or about the city.

"It was a different Oxford in those days," he says, "from anything that a visitor would now dream of. On all sides, except where it touched the railway, the city ended abruptly, as if a wall had been about it, and you came suddenly upon the meadows. There was little brick in the city, it was either grey with stone or yellow with the wash of the pebble-dash in the poorer streets. It was an endless delight to us to wander about the streets, where were still many old houses with wood carving and a little sculpture here and there. The Chapel of Merton College had been lately renovated by Butterfield, and Pollen, a former Fellow of Merton, had painted the roof of it. Many an afternoon we spent in that chapel. Indeed I think the buildings of Merton and the Cloisters of New College were our chief shrines in Oxford."

Dixon, who had been up a term already, says that he

remembers being taken by Morris "to look at the Tower of Merton."

And not only did their love for art bind Morris and Edward to each other especially, but in religious feeling also they lived a separate life, for the Pembroke set had little interest in the Church polemics which at that time so engrossed the two friends. In this matter they met with greater sympathy from a few men of their own College, with whom, having discovered a common ground, they eagerly conversed upon doctrinal points.

Faulkner, Edward's new friend, was a powerful man, physically, mentally, and morally. Unlike any of the others, his gift was for mathematics and physical science, while his remoteness from things theological was complete. There was about him a special manliness, singleness of mind, and fearless honesty. He had great natural skill of hand and sympathy with the executive side of art, but no power of design so far as I know.

In all the happiness of his first intercourse with Morris, Edward remembered the absent Cormell, and tried, so far as letters would do it, to keep him abreast with the new life in which he found himself. On May 1st he writes: "I am well pleased that our taste in poetics is concurrent. If Tennyson affords you as many hours of unmitigated happiness—I speak without affectation here—as he has to me, you will look with gratitude to any who helped you to appreciate him. When I take up the works of any other poet, save Shakespeare only, I seem to have fallen from the only guide worth following far into dreamland. There are some passages here and there so strangely accordant to that unutterable feeling which comes on one like a seizure at certain times, and which Schlegel writes of under the term 'Sighing after the Infinite,' that it is sometimes an inexpressible relief to know and be able to utter them aloud, as if the poet had, in an inspiration, hit upon some Runic words to give voice and form to what were otherwise painfully ineffable. Of these I think one song in the Princess is remarkable. 'Tears, idle tears, I know not what they mean,' is of this kind. In some hot dreamy afternoons I have thought upon it for hours, until I have been exquisitely miserable. Our old favourite, the 'Bugle Song,' is another, and incidental passages over all the poems are of the same strange nature.

"In answer to your question I understand '(dreary) gleams' to be a substantive in apposition to 'curlews.' I know nothing of the flight of curlews, but you may take Tennyson's word for it, they 'gleam.'

"If you can get hold of a book called 'Poems by Alexander Smith,' read them by all means. He is a very promising poet indeed, and his objective writing is almost incomparable, although his aim is evidently more subjective and metaphysical. There, however, are depths only reached by one—our great Dramatist. Smith is a very young man, and strange to say his work has met with most flattering reviews in all the leading dodges—cf. Westminster especially. I bought it the other day, and so enraptured Fulford that he dashed off and got one directly. By the bye, he is in the Schools on Thursday next—pray for his success.

"Yesterday my uncle Catherwood came up to see me; so I am in for a few days lionizing.

"10 o'clock, evening. I have just been amusing myself by pouring basons of water on the crowd below from Dixon's garret, such fun, by Jove.

"Macdonald one of the lapsed!! 'Good Evans!' as —— says, can it be? Poor fellow, I pity him from the innermost recesses of my heart. Don't let him influence you, Crom. Remember, I have set my heart on our founding a Brotherhood. Learn Sir Galahad by heart. He is to be the patron of our Order. I have enlisted *one* in the project up here, heart and soul. You shall have a copy of the canons some day.

"(Signed) General of the Order of Sir Galahad."

This outburst of enthusiasm about Tennyson was not spasmodic, but represents, broadly speaking, what Edward felt first and last; for if at any time the poet ever wrote what he valued less, the glorious gifts before received were still returned to with fresh gratitude. Some words written after the death of Tennyson in 1892 may fitly go with these of so many years before. The undertaker element of the funeral in Westminster Abbey had jarred him to the quick, and he breaks out: "O but yesterday was so flat and flattening. I'll never forgive the Queen for not coming up to it, and I wish Gladstone had. And there should have been street music, some soldiers and some trumpets, and bells muffled all over London, and rumbling drums. I did hate it so heartily, but as he sleeps by Chaucer I daresay they woke and had nice talks in the night, and I have spent much of the early dark morning making up talks for them; I suppose he'll be hurrying off to Virgil soon. I wish I hadn't gone."

The mention of a "Brotherhood" sounds as if the idea of it had been cherished for some time, but Mr. Price does not remember its being named before the Oxford days. There is no doubt that in the beginning Edward hoped to form amongst his friends a small conventual society of cleric and lay members working in the heart of London, such as that suggested in Hurrell Froude's Project for the Revival of Religion in Great Towns, and in this restricted scheme the Pembroke set never took any part. The "one" enlisted in the project was of course Morris.

This visit of Mr. Catherwood's was the last time he and Edward met. Before the end of the month that kind uncle and friend was dead.

Another letter to Mr. Price continues the subject of the curlew-verse in Locksley Hall which had been a puzzle to Cormell, but of which Edward's sense of light and shade at once made a clear picture.

"Mine is the last edition but one and reads:

> 'Tis the place and all around it, as of old the curlews call,
> Dreary gleams about the moorland, flying over Locksley Hall.

I repeat my explanations—'dreary gleams' is in apposition to 'curlews.'

. . . . . as of old the curlews call,
Dreary gleams (are they) about the moorland, etc.

Dreary, because prognosticating the coming storm—gleams, because their flight, thrown in relief by the dark background of the sky, is best expressed by that word—sometimes lost in the blackness of a cloud, and suddenly becoming visible as they strike an angle of light. On such matters cf. Ruskin, Modern Painters, vol. i., 'Clouds'—he is the most profound investigator of the objective that I know of: the whole work is evidence of a painfully careful study of nature, universally and particularly; in aesthetics he is authority. Above all things I recommend you to read him, he will do you more good in twenty chapters than all the mathematics ever written."

Further on, he answers at great length a charge brought against Tennyson, of not being always correct in his metres.

"In my opinion that unfettered element in his metre is one of the very greatest charms and characteristics in his style—it is that whereby he most of all shews his power in making words themselves a vehicle not of his descriptions only but of that very nature he describes, a kind of onomatopoeia not in isolated words but in the whole run of the poem. In external nature you never see that cloying, satiating evenness whereby you would trammel her best interpreters; 'ever-varying' is of all epithets the most common to her. What should you think of a mountain range, with every mountain of the same height, the same conical shape, or of a country with roads intersecting at right angles? Of course you would be very much disgusted. We find nature harmonious only in fragments, and as we find her we must take her. I beg of you to read again the 'Dying Swan.' In the first few lines of it you have the character of the country as clearly before you as if you had read volumes of Lincolnshire topography, as to the third part, I never saw its equal—one might write commentary after commentary and never have finished dilating upon its inexpressible truthfulness.

Read too the 'Vision of Sin' and hosts of others up and down the book, and acknowledge that to express nature faithfully we must follow her own rules of language, now in even cadences, and now in rugged outbursts. I cannot see the least objection to your example from the 'Oriana' —the whole poem is ejaculatory, wild, passionate, despairing, gasped out at intervals; it would be unnatural to insist on the right ictus everywhere. The misery is fresh upon him and he is frenzied for the time. In Locksley Hall the hero has no reproach for himself, he can look calmly at his own past, he can resolve for the future, and where is more perfect metre than in that? Metre and rhyme are only accessories, faithfulness and truth and beauty are necessaries—if they are not compatible everywhere, the former must be sacrificed, never the latter—and so Tennyson always writes.

"If you want correctness take Pope and Dryden (and a dried 'un he was) but you must take their chilliness too: read Moore, but you must swallow also his namby-pamby drawing-room young-ladyism.

"Yes, we'll read Keats and Shelley and Coleridge like one o'clock when I get back."

A Balliol man with whom Edward was acquainted did him the lasting service of introducing him to Mr. MacLaren's fencing rooms and gymnasium in Oriel Lane. In a letter to his father dated April 27th he says: "I continue my fencing lessons &c. and feel almost unutterable benefit from them; my strength grows perceptibly and MacLaren promises to send me forth a very different object to what I was when I entered."

This was not all that he found there, however, for in Mr. MacLaren he gained one of the truest friends he ever had, and one whose eyes discerned his pupil's genius from the first. Mr. Price speaks of him as having been "fascinated" by Edward and Morris. He was about a dozen years their senior, a cultivated man of the highest character and with warmth and tenderness underlying reserve of manner. His home at Summertown, then a small village separated by a stretch of country road from Oxford, was a sanctuary seldom opened to the outer world. A low white house with its rose-covered veranda and a garden like a small Paradise shut in with white walls contained all that was dearest to him, being shared by a gifted young wife, then scarcely more than a girl. The notes say: "MacLaren interested us greatly, and we him, I suppose, for he did an almost unheard-of thing, inviting us to his home at Summertown, where we went three or four times in the term to dine with him, and his talk was admirable and his tastes inclining greatly to poetry. I think our enthusiasm was always a pleasure to him, and he aided and abetted us in all the inclinations of our hearts." It was when Edward began, as he soon did, to make studies of landscape and foliage in the country round Oxford, that MacLaren recognized his power, and the unfailing belief and encouragement that he gave in these early days were never forgotten.

The following letter to Mr. Price, written, in the character of "Cardinal de Birmingham," during the Long Vacation, shews, however, that Edward himself was not yet awake to the knowledge of his own special gift: Ecclesiasticism still comes first, though the way in which he unburdens himself to his friend of disappointment and disturbance of mind, owing to the lack of Christian unity with which he had met, shews how swiftly he was coming to conclusions for himself, and that no particular division of the Church was likely to hold him long.

"EDOUARD

"Cardinal de Birmingham

unto our trusty and beloved brother, Cormel, of the Order of St. Philip Neri elect. Health and Peace.

"In our most hearty wise we commend us unto you, dear brother, and for this same your loving epistle, howbeit it came tardily, we do thank you much. Indeed we had well nigh despaired of your courtesy in this matter, making therewithal many excuses for you of our charity.

"But now with the burden of many things upon us, we

do hold ourselves bound unto you for a season, and the more readily for because we see our brother in grievous need of our ghostly counsel and advice; the which moreover we would give in all modesty and gentleness, even as communing with ourself.

"And that our epistle come not unto you as it were a Homily full of harsh conceits of our Philosophy, we will advertise you somewhat of the estate of matters in our Province, Spiritual and Temporal, and, as far as our poor erudition in such matters, of the advancement of Literature.

"First of things Spiritual and Temporal in our jurisdiction; and briefly, for herein is such deep cause for sorrowing that we would not willingly pain you by baring it; for we be all so crammed with foul heresy, and discord, and prejudice, and bigotry, and all uncharitableness, that our very air, wherein we breathe, reeks thereof. And with all this bitterness so little of knowledge, or sympathy, or liberty, wherein this strange land doth so boast itself, that the contemplation is most pitiful. Nor this on one side only, or of one party only, but all conspire together, as it were of purpose, to choke up the only passage unto Truth in these days, even the suspense of judgment, afore all things necessary unto the attainment of τὸ ἀληθές.

"Now we beseech you look one moment at our racked diocese. The Oratorians, like Ishmael, with their hands against every man, and every man's hand against them; yet be they of all men by nature most peaceful, by education most contemplative, by discipline most philanthropic. Our dear brother of Sackville [the Rev. J. M. Neale, Warden of Sackville College, East Grinstead] will carry out his threat against the rector of St. Martin's, [the Rev. J. C. Miller] and though his cause be urgent, and the offence most palpable, yet shall he do us little good and greater harm. Our dear Latimer [the incumbent of St. Paul's, Birmingham] is away, and meantime the pulpit wherein he preached positive doctrine, most firmly and withal most gently, hath become a rostrum for negative declamation against all others; Eclectics, Syncretics, Rationalists, Pantheists, Atheists, and all names that are named in this age of 'isms.' These men not discerning that, because the time is urgent and dangers thicken, our people most chiefly desire to know what they must believe, and afterwards, when they shall be well-advised of that, also what they must avoid—not but that under an expert man the two teachings, positive and negative, may go hand in hand, but where, as is oftenest found, they be mediocre men, then the former first and by no means the latter. Therefore comes it that our preaching is unprofitable, nay absolutely ruinous to unity, and tending to Infidelity. For what shall it profit the unlearned to know arguments against eclecticism or rationalism or the rest? Granting, what is relatively impossible, that he will remember and use those same arguments aright, if he be at any time assailed by their supporters, yet will he not thereby, trusting in himself, and failing to seek counsel of his spiritual adviser, break one only remaining link between them and divorce what God did join together? And by the unlearned I mean not the poor, but the mass of men. On the other hand what shall this declamation profit the learned man? Will dogmatical condemnation of other creeds disprove them? Because one saith of Romanism that it is anti-Christ and corrupt, is it therefore so? or of Rationalism that it is senseless, is it therefore so? Nay, but they who advance both these most opposite opinions are not men to be so dealt with. Therefore they are unprofitable to the man who asks the 'why' and 'wherefore' of these things, who philosophically asks the διότι and takes not the mathematical ὅτι, the *ipse dixit* of everyone.

"But of this enough. Of Temporalities we will premise some few things, and then to more lofty converse.

"Our eccentric and most excellent friend Fulford hath been with us somewhat of late. Of a truth he is a most wild genius—here now, and far off in a moment, culling the sweetness of every flower around him. Full of wisdom, yet lacking knowledge; of the finest sense of imagination and good taste in what he lists; the only man we know who lives to live. And the contemplation of him is an excellent study; for his carelessness of cares makes him a merry companion, a sympathetic friend, and the most charitable of all censors.

"And in truth we begin more and more to see the final futility of the cramming system of education in this day. The age is utilitarian indeed, and every public speaker feels bound to remind his hearers of it in every oration, but truly it is at the sacrifice of their hearts' blood and their children's too that men are purchasing this possession. More and more is the age losing sight of the end and aim of man's existence, and of the legitimate means thereto. It will not learn that it is wisdom and not knowledge that is to be attained, the mind and not the body that is to be considered; that that only is an education, wherein the man is cultivated, not as an instrument towards some ulterior end, but as an end unto himself alone, ἁπλῶς, absolutely as a man, not τινί, relatively as a professional man.

"But of this when we meet κατ' ὄμμα, for we must enlist you, dear brother, in this crusade and Holy Warfare against the age, 'the heartless coldness of the times.'

"Macdonald and Heeley did us the honour of a visit yesterday. We talked much of all subjects—Transcendentalism and all the host of German systems—we discussed together calmly on dangerous ground; ourself ventured on a relative defence of the Jesuits and met with no opposition whatever, to our great surprise. In the evening your sisters favoured us with a fleeting call, and the Lady Abbess of the Convent also. Our topic was celibacy, wherein ourself was exposed to all but personal violence.

"In literature we have dealt but little since your departure; nay, we crave pardon for this our presuming on the subject, because we might be better schooled of you; howbeit some few things we must say.

"Our brother, the Cardinal Archbishop of Westminster, has re-published his essays from the Dublin Review. They are chiefly on Taste, some few on polemics—learned and spirited. There is a remarkable one on Sacrilege and its curse; proving statistically that Monastery and Abbey lands have never continued, in any one case of all through the length and breadth of this land, in any family for the three generations of father, son and grandson with the link unbroken. We remember Neale has a preface to one of his books to the same intent; the fact is more than curious, it is startling.

"Ruskin has published the second vol. of his 'Stones of Venice,' entitled 'Sea Stories.' His style is more wonderful than ever; the most persuasive oratory we ever read. His acme is to come. There never was such mind and soul so fused through language yet. It has the brilliancy of Jeffrey, the elegance of Macaulay, the diction of Shakespeare had he written in prose, and the fire of—Ruskin—we can find no other.

"We are less pleased with Hallam this second reading. One thing must not be forgotten, he did some little justice to the schoolmen and Middle Ages when an ignorant Literature and a profoundly ignorant people joined in one stolid senseless cry against them.

"Now dear Brother we must say farewell. On Monday, nomine + Jesu, we depart for the metropolis, whence you shall hear from us.

"+ EDOUARD
"Cardinal de Birmingham
"O. J.

"Given under our hand
"at our palace.

"Ides August, MDCCCLIII."

"Touching the matter whereof you ask our counsel and advice, hear.

"We shall give no frivolous account or explanation whatever, or enter into any disquisition as to the nature, tests, or evidence of any symptoms whatever, metaphysical, psychological, ethical or physical.

"You have as yet taken no vows, therefore you are as yet perfectly at liberty to decide your own fate.

"If your decision involve the happiness of another you know your course, follow nature, and remember the soul is above the mind, and the heart greater than the brain; for it is mind that makes man, but soul that makes man angel. Man as the seat of mind is isolated in the universe, for Angels that are above him and beasts that are below him are mindless, but it is soul that links him with higher beings and distinguishes him from the lower also. Therefore develope it to the full, and if you have one who may serve for a personification of all humanity, expend your love there, and it will orb from its centre wider and wider, like circles in water when a stone is thrown therein.

"But self-denial and self-disappointment, though I do not urge it, is even better discipline to the soul than that.

"If we lose you from the cause of celibacy, you are no traitor; only do not be hasty.

"Pax vobiscum in aeternum.

"EDOUARD."

The serious postscript to this letter throws a light upon half-jesting references to celibacy and misogyny made elsewhere. Underneath them was deep feeling, and the inner circle knew this, but to the outer world a veil of exaggeration was presented which bore the handling of those who only laughed or wondered.

About these first Oxford days there is a note of Canon Dixon's, which I will give here as a memory too intimate for comment. "I believe," he says, "that early in Oxford Edward experienced a great inward change. He said to me and Morris that he knew the time when he felt his heart burst into a blossom of love to his friends and all the men around him. I have often thought of the earnest and excited manner in which he said this. As well as I can remember that was the expression he used. Certainly at the time he began to shew a more decided and stronger character than at school; though still full of vivacity and amusement."

During his visit to "the Metropolis," alluded to by the Cardinal de Birmingham, Edward went to Walthamstow to see Morris. It had never occurred to them to mention to each other what their homes were like, so he had no idea whether his friend lived in a large house or a small one, and when he saw it, in comparison with his own, it seemed to him magnificent. Morris's father had been dead some years, but his mother welcomed Edward kindly, and seeing his affection for her son would willingly have told many stories of his childhood; but at this Morris chafed so much that the anecdotes had to be deferred. Three happy days they spent together, talking as they wandered about the flower and high-walled kitchen gardens, or reading in the deep window seats of a landing on the big central staircase, where many books were kept.

About this time, my father's term in Birmingham came to an end, and he was appointed to go to London, at which we children were greatly excited. I have said that Edward came to bid us good-bye before we left, and how well I remember the visit. It was only through our brother that we knew him—there were no friends in common at whose houses we might have met, and we did not see him except at long intervals—yet the profound impression made by those rare meetings was never lessened by his absence, and as the train passed slowly through the tunnel of the Great Western Railway at the beginning of our journey to London, I grieved in the darkness because I was leaving the place where he lived.

On returning to Oxford in October, Edward and Morris found to their great satisfaction that they could both get rooms in College. I do not know where Edward's were, but he spoke of those that Morris had as being "pleasant ones overlooking Exeter Garden and the Schools, in a little quadrangle that was called Hell Quad. You passed under an archway called Purgatory from the great quadrangle to reach it."

The evenings at Pembroke began again, and also the correspondence with Mr. Price. Early in the term Edward writes of the joy he has in receiving news of his friends in Birmingham: "the delight one experiences here on returning from Chapel and finding a letter from home is unequalled in the whole range of correspondence." He wrote constantly to his father and Miss Sampson, with a tender anxiety expressed that they should be "happy." He could not know that his absence had taken away the light of the house.

"My readings as yet have been very limited," he says, a little later, "not fit to talk about in fact. One thing I am almost ashamed to mention—viz. the spell that man Poe throws round me. His book of horrors is by me now. I know how contrary to all rules of taste are such writings, but there is something full of delicate refinement in all that hideousness. The charm is only temporary—in a day or two he will lie neglected, as such ephemeral works always are, but at present he is lord of the ascendant.

"If you meet with the volume just published with all his tales in, read particularly that in which he exemplifies his notion of analysis of and identification with another's thinking: they are, 'The Murders in the Rue Morgue,' and 'The Purloined Letter' more especially. 'The Gold Beetle' you know—it is a beautiful story. 'The Descent into the Maelstrom,' 'The Pit and the Pendulum' (especially this), and several others are marvellously startling. 'The Fall of the House of Usher' is very grand, almost my favourite. Some I think very objectionable, such as 'Mesmeric Effects,' 'The Black Cat' and one or two others."

In spite of this forecast of indifference, Edward's estimate of Poe's work always remained high, and a harsh and inaccurate memoir published after Poe's death gave him acute distress. Talking of it not many years ago he said that the day when he read it was one of the most miserable of his life. "It happened to be a wet day, and I felt unfit for any mortal thing after reading it. I went into the kitchen to try and get some comfort out of baking and the ruddy glow of the fire, but it wouldn't do—what did anything matter if one who wrote such beautiful things could behave so?" I remember his joy in 1874 on the appearance of Mr. Ingram's edition of Poe's works with a "Life" which refuted these accusations, and how he hastened to get the book.

"To pass to extremes," the letter goes on, "have you seen Archdeacon Wilberforce's last work on the Holy Eucharist? I am now engaged in reading it at meal times. It has been spoken of, and I readily assent, as the most controversial and truly theological work that has come out for ages. It makes up his series now, viz. The Incarnation, Holy Baptism, and this. It will be a book for you in after time."

The influence of Wilberforce upon both Edward and Morris was very great, and when, at the time of his secession to Rome in 1854, he published his Enquiry into the Principles of Church Authority, he all but carried them with him. From Wilberforce the letter turns again to answer something that Cormell must have said:

"Don't be afraid, Crom, of being independent in thought. It is a prerogative of man. This is the time for us to think highly of our species, to dream of development and the Divinity of mind; we shall soon wash away such fancies in the Lethe of getting our bread. Your own feelings will utter the μηκέτ' ἐσέλθῃς and you can fall back upon Faith. Oh! it is a glorious thought, that in our nature's ruin we yet possess our identity and stand isolated in revealed Creation as the Beings with Mind. It is grand to be in such peril as we are—I speak not lightly—to be born to free will; more independent than Angels, for they cannot err by reason, having all things by intuition; higher than brutes, for they are impelled by the laws of instinct, to our observance inevitable; partaking of the nature of both, and with mind for our proper own, we ought not to shame our natures as we do. What a grind, you say—nay, I mean it all."

There are two more letters written in this Michaelmas term, and both bear the same date, November 8th. One is to Cormell Price and the other to Harry Macdonald, who had remained in Birmingham in order to continue his school life there. They had started a manuscript School Magazine, a scheme which had Edward's sympathy. But the Head Master judged, perhaps rightly, that it was likely to interfere with their school work, and suppressed it after one or two numbers. The reasons he gave for this step were considered by the boys as unsatisfactory as the act itself, and when at the same time he warned them vaguely of some influence proceeding from Oxford which he mistrusted, they were very indignant.

The letter to Price comes first, and enters on the subject at once:

"First, let me communicate with you on the suppression of the Press. It is an assault upon your liberties, which at another time might be a signal for arms. It is an act of high treason against the Great Republic of Literature, a most unwarrantable exertion of despotism, which cannot be reprehended in language half strong enough. It is inconsistent, because inquisitorial in a land that acknowledges no Inquisition—it is self-destructive, like all tyranny, because it dreads investigation, and yet invites it—it is impotent because unjust and unreasonable. But you must submit, comforting yourselves with the assurance that

The tyrant's cruel glee
Forces on the freer hour."

The letter ends with, "I heard Pusey on Sunday—a magnificent sermon, profound and exhaustive, on Justification. He came out now and then gloriously—full of liberality. It lasted close upon two hours."

To Macdonald he begins:

"A letter from Crom has wrought an impulse, which I do not attempt to strive against, bringing with old memories a yearning to communicate with you, and so with poor materials and no capacity for invention this morning, I purpose opening a correspondence which with your good pleasure shall not cease.

"I have written also to Crom, and expressed my sympathy with him on the suppression of the Hebdomadal,—sympathy which I would offer you too as co-editor. Whatever heresy the article in question may have inculcated, it was unfair and undignified to take such proceedings—unfair because it involved in that suppression much that might have become beneficial, and undignified because it hinted at a fear that 'absurdity and conceit' would subvert obedience: the argument is either very lame, or the discipline of the school at a very low ebb.

"The statement that 'men who have shewn a turn of mind for general knowledge have never come to any good in the world' remains after all but a statement, not worth refutation—no one would certainly number its author in the obnoxious category—but we will hope it was simply meant for a rhetorical climax.

"We know indeed, and may deplore that individual progress now is not what it was in former times, that the cultivation of the individual is drowned and overwhelmed in the progress of the species; we know that every tyro now is acquainted with more truths than ever Aristotle mapped the way for, or Plato dreamed of; but the difference between them and us shews that 'the march of intellect' is no inseparable concomitant with the 'march of science,' that there is, in fine, no proportion between the possession of facts and the development of mind, for the latter is the fruit of profound concentration of all the soul's energies, while the former is but flower-culling. It is absolutely true, I suppose, that the gaining general knowledge in youth is not incompatible with concentration; but relatively it is not true, because not practicable. Society compels us, if we are to take any stand therein, to keep up with the time, and we are not here to grumble with the age, but adapt ourselves to it: the earth is brimming too full of humanity to allow room for asceticism and seclusion, which are necessary conditions of individual advancement. In old times men had it at command, but we have not; the times and the seasons require more of us than pedantry; and therefore I think the late act and the reasoning which led to it, to be a vast mistake. How far Oxford men deserve this suspicion of tampering with the established teaching I shall not say—none that I wot of would take the trouble, to begin with.

"The suspicious characters intended by Oxford men sug

gest Fulford, of whom, as more especially a middle term between us, I shall speak now—and, to begin with a rhapsody, what a glorious little fellow he is! Our subjects of private communication and thought this term have been those branches of psychology treating of the affections—a subject which we have elaborated very satisfactorily, in spite of constant interruptions on the part of un-sentimentalists such as Morris and Faulkner. The name of Fulford again suggests 'table-turning,' and this, mesmerism in general. Have you seen the article thereon in the Quarterly this time? it is well worth reading, and would interest you. The Quarterly reminds me of reviews in common, with all of w^h I am intensely disgusted, and never purpose reading a review on any man's work, if possible, before the work itself. The vulgar criticisms poured on Ruskin's last work from all the presses are abominable. No one half understands him yet, he leaves them all behind in his star-flights, grovelling on the earth—and then they complain when he is past the cloud regions that they cannot see him or that he is obscure. By his eloquence, the vehicle wherein he travels, they are all spell-bound, as who would not be, for surely man never wrote like him yet—but though they appreciate the form more or less, they cannot reach the matter.

"In this last work he transcends himself in diction, more Saxon pure and simple than ever—in prose what Tennyson is in poetry, and what the Pre-Raphaelites are in painting, full of devotion, and love for the subject, Insular and Northern in all their affections, giving us the very ideal of Teutonic beauty.

"You have heard of course of the resignation of Maurice at King's Coll: London and the writings w^h led to it. It is a hard question to decide upon, but I am very sorry—for the Christian Socialists, if Maurice and Kingsley are fair examples, must be glorious fellows."

There had been a letter about this time in the Guardian from the Rev. F. D. Maurice, on the subject of the charges brought against him by the Principal of King's

College. The chief of these charges was his denial of the usual meaning of Eternal Punishment, and a few days later the Council of the College declared the two chairs he held to be vacant.

Fulford also was in correspondence with my brother at this time, and through his letters there are occasional glimpses of the Birmingham set.

"We have fallen at once into our old habits: we assemble nightly in Faulkner's room and drink tea as regularly as ever, but the Tales from Household Words or scenes from Shakespeare or imitations of the Dons have given place to the more exciting amusement of chaffing——, who during his absence of two terms from Alma Mater has nursed up his gullibility to a degree that would do honour to half a dozen freshmen, all sons of clergymen, educated privately by their fathers. He has been moving tables, books, papers (whatever he can lay his hands on) in a surprising manner since Monday, when we initiated him into the mystery, and made the table (in obedience to not-involuntary muscular motion) pronounce the most glorious things concerning him, of which the roof and crown was that he was a musical and poetical genius. No wonder he moved all sorts of things by himself after that." In the same letter Fulford tells of having been to see Heeley at Cambridge, and of the impression that Cambridge men made upon him. They appeared to be harder readers than the men he knew at Oxford. They all talked "shop," he adds, "to a fearful extent, and perfectly surprised me by their knowledge of University matters, accustomed as I am at Oxford to such utter indifference to them even in such a know-everything as Jones."

But this indifference on Edward's part arose from deep disappointment, and it was long before he could accustom himself to the reality of Oxford. The daily work for the schools, he says, speaking of himself and Morris, was uninteresting to them, and made absolutely desolate by the manner of teaching—"but little by little we fed ourselves with the food that fitted us."

The mention of table-turning reminds me that whilst we lived in Birmingham, Fulford had seen something of it at our house, for we children had heard of it and tried it, with what are still to me astonishing results. The power, whatever it might be, was discovered whilst our parents were from home, and duly reported to them on their return as treasure-trove. Our father said something like, "Well, well, my children, if it ever does it again, call me"; so one day, when he was safely within the double doors of his study, we set to work. We had no theory about it, and were only curious each time to see what would happen. The table, a large round one, did not fail us now, but seemed to awaken just as usual, turning at first with slow heaviness and then gradually quickening its pace till it spun quite easily and set us running to keep up with it. "Call Papa!" was the word, and a scout flew to the study. He was with us at once, not even waiting to lay down his long Broseley pipe. Incredulity gave place to excitement at the first glance, but, to convince us of our self-deception, he cried out, "Don't stop, children," and leapt lightly between us, pipe in hand, upon the middle of the table, thinking to stop it in a second. His weight, however, made no difference—the table turned as swiftly and easily as before, and we ran round and round with it, laughing at our amazed father.

And not only tables did we turn, but other objects also, especially a very communicative tea-urn with which we established a code of rapping. Our removal to London put an end to these *séances*, but none of us ever understood the things we saw at them.

The next trace I find of Edward is an account sent to his father of a day during the Christmas vacation, when he was with his aunt in London, and they went together to see her friend, Mr. Lewis, the well-known chess-player; but I have no clue to the gentleman whom he met there. It is curious to feel the power of Oxford over him in spite of his quarrel with the place, and the *esprit de corps* that rises when speaking of it.

"At Norwood I spent a delightful day. Mr. Lewis himself is a profoundly talented man—the greatest chess-player in Europe, they say—and I met, and argued with, an old friend of Burney, Lamb, Hazlitt, Coleridge, &c. &c.: a most glorious fellow—with eyes that have haunted me ever since, who took to me desperately, and pressed me to come and argue with himself and his son—a student at Heidelberg—in metaphysics, aesthetics, educational or theological questions. Of course I thanked him profusely, but though he was polite enough to compliment me and call himself vanquished, I should have little disposition to sully the glory of Oxford in appearing as her champion before two such knights."

This incident confirms Mr. Price's account of Edward's strong natural bent towards logic and metaphysics; and the cordiality of his antagonist, who professed himself vanquished, makes one believe that he was, as I have heard, never captious in argument and quite free from pedantry of terms, so that those who did not know at what cost of study and training he had strengthened his natural ability were astonished by his skill in disputation.

But now his great pleasure was in the society of one with whom no hour was wasted in dispute. The particular kind of help that he needed at that particular time came to him through the sympathy of Morris, and they literally talked together day and night of the things that lay near to their hearts. Their intercourse, however, was too vital to lead them hand in hand round a circle, and by the time their first year at Oxford was over, they had begun to deal with much that had previously been unquestioned.

When they met again in the New Year this is how Edward, with just confidence in the generosity of his first friend, writes to him of the second who had become so dear.

"Morris has a deal of my time. He is one of the cleverest fellows I know, and to me far more congenial in his thoughts and likings than anyone it has been my good fortune to meet with—his taste and criticism in Art and Aesthetics generally I should any day infinitely prefer to

Fulford's, who you know was my old ideal in such subjects. He is full of enthusiasm for things holy and beautiful and true, and, what is rarest, of the most exquisite perception and judgment in them. For myself, he has tinged my whole inner being with the beauty of his own, and I know not a single gift for which I owe such gratitude to Heaven as his friendship. If it were not for his boisterous mad outbursts and freaks, which break the romance he sheds around him—at least to me—he would be a perfect hero.

"How I am grinding you, poor fellow! well, briefly, come and see him and hear him, not in the smoke room or in disputations (the smoke room of intellects) but by the riverside and on the highways, as I alone have seen and heard him."

CHAPTER VI

1854

When shall I arise and the night be gone?

THE year 1854 was a marked one in Edward's life, for the passing away of old things and the coming of new moved him profoundly.

As a rule, ordinary matters only were treated of in the letters home, which were written with fair regularity once a week; but there is a letter at the end of January in which the barriers of difference in age and of close relationship give way before a passion of enthusiasm, and like a child throwing himself into his father's arms, he breaks out with this midwinter ecstasy:

"I have just come in from my terminal pilgrimage to Godstowe ruins and the burial place of Fair Rosamond. The day has gone down magnificently; all by the river's side I came back in a delirium of joy, the land was so enchanted with bright colours, blue and purple in the sky, shot over with a dust of golden shower, and in the water, a mirror'd counterpart, ruffled by a light west wind—and in my mind pictures of the old days, the abbey, and long processions of the faithful, banners of the cross, copes and crosiers, gay knights and ladies by the river bank, hawking-parties and all the pageantry of the golden age—it made me feel so wild and mad I had to throw stones into the water to break the dream. I never remember having such an unutterable ecstasy, it was quite painful with intensity, as if my forehead would burst. I get frightened of indulging now in dreams, so vivid that they seem recollections rather than imaginations, but they seldom last more than half-an-hour; and the sound of earthly bells in the distance, and presently the wreathing of steam upon the trees where the railway runs, called me back to the years I cannot convince myself of living in."

A different side of his nature appears in a letter written shortly after this, where some questions from Cormell about University matters are answered in detail with the same practical judgment that helped many another friend in later life.

"As to scholarships generally, I should think there are little grounds for argument anyway, either for chance or probability or anything. They depend entirely upon the men who present themselves for candidates, subject to a certain standard only, and of course fluctuate continually. The idea of the stiffness of University scholarships has very likely deterred many from trying, and so the competition has been less; otherwise I have not heard that the last two or three have been shady. The scholarships at Queen's are good, but this College is now the Brasenose of old times, very fast indeed. And 'Demyship' is a name peculiar to Magdalen, leading finally I believe to a fellowship; most counties in England have one or two there.

"The chief points will be the Latin writing and accuracy of translation. In both, the first aim must be to render the meaning of a passage as plainly and perspicuously as possible: then ornament of diction, periods, antitheses, &c. may come in, but above all let the first attention be given to the matter, not the form of either.

"Terseness is the characteristic of Latin, and terseness therefore is desirable for Oxford Latin. Tacitus is better than Cicero if it were possible to follow him. In translation from Greek look well to the particles; they are here supposed to be connecting links between sentences &c. not meaningless nonsense for filling up, to be translated at random by 'forsooth,' 'but,' 'indeed' &c. I should imagine these two are the chief things to be observed."

Later on he writes that it has been a rambling term with him altogether, but certainly the happiest he has yet spent, that every hour has been full of some employment or another, and that he has "fallen back upon drawing and intends to cultivate it to some extent." Macdonald, who went up to matriculate in March, found him busy making designs from the Lady of Shalott.

The custom, which lasted all their lives, of Morris reading aloud to Edward, had already begun, and the Notes tell how in this way they both came to know Ruskin's Edinburgh Lectures soon after they were printed.

"I was working in my room when Morris ran in one morning bringing the newly published book with him: so everything was put aside until he read it all through to me. And there we first saw about the Pre-Raphaelites, and there I first saw the name of Rossetti. So for many a day after that we talked of little else but paintings which we had never seen, and saddened the lives of our Pembroke friends."

Presently, however, to their joy, Millais's "Return of the Dove to the Ark" came down to Oxford and was to be seen at Mr. Wyatt's shop in the High Street, "and then," Edward said, "we knew." But still they knew nothing about Van Eyck or Giotto and the Italian painters, and nothing also of the art of painting. A little longer and all this would come to them, for now days counted for weeks and weeks for months.

Early in the year, he had spoken of being happy—he was "beginning to forgive Oxford, and the fidgets of rebellion were over"; but deep reflection followed, and the ground on which he had hitherto stood so firmly began to fail. Mr. Price speaks of the religious perplexity that Edward went through this year as being nothing less than agony. At one time in his distress he was all but ready to silence questioning and accept the tenets of the elder Church *en bloc*; at another he went for counsel to Newman's old friend and disciple, Charles Marriott, the learned and saintly Vicar of St. Mary's. This interview gave some relief, but the whole-hearted, enthusiastic and unenquiring days were gone.

During part of the Long Vacation, as if to give Edward

breathing space for communion with his own soul, Morris was abroad and Cormell away from Birmingham, so that after he had paid his usual visit to his aunt in London, he found himself alone in the quiet of his father's house.

A letter written thence shews that he had already begun a scheme of work which was the first step in his artistic life: it was a series of pen-and-ink designs made at the suggestion of his friend Mr. MacLaren.

These drawings were intended for illustrations to a volume of Ballads upon the Fairy Mythology of Europe, which MacLaren had written with the intention of publishing immediately; and no greater proof of confidence could have been given than his determination to put off the appearance of his book until it could be illustrated throughout by the experiments of an unknown man. He had evidently asked Edward to come and visit him at Summertown, and the answer is: "Thank you a thousand times for your kind invitation. I almost fear it would unsettle me to leave home again, and I am quiet now: already I have refused three similar invitations, one to Cambridge, one to Leicester, and one to Hereford; but if I had accepted any it would have been yours, from priority of engagement, and sympathy in our common work." Unfortunately the last sheet only of this letter can be found. In it he gives an account of a visit to the Royal Academy Exhibition, which was made memorable that year by Holman Hunt's pictures of "The Awakened Conscience" and "The Light of the World." The fragment that remains begins thus:

"Landseer has drivelled his time away on another group of the royal family in Highland costume—will he ever learn that the subject is not remarkable for conception, or capable of a counterbalancing beauty of execution, that it should be repeated every year? Maclise has managed to cover an acre of canvas with mangled bodies, and a host of meaningless faces in steel helmets,—and all to illustrate a fact in history about which the less said the better. [The Marriage of Strongbow and Eva.] There is a pleasing picture of Bertrand de Born the warrior-troubadour of the

XIII century singing to his harp by moonlight—he was a demon in real life, why should he be canonized by the painter? Altogether, what with silly unmeaning subjects, and those of more questionable character, devoted to the hero-worship of traitors and robbers, or the prettiness and romance of a heartless religion, I saw that the Pre-Raphaelites had indeed come at a time when there was need for them, and resolved after my little ability to defend and claim a patient hearing for them.

"I had only time to visit Sydenham once. From the fuss and nonsense I had heard in conversation about it, as if the world had been ripening and developing to one end, to wit, the Crystal Palace of 1854, I was prepared to be thoroughly disgusted, but no,—many things pleased me, and I could pardon others, but as an entirety we must boast little of it, or future generations will say, 'Was this their great palace they talked so much about, poor fools!' When they have built themselves an architecture in the enduring stone worthy of their time, and covered it with carving and bright colour, they will indeed have cause to laugh at the large hot-houses of our day we poetically call Crystal Palaces. As I looked at it in its gigantic wearisomeness, in its length of cheerless monotony, iron and glass, glass and iron, I grew more and more convinced of the powerlessness of such material to effect an Architecture. Its only claim to our admiration consists in its size, not in those elements in which lies the true principle of appreciation, form and colour: its form is necessarily rigid and mechanical, its colour simple transparency and a painfully dazzling reflection: it is a fit apartment for fragrant shrubs, trickling fountains, muslin-de-laines, eau-de-Cologne, Grecian statues, strawberry ices and brass bands—but give me 'The Light of the World' and the apse of Westminster."

This mention of Grecian statues together with eau-de-Cologne recalls to me the fact that it was not till many years after the date of this letter that he turned seriously to the study of Greek art.

Then follow a few simple words to his friend explaining

why he had not written before. "One thing that prevented me writing was the heart-aches and love-troubles I have been getting into. It will not do to write about them, but I could tell you anything: this ought to have been stated as my real excuse, for no rheumatisms in the head would really have prevented me writing. You will know how to make excuses for this, you will remember how life and the things of life dwindle and fade away at the time, but I am quite awake now, anxiously expecting your next letter with advice about the great design. I shall have made some progress before you write which shall be duly notified in reply."

In October also, just before they were to meet at Oxford, there is a letter to Cormell acknowledging one from him, and saying, "You wrote at a time when I was suffering greater mental troubles than I ever remember. I am bound to say this much, that you may know it was not from inattention or carelessness that you have not heard from me before, but only from having no heart to write a merry letter and too much friendship to pour my sorrows into your ear."

The unknown troubler of his heart moves across this mirror of the past and disappears; nor was the destruction of the celibate ideal involved in the experience, for in the letter just quoted he continues: "The Monastery, Crom, stands a fairer chance than ever of being founded—I know that it will be some day."

Never at any time in his life did his ordinary manner betray to others the sadness to which, in common with all sensitive natures, he was subject. This was, I believe, owing partly to a principle which I find formulated in one of his late letters: "I hold it a point of honour with every gentleman to conceal himself, and make a fair show before people, to ease life for everyone,"—and partly to the cheering effect that companionship always had upon him. Thus, in the same letter which hints at his trouble, he writes the following bright account of his relations with Cormell's family.

"I think it was this day week that Miss Sampson, Fulford and I spent an evening at Spon Lane, very pleasantly indeed, as the little man observed. By the bye, Crom, you'd better mind and ask his intentions. Monk as I am and unlettered in the world's etiquette, it seemed very improper of him presenting a rose to F. There is a language of flowers, I hear, and you had better make it out and see what he means—but this is digressing. So very pleasantly passed the time that my father was quite enchanted with the bare relation of the visit. So on Sunday I again stormed Spon Lane with him, whereupon another very pleasant evening followed, to the entire oblivion of our visit's object, so the next day I had to go over again."

Yet I know that it is an allegorical portrait of himself which exists in an early drawing that I will try to describe. It shews the figure of a man seated in mournful dejection before a desk where lies an unfinished drawing of an angel. A small broken statue of an angel also lies at his feet. The man's eyes are closed, and his head rests wearily upon one hand, while in the other he holds an hour-glass from which but few of the sands have run. The background is of heavy rain falling into a dark sea, and underneath it is written, "When shall I arise and the night be gone?"

Before the Long Vacation was over, the quiet of home had done its office, and he was eager to be gone again. The postponement of term for a week made him angry, and he wrote to Cormell saying how ardently he longed to be back "with Morris and his glorious little company of martyrs."

Morris had written on his return from France, full of enthusiasm about the churches he had seen—Beauvais, Amiens and Chartres; he had a new world to tell of.

By good fortune at the beginning of the October term the friends were able to get fresh rooms in College next door to each other. "All day long I have been hurrying about," Edward writes to Miss Sampson, "seeing after the removal of my property, so that I might not lose half of it. My new rooms are a great improvement upon the old ones—you must contrive this term to come up and see them." They were in the part of Exeter known as the "Old Buildings," long since taken down. "Tumbly old buildings, gable-roofed and pebble-dashed, little dark passages led from the staircase to the sitting rooms, a couple of steps to go down, a pace or two, and then three steps to go up—your face was banged by the door, and then, inside the rooms, a couple of steps up to a seat in the window, and a couple of steps down into the bedroom—the which was bliss," say the Notes.

Here, when they were alone together in the evenings, the friends read Chaucer, and in the daytime they went often to look at the painted books in the Bodleian. Old chronicles too they devoured, and anything of any kind written about the Middle Ages, yet somehow missed for a little longer the two great books that afterwards filled so much of their lives—the Morte d'Arthur and the Tale of the Niblungs.

There was another atmosphere about the evenings in Faulkner's rooms at Pembroke. All the men there met, as Canon Dixon says, "on the common ground of poetry and indefinite artistic and literary aspiration," and they all had the idea of doing something for the world in their generation, but it was "with larger, other eyes" than the rest that the two Exeter men regarded the beauty of the visible world.

It would have been unnatural and impossible for half-a-dozen friends who saw each other daily to keep their intercourse for ever at high-water mark, and no studied seriousness was added to that which each felt in his own way as he looked forward to life. They had their jokes, their bear-fights, and their arguments, they chaffed and talked slang, and many an evening passed in laughter.

With the appearance of Cormell Price at Brasenose in October (Harry Macdonald had gone up six months before with a Corpus scholarship), the Birmingham set, to which Morris now definitely belonged, was complete.

The welcome given to Cormell by Morris delighted Edward: "Morris loved him from the first," he says, "and was always fond of him and tender about him, as we all were." They carried him to the gymnasium and introduced him to MacLaren, but Edward's own attendance there was not very regular at this time, owing to the great fatigue that he began to feel after exercising. His power of walking also failed, and he complained of headache, brought on, as he supposed, "by over excitement." Writing home, he exclaims that Morris still continues the most clever, glorious fellow in or out of Oxford, and says that they are more together this term than ever.

But how can a woman hope to describe the life of men at college, since she can never have seen it as it really is? The thing is impossible. Nevertheless that life has always been a centre for many thoughts and imaginings of women, who make for themselves pictures of it according to the degree of their respect or admiration for the men they know. Those of whom I write were eagerly followed by the hearts of mothers and sisters and friends, and it is from the point of view of some of these that I must speak, if I am to make the time alive to any one.

In the first place I will notice that though each member of the "set" was as different from another as possible, they all made upon us the impression of being gifted, interesting, and amusing beyond words. That we thought them good, goes without saying. Some of us chose Fulford, some Edward, some Cormell Price for lode-star. I did not know Dixon and Faulkner sufficiently well at that time to see their reflection in the eyes that followed them. My brother had several very dear women and girl friends besides his mother and sisters, nor do I doubt that each one of the Brotherhood was blessed in the thoughts of some heart, known or unknown to himself.

They had no conquering airs with women, but were either frank and pleased in their society or shy and humble. I am confident that the mystery which shrouds men and women from each other in youth was sacred to each one of them.

To me that group will never grow old; still I see them

in my mind as I did then, the thought of one bringing up that of the others, all ardent, all filled with enthusiasm about something or some one.

Fulford alone seemed occasionally to stand outside, looking at himself and the others, and would talk or write of it, never so happy as when analyzing his own or a friend's character. In early Oxford days he used to write long letters to my brother, who was still at school, giving him descriptions of University life in a rather prepensely *blasé* style, though sometimes enlivened by humour and an interest that he could not disguise. Once he took the pains to send Harry a long dramatic account of an evening at Pembroke, in which some "chopping-block" from the outside, whose name (X.) I do not recognize, is made to draw out the peculiarities of different members of the set by a string of questions so wide of any mark and yet so fishing for second-hand information about books he was supposed to be reading up for himself, that Fulford rises to an ecstasy of delight in his own story. Dixon, Edward, Fulford, Faulkner, and the unknown one are represented cosily drinking tea by firelight when the scene opens, and the buzzing talk of X. rouses the others one by one from their quiet comfort. At first Edward and Dixon play into each other's hands by seriously answering all his questions in the most abstruse and technical terms, while Fulford seems to hop round the three, egging them on, and Faulkner keeps a long-suffering silence, but when X.—bewildered by a solemn explanation which he has brought upon himself from Dixon of the term "Intellectual Transcendentalism"—says, "Would you mind saying it over again? I didn't quite catch it," Faulkner springs up with a bitter cry of "No! No! Don't. You shan't!", and engages in a bear-fight with Edward. The bore triumphs, however, by going on with the conversation when the bear-fight is over, and finally leaves with an apology for deserting them so soon.

To this may be added Edward's own recollection of evenings at a later date. "We chatted about life, such as we knew it, and about ghosts, which Dixon believed in religiously but Faulkner despised, and many an evening we wound up with a bear-fight, and so at 11, home to Exeter and bed." "Exit *he* to Exe*ter*" was remembered as his form of farewell one night.

Intercourse with Heeley was kept up by letters to and from one or other of the Oxford set, and by the exchange of flying visits. It was a great disappointment to him that none of his most intimate friends at King Edward's School joined him at Cambridge, and when Macdonald got a scholarship at Oxford he expressed himself warmly about it to Price: "I would have given almost anything to have had Macdonald up here. No fellow has ever had more influence on me: at least on certain parts of the 'Me,' and no fellow's influence has been more advantageous." In this same letter he speaks to Cormell of his "ill success in starting a correspondence with Jones, whose loved idea (cf. Abelard & Heloisa) lies mixt with yours in my mind," and desires that when next Cormell sees Edward, he will touch him up on the subject "as with the touch of a gnat."

Between Fulford and Heeley, who both really enjoyed writing, there was a voluminous correspondence, and in one of his easy-going letters to my brother, Wilfred scribbles away, "When we are all great men, I think of publishing a volume or two of letters between yourself, Fulford, Dixon, Valentine and myself. Fancy. Early records and correspondence of Mr. Justice Macdonald, Mr. Valentine, Editor of the Meteorosophist, R. W. Dixon, Esq. Poet Laureate, Sir William Fulford, Bart., M.A., M.P., and the Rev. W. L. Heeley, Domestic Chaplain to Baron Skinflint." But he was wrong in every case.

To the families of the different men news of the set was distilled by letter, by anecdote, by rumour, and in vacation by glimpses of themselves, always memorable to the home-dwellers. The following extract from a diary of 1854, kept by a young sister of Cormell's, is too innocent in its extravagance to be laughed at, and is worth something as shewing Edward's early certainty of a great future for Morris, as well as the hero-worship for himself that had grown up in a household where there was no glamour of strangeness about him, and he was a kind of adopted brother.

"Sep: 18th. Jones came to tea. He is the most clever and the nicest fellow I ever knew. He says he thinks Fulford will be a 'star' and he is sure Morris will be, and I am sure Jones will be, in drawing—he draws splendidly and is inexpressibly splendid." Morris was as yet only a name to her.

The tension of mind and feeling in which this year passed is not visible in any of Edward's home letters, which arrive as often as usual, and seem eager for news in return.

In one of them there is a tender message to an invalid sister of Cormell's: "Remember me very kindly to her," he writes, "and say that I often talk with her brother about home, and that with all our excitement among things new and old up here we find many a quiet hour to think of those who think often of us." His widowed aunt, too, in her lonely London house was often in his mind. "Whatever time I may have beyond my home duties," he says to his father, "must be devoted to her. She must at times be very lonely—reduced to amuse herself by reading my old letters over and over again."

The anxiety and self-searching that underlay this smooth surface of affection and sympathy for others were too deep to be spoken of even with Morris. "Slowly, and almost insensibly," he says, "without ever talking about it, I think we were both settling in our minds that the clerical life was not for us, and art was growing more and more dominant daily." No wonder if at times during such a crisis all things seemed dark to him and physical health failed; but this slow, wide-eyed discovery of where his place and duty in the world lay was the beginning of dawn.

CHAPTER VII

1855

Lo, the winter is past, the rain is over and gone.

"YESTERDAY I went such a beautiful walk with Morris and Smith—he is another who is to join our brotherhood," wrote Edward in November, 1854; but in May, 1855, Mr. Price says: "Our Monastery will come to nought I'm afraid; Smith has changed his views to extreme latitudinarianism, Morris has become questionable in doctrinal points, and Ted is too Catholic to be ordained. He and Morris diverge more and more in views though not in friendship."

The words "too Catholic to be ordained" we may presume to mean that Edward was no longer loyal to the Church of England, but they do not suggest what was the fact, namely, that another inmost religion was gradually taking the place of every form that had gone before it.

"Divergence in views but not in friendship" exactly expresses what happened and was bound to happen from time to time between two such men as Morris and Edward; but divergence of aim, never. With the abandonment of the clerical ideal went also the first proposed scheme of a brotherhood, but from the ashes of the old the new was born. Before this, however, there was a time when in the deep unrest of his spirit Edward would gladly have cut his way out of the *impasse* in which he found himself at Oxford by accepting one of the commissions offered by Government to the University during the Crimean War. "I wanted to go and get killed," he said, but he was rejected on the score of health, and deliverance was accomplished otherwise.

At the end of May Edward ran up to London to see the Royal Academy Exhibition, carrying Mr. Price with him to his aunt's house. For the lonely little lady this was great happiness, and thenceforth Cormell became one of her chief favourites. When they left her she writes to him, "My dear Edward seems very desirous that I should make a 'pet' of you, and to tell you the truth I do not think I should find much difficulty in so doing. You have no idea how much I miss you both; after you were gone I went into your room and it looked so desolate that I could almost have shed tears!" And Morris came up to town also, for the Notes say: "When I was in London visiting my aunt, Morris and I went across to Tottenham to the house of a Mr. Windus, who was said to have some pictures of the Pre-Raphaelites, where we spent a happy morning. It was there that we first saw a picture by Madox Brown, called 'The Last of England,' and a beautiful little picture of a lady in black by Millais which I have never seen since, and some drawings by Millais; and we came away strengthened and confirmed. It must have been at the end of the summer term of this year that we got permission to look at the Pre-Raphaelite pictures in the house of Mr. Combe, the head of the Clarendon Press at Oxford, and there we saw two pictures by Holman Hunt, 'The Christian Missionary wounded in the Fisherman's Hut' and a portrait of some surpliced friend of the Combes in Oxford, with part of the Cloisters of New College for a background. But our greatest wonder and delight was reserved for a water-colour of Rossetti's, of Dante drawing the head of Beatrice and disturbed by people of importance. We had already fallen in with a copy of the Germ, containing Rossetti's poem of the Blessed Damozel, and at once he seemed to us the chief figure in the Pre-Raphaelite Brotherhood."

For the Long Vacation they made a happy plan of going to North France to see the churches of which Morris had brought word the year before; but first, as soon as term was over, they agreed to accept an invitation from Heeley and go to see him and Cambridge.

"There was nothing much in this journey," Edward says; "but for some reason I remember every moment of it, from my hunting long in the shops in the Strand and elsewhere to find some portrait or other of Tennyson, whom I had never seen and whose aspect was unknown to me, and getting a bad little print which had to content me. And then I met Morris at the Railway. Our talk was of old French Chronicles, and I remember everything on the journey. That first evening in Cambridge we went before any other place to see the little round Church [St. Sepulchre's]; and there Heeley showed us the first edition of Tennyson's poems with the Hesperides in it, and the earlier Mariana in the South, to our great delight and content. Three or four very happy days we passed."

Soon after this Cambridge visit my own recollection of Morris begins. At the Royal Academy, where Wilfred Heeley had taken me, we saw him standing before Millais's picture of "The Rescue," examining it closely: as he turned to go away, Heeley said "That 's Morris," and introduced us to each other; but he looked as if he scarcely saw me. He was very handsome, of an unusual type—the statues of mediaeval kings often remind me of him—and at that time he wore no moustache, so that the drawing of his mouth, which was his most expressive feature, could be clearly seen. His eyes always seemed to me to take in rather than to give out. His hair waved and curled triumphantly.

By this time his reputation as a poet had been established amongst his friends at Oxford by some verses, the first he had ever written, of new and singular beauty. The way in which he answered the enthusiasm with which they were hailed tells more about him than any description could. "Well, if this is poetry," he said, "it is very easy to write." And though for some time he continued to produce a fresh poem almost every day, he did not give up any other work that he was about, but simply added poetry as the blossom of it all.

"Topsy is writing such a beautiful story," says Edward in a letter home, "so glorious you cannot think; when it is finished you shall see it." The name of "Topsy" was given to Morris by Edward, and finding favour in the intimate circle, it soon became much more closely identified with him than his own proper one of William, which no one at Oxford ever used. Edward, on the other hand, was a man whom friends readily called by his familiar Christian name, Ted, or, in later years, Ned.

The tour in France was intended to be a walking one, for the sake of economy necessary for Edward, and Fulford and Price were both asked to join it, but finally Cormell was unable to come.

On July 18th, the day before they started, Edward called at our house in Chelsea, when I was out. Returning home I missed him so narrowly that I distinctly saw him walking away down the street as I reached my own door. "Jones and Morris and Fulford were going to France to-morrow," I was told; "Jones had just been to call." I knew it.

Faulkner and Heeley and Macdonald spent the evening with Edward and Fulford, who were to meet Morris at the train next morning, and then the two travellers went for the night to a small hotel near the railway station. Fulford had brought a volume of Keats with him and read some of it aloud before they slept.

They crossed by Folkestone and Boulogne, going straight on to Abbeville, where they arrived late in the evening; but after a short night Morris called the others early to wander about the town till breakfast. In the afternoon they left again, having seen streets, houses and churches all beautiful in fresh and foreign ways, and, from the tower of St. Wolfram's, such a panorama of the high-pitched roofs and irregular streets of the town and the low hills and bright fields of the country round as made them loth to come away. Short as their time was, however, Edward managed to make a drawing in one of the streets.

Amiens was reached and an hour spent in the Cathedral

before dinner, the pilgrims returning to it afterwards. "Morris surveyed it with calm joy," writes Fulford, "and Jones was speechless with admiration. It did not awe me until it got quite dark, for we stayed till after nine, but it was so solemn, so human and divine in its beauty, that love cast out fear."

Fulford's attitude of vigilance to mark his own sensations, and his interest in the enthusiasm of the other two, are preserved in letters which he wrote during the tour. Morris wrote to Cormell, and in his Notes Edward has completed a picture of the time.

The walking part of the tour soon came to an end, for Morris was uncomfortably shod and fell lame at Amiens, "filling the streets with imprecations on all bootmakers." He bought a pair of gay carpet slippers to try if those would be easier, and in them gallantly continued the journey for ten miles, but at Beauvais, as he was quite footsore, they gave up all further idea of walking.

On Sunday morning the 22nd July they attended High Mass in Beauvais Cathedral, and the impression made upon Edward by the service may be seen from the following passage in a letter written more than a generation afterwards:

"Do you know Beauvais, which is the most beautiful church in the world? I must see it again some day—one day I must. It is thirty-seven years since I saw it and I remember it all—and the processions—and the trombones—and the ancient singing—more beautiful than anything I had ever heard and I think I have never heard the like since. And the great organ that made the air tremble—and the greater organ that pealed out suddenly, and I thought the Day of Judgment had come—and the roof, and the long lights that are the most graceful things man has ever made.

"What a day it was, and how alive I was, and young—and a blue dragon-fly stood still in the air so long that I could have painted him. Oh me, what fun it was to be young. Yes, if I took account of my life and the days in it that most went to make me, the Sunday at Beauvais would be the first day of creation."

Morris in his wonderful way knew everything about every place they went to, and the thought of the mischief that was being done in Paris to Notre-Dame, and how miserable it would be to see, made him urge his companions to go straight from Beauvais to Chartres, missing Paris entirely. "But I wanted to see the pictures in the Louvre," says Edward, "and Fulford wanted to see Paris, and after all there was the Hotel Cluny with which to pacify Morris"; so, after attending Vespers at Beauvais, to Paris they went, and the next day Fulford says that they worked hard at sight-seeing for sixteen hours. At the Beaux Arts they found to their delight no less than seven Pre-Raphaelite pictures, and stayed looking at little beside them for half the day.

In the evening, by Edward's particular desire, they went to the Opera, for he had never seen one, and heard Alboni in Le Prophète. "Jones was perfectly enraptured, but Morris seemed a good deal bored," reports Fulford.

They found the sculptures of Notre-Dame, as Morris had foretold, half taken down and lying in careless wreck under the porches, and "for the first time saw some of the secrets of restoration."

In the Louvre Morris made Edward shut his eyes and so led him up to Angelico's picture of "The Coronation of the Virgin" before he allowed him to look, and then he was transported with delight. But "Morris was fidgetty" all the time they were in Paris, so after three days they hurried away and went straight to Chartres.

"There we were for two days, spending all our time in the Church, and thence made northwards for Rouen, travelling gently and stopping at every Church we could find. Rouen was still a beautiful mediaeval city, and we stayed awhile and had our hearts filled. From there we walked to Caudebec, then by diligence to Havre, on our way to the churches of the Calvados: and it was while walking on the quay at Havre at night that we resolved definitely that we would begin a life of art, and put off our decision no longer—he should be an architect and I a painter. It was a resolve only needing final conclusion; we were bent on that road for the whole past year, and after that night's talk we never hesitated more. That was the most memorable night of my life."

What need for us to follow the journey further, now they have reached its goal?

Soon after their return to England Morris went down to stay with Edward in Birmingham, and the little house in the Bristol Road shone with joy at their presence. Most of the Oxford set, together with Wilfred Heeley, were then living within a few miles of each other, and the men met every day.

A diary of the time, kept by Mr. Price, fortunately remains, through which one can see them all in the far distance, beginning with Sunday, August 26th, when Cormell went up to the Bristol Road to see Edward and found Morris there, "wild and jolly as ever," and they had "much talk about Maud." They seem to have held one long conversation, only interrupted by the night's sleep.

The Prices were now living altogether at Spon Lane, West Bromwich, but distance did not prevent the friends from making their house a frequent trysting-place where the eager interest and gay spirit of the girls kept everything at its brightest. A great deal of reading aloud was done there, chiefly by Fulford. The Palace of Art, Vision of Sin, and Oenone are all mentioned as being read by him in one evening. The young people used to gather round a small oak table to listen, and there was a world of conversation afterwards about what they had heard.

But when the men were alone, much of their talk was of a scheme that for some time past had been taking the place of the first proposed brotherhood and whose details they now threshed out and sifted. It was an idea, suggested by Dixon, of their all joining together to start a magazine, which would be at once a medium for the expression of their principles and enthusiasms and also an assured place for the publication of original work. The whole set welcomed the plan, and Heeley promised help from Cambridge, but innumerable spoken words had to precede the written ones.

What preparation of the heart of man could have been better than this, recorded by Mr. Price after one of their conversations: "It is unanimously agreed that there shall be no shewing off, no quips, no sneers, no lampooning in our Magazine"? Politics, they resolved, were to be almost eschewed, and the contents of the magazine were to be "mainly Tales, Poetry, friendly critiques and social articles."

They went long walks, talking as they went. One gloriously fine day it was to the Lickey Hills; "Art the chief subject going out, Keats coming back," says the diary. Then, for a change, next day, Edward and Morris carried Mr. Jones and Miss Sampson to Spon Lane, and the evening passed merrily, "talking of trifles." A meeting at Heeley's house is mentioned, where conversation fell chiefly upon Carlyle and Tennyson,—Past and Present and the French Revolution were in their hands that Autumn—and again, before Morris' visit came to an end, we see them at Spon Lane, where with prophetic interest Morris and Cormell talked long together of "the organization of labour." Then there were quiet times when Edward and Morris were alone and communed with each other in their own world of imagination. About this world which never failed him Edward once said, "Of course imagining doesn't end with my work: I go on always in that strange land that is more true than real." He had lately found a treasure belonging to that land over which he and his friend now rejoiced together.

It was Southey's reprint of Malory's Morte d'Arthur: and sometimes I think that the book never can have been loved as it was by those two men. With Edward it became literally a part of himself. Its strength and beauty, its mystical religion and noble chivalry of action, the world of lost history and romance in the names of people and places—it was his own birthright upon which he entered.

"I remember I could not buy the precious book," he writes thirty-five years afterwards. "I used to read it in a bookseller's shop day after day, and bought cheap books to pacify the owner, but Morris got it at once and we feasted on it long." After nearly three weeks together in Birmingham Morris went on to Worcester, and Edward started for a long-delayed visit to Harris Bridge, but "the precious book" seems to have been left with him, for when he was back again at home Mr. Price's journal says, "over to Birmingham, round and round the garden with Ted, reading the Morte d'Arthur, the chapters about the death of Percival's sister and the Shalott lady." Then the talks began again, though Morris was not there, except by letters, which he sent often. In one of these letters he evidently spoke about leaving Oxford before taking his degree, for on September 28th Cormell puts succinctly in his diary, "Wrote to Morris two sheets abusing him roundly for thinking of leaving Oxford"—to which Morris answers in his own direct way, "Thank you very much for taking so much interest in me, but make your mind easy about my coming back next term, I am certainly coming back, though I should not have done so if it had not been for my Mother." Dixon too was writing frequently, so that absence was bridged over and the little constellation moved steadily along in its appointed course. Occasionally the evenings were varied by going to the theatre, but generally their own company sufficed them.

One night they are at Fulford's home, talking about dreams and ghosts, and Fulford reads them a story he has written for the yet unnamed magazine. Then the talk swings round to "health in mediaeval times compared with modern."

On October 6th the same post brings letters from both Morris and Dixon, "both sick of aimless, theoretical lives," and by the 13th the whole set, more truly a Brotherhood than ever before, meet in Oxford for what proved to be their last term together. Fulford, who was hesitating about taking orders, had tried the experiment of being a master in a boys' school at Wimbledon, but came back to "coach" Morris for his degree, and Heeley, who had left Cambridge and passed the East India Civil Service examination with distinction, was a great deal with them.

Dixon was living out of College at this time and his rooms were now the usual place of meeting. Dr. Birkbeck Hill, then in his second term at Pembroke, has written sympathetically of evenings that he remembers there; recalling "a little front parlour in a small lodging house in Pembroke Street" as the background of a group of eager young men who were discussing the forthcoming first number of the Oxford and Cambridge Magazine. "It was a new world into which I was brought," he says. "The subjects I had always heard discussed were never discussed here, while matters on which I had never heard anyone speak formed here the staple of the talk."

I cannot help lingering over these days, so affecting in the mingled light of the past and present. Let us take up the story at the first day of term.

"Topsy met me at the station," says Mr. Price: "drove to Dixon's, where were Fulford, Ted, Mac, Hatch, and James Price. Talked about the grind and all topics."

The following day was Sunday, and after Morning Service the men adjourned to Morris' rooms, where "John Oakley came in." This was a man well known and loved through his life for his powerful and genial nature, and remembered by a world larger than the circle of his personal friends as President of the Union at Oxford, hardworking clergyman in the East End of London, and afterwards Dean of Carlisle and of Manchester.

In the evening they met again at Dixon's, where they "talked on a myriad subjects and Ted read some 'Yeast.'" Alton Locke, Hypatia, and Westward Ho! had all been welcomed gladly by the set. Hood too was well known and valued. One night, after Fulford had read Miss Kilmansegg aloud, they all agreed that Hood was underrated. "More humour than wit this night: the fun became rampagious" suggests practical jokes with Edward in the foreground. "Most of the set in a very stupid humour" is another frank verdict. "Ted thinks of leaving Oxford and beginning painting at once," is an entry before the term was a week old, and some words from a home letter of Edward's about the same time may be taken with it: "All the fellows here are quite well; I meet them every day in the evening and sometimes oftener. Altogether the evenings pass pleasantly, but many of us are sadly tired of Oxford I think."

After the night at Havre, Edward and Morris had been of one mind in wishing to leave Oxford directly and go, the one into an architect's office and the other to his painting; but clear as their knowledge was of the way they meant to take, they could not follow it so ruthlessly. Their parents had to be reckoned with—not as mere obstructions, for they loved them—and we have seen the conclusion to which Morris came. There is no account of how Mr. Jones received the news that his son was to be an artist instead of a clergyman, but it is certain he would not long oppose anything which that son desired. Edward carried his difficulty to his firm friend outside the set at Oxford. "I dine at MacLaren's to-day," he writes, "to talk over future prospects and my profession. I want to get the matter settled if possible soon, for it is so wearing not to have a clear object before one." By the end of the term his final declared intention is, "I shall take my degree next June, and commence at once to get a living."

To Edward I believe the most important thing that happened this term was his meeting with Rossetti's illustration to The Maids of Elfenmere, just published in Allingham's Day and Night Songs. For him it cleared up the question of what a modern drawing could be made to express and with how much beauty, and at the sight his own imagination burned within him and he became bold to use it. From what he said at the time about this design he never swerved: "It is I think the most beautiful drawing for an illustration that I have ever seen; the weirdness of the Maids of Elfenmere, the musical timed movement of their arms together as they sing, the face of the man, above all, are such as only a great artist could conceive."

I hesitate to speak about the technicalities of art or about pictures which are their own expounders, but the spirit of Edward's work was a part of himself and my knowledge of him helped me to understand it, so that I feel it is possible to lay one's finger on his earliest work and say: "This was done before and this after he had seen The Maids of Elfenmere."

The designs which were made for Mr. MacLaren's book remain in the possession of his family and are of the most curious interest. The scheme included a frontispiece, title-page, illustrations and ornamental letters. They were begun early in 1854 and carried on for about two years and a half, and in the series may be traced his development from the time that he first went into the Wytham woods to draw leaves and branches until the day when he discovered that the human form was the alphabet of the language he was henceforth to use.

Mr. MacLaren's daughter has repeated to me a story about Edward while he was engaged on this work, which she often heard her father tell. One early morning he was awakened by gravel being thrown at his bedroom window, and looking out saw Edward standing in the garden below with a haggard face. "What 's the matter? what do you want?" "Mac, you must come down—I've been up all night over it, and this drawing won't come right—you must come down and look at it and see if you can say where it 's wrong." MacLaren went down, and with eyes freshly brought to bear upon the drawing saw something that he was able to suggest before his friend turned again to walk back to Oxford.

The visit to Harris Bridge in September had been a pleasant one to Edward, especially in renewing friendship with his cousin Maria Choyce. After his return he writes to her:

"It was a very happy week I spent with you, and I often recall it, day by day, as it went by so tranquilly, so differently from the ordinary course of my life: and among many plans and hopes for future months, not the least in pleasurable forethought is the purpose of again seeing you at Harris Bridge, and carrying on our old conversations that were so soon broken, with better store of knowledge and deeper sympathies."

He intended to begin a regular correspondence with her again, but writing dwindled before painting, and the intention came to nothing. In one of the letters he did accomplish he speaks of his present position and changed views for the future. "And I am to be, Heaven knows what, a painter I hope, if that is possible—if not, why anything so it be not a parson. Save me from that, for I have looked behind the veil." These words recall others occasionally heard from him in later life, about the "material" of which clergymen were made as he saw it in Oxford. The kind of artist he looked forward to being was "probably a poor and nameless one—very probably indeed." An account he gives to her of the Magazine fortunately carries on its history from the point already reached.

"Shall I tell you about our Magazine, as you are so good as to take an interest in it? In the enclosed envelope I have sent you a prospectus. It appeared in nearly all the magazincs of the month, and will be in the Quarterly reviews of January and in the Times. We have thoroughly set ourselves to the work now, banded ourselves into an exclusive Brotherhood of seven. Mr. Morris is proprietor. The expenses will fall very heavily upon him, I fear, for it cannot be published under £500 per annum, exclusive of engravings which we shall sometimes give: he hopes not to lose more than £300, but even that is a great deal. Not one Magazine in a hundred pays, but we are full of hope. We have such a deal to tell people, such a deal of scolding to administer, so many fights to wage and opposition to encounter that our spirits are quite rising with the emergency. We shall restrict ourselves to our present contributors, and not receive any indiscriminate contributions, for we wish to keep before us one aim and end throughout the Magazine, and I question if we should find many to join us in all the undertaking, and answer for all our opinions.

"Two of the most able young writers of Cambridge have joined us, and for three of our Oxford contributors I should look long up and down the world before I could name their peers. Our first number will contain:

Sir Philip Sidney — to be continued through six months	by Mr. Heeley.
Alfred Tennyson & his Poems—through 3 numbers	by Fulford.
The Cousins, a Tale	by me.
Story of the Unknown Church . .	by Morris.
The Rivals, a Tale	by Dixon.
Notice of the Song of Hiawatha . .	by Macdonald.
Essay on The Newcomes . . .	by me.
Notice of Kingsley's Sermons . .	by Heeley.
Winter Weather, a Poem . . .	by Morris.

"I have not gone on with the tale I began at Harris Bridge: that must be in reserve for a long time. In the next number we shall have:

Continuation of Sir Philip Sidney.	
" " Tennyson.	
A Northern Tale	by me.
Essay on French Churches . . .	by Morris.
The War	by Dixon.
Review of Macaulay	by Heeley.
Essay on Carlyle	by Vernon Lushington.

and something else undecided—and I hope an engraving. Of course I am established as permanent artist to the Brotherhood. As the months go on we hope to treat about everything, to have articles on all the great men living or dead. In the March number I shall introduce Ruskin and in the April Fouqué. We have bound ourselves to continue it for one year, and then if it does not turn out such a very great failure we have no limits to its continuance. It will go on till we are all dead, I hope, and perhaps afterwards. I will send you the first number and then you shall please yourself about taking it in. You will find a deal of it very dry sometimes, but you will not mind that. For my part I have not much esteem for things done without labour.

"Watch carefully all that Morris writes. You will find one of the very purest and most beautiful minds on earth breathing through all he touches. Sometimes I even regret that he is my friend, for I am open to the charge of partiality by praising him so, and if he were a stranger I know I should detect him in a heap of others' writings, and watch for something very great from him, as I do now. Fulford also—in all he writes you may place every belief, he is a hard and deep thinker with a perfectly magnetic influence over truth, drawing it to him, and selecting it where others would constantly miss it. He does not write so poetically nor beautifully, or rather pictorially, as Morris, but in argument he is triumphant, you will soon detect him.

"Dixon is another fine fellow, a most interesting man, as ladies would say—dark-haired and pale-faced, with a beautiful brow and a deep, melancholy voice. He is a poet also. I should be sorry to dash the romance of his character, but truth compels me to say he is an inveterate smoker.

"Heeley is an awful fellow—knows everything, so as to have taken the place of the proverb 'The deuce knows,' and invested it with his own personality, 'Heeley knows.' Huge moustachios, not handsome, very awkward, covered with honours at Cambridge.

"Macdonald is at present only a complement. When we have filled our staff to completion he will retire, and two giants come in his place, Faulkner, on whose youthful brows hang the heaviest laurels Oxford has given for years, and a great Cambridge man named Lushington, to whom I have not yet been introduced. He is already an author and I hear a very very fine fellow.

"Such is our little Brotherhood. We may do a world of good, for we start from new principles and those of the strongest kind, and are as full of enthusiasm as the first crusaders, and we may perish in a year as others have done before. Well, if we are wanted I suppose we shall remain, and if not, what have we to want? Nothing, I know, for I can safely affirm for all that no mean and contemptible desire for a little contemporary fame, no mere purpose of writing for writing's sake has prompted one amongst us, but a sole and only wish to teach others principles and truths which they may not know and which have made us happy."

At Rouen Edward and Morris had found the Tauchnitz edition of Thackeray's latest book, The Newcomes, and the enthusiasm with which they read it resulted in the essay which Edward marks in this letter as one of his own contributions to the first number of the Magazine.

In after years he was very sensitive about these early writings, and if it had been possible would have wiped out every word, but the literary power which he disclaimed was proved at Oxford by the frequent "posting" of his name on the gate of his College for English Essays and was shewn always in private correspondence. After he became a painter he seemed to feel a kind of jealousy at the employment of any other means of expression than painting, and deliberately curbed the use of words in public, so that nothing would have induced him to make a speech or write an article.

His Essay on The Newcomes need not be discussed here, but some words in it so clearly put this point of the language of art that I will quote them. "When shall we learn to read a picture as we do a poem, to find some story from it, some little atom of human interest that may feed our hearts withal, lest the outer influences of the day crush them from good thoughts? When will men look for these things and the artist satisfy them?" And in another place, speaking especially of illustrations to books, he writes: "An artist should be no faint echo of other men's thoughts, but a voice concurrent or prophetical, full of meaning."

As to the story of The Cousins, Canon Dixon's memory brings back the scene of its being first read before the Set, and shews us for a moment the whole group. He says: "The first notion I had of E. B.-J.'s literary power was at the time of the starting of the first number of the Oxford and Cambridge Magazine. I had written my tale of 'The Rivals,' and read it one evening to the assembled Brotherhood in my room in Pembroke Street, and it had been received in a manner of which I need here say nothing. Morris had written his 'Story of an Unknown Church': and it had been read, and received in a way of which I remember nothing but my own admiration: but when it was read I cannot recall. A few days afterwards I met Fulford, who said, 'He has written such a gorgeous tale, that man.' He meant E. B.-J. In the evening of the same day (I think) we met in Fulford's room and E. B.-J. read 'The Cousins.' We were all as if dumb at the end of it. I felt the commanding beauty and delicate phrasing, and also the goodness of heart that the writing shewed. I had no notion before that E. B.-J. was gifted so highly for literature. His reading of it was very fine. As soon as he could, he rushed out and left us.

"He afterwards wrote for the Magazine a northern story. I think it was called 'A Story of the North.' My opinion of this was not quite so favourable. It seemed to me too fierce (in style) for the matter; and more laboured than 'The Cousins.'"

There is a frank entry about this time in Mr. Price's diary: "It is observable that less sentiment is uttered than aforetime by us—reserved, I suppose, for paper." Faulkner's double first in Greats, just taken, explains the "laurels" mentioned in Edward's description of him.

The Vernon Lushington spoken of, since well known as Judge Lushington, is so pleasantly drawn in the following description of him by Heeley when they were undergraduates together, that one sees why the Oxford Set must have welcomed him gladly as a contributor.

"One of the jolliest men I know in Trinity is Lushington, son of Dr. Lushington (a great man in the Ecclesiastical

Courts). The young Lushington has been a middy for three years, cruising about the Indian Ocean, having *rencontres* with Arabs &c., then he comes to Cambridge and takes up arms against a sea of troubles, classical and mathematical. He is thoroughly frank, open and sailorlike, earnest and enthusiastic, extremely Radical, but not wildly, taking a great deal of interest in all questions of political economy and moral philosophy, an ardent admirer of Plato, Wordsworth, and especially Ruskin."

But in spite of such companionship at Trinity, Heeley kept a longing eye on the life of his old schoolfellows at Oxford. "I wish," he wrote to one of them, "I had fallen into a set as you have, but I know many men and few well. I wish more than ever that I had something in common with other men beyond common fondness for literature and such things."

Morris took a pass degree, and after that began at once to make arrangements for entering the office of Mr. Street the architect, who was then living in Oxford. This was all settled by the beginning of December, to Cormell Price's great comfort, for Edward did not intend to keep residence next term, and life at Oxford without both his chief friends was not to be calmly contemplated.

So far as I can gather, Edward's plan was to go up to London at the beginning of the new year for a visit to his aunt, and then to return to Birmingham and pass the next two or three months quietly at home, reading for honours. It was unknown to him when he came down to spend Christmas with his father that he had in reality left Oxford.

CHAPTER VIII

ANNUS MIRABILIS
1856

ONE wet morning in January, 1856, Edward found his way to Walpole Street, Chelsea, where the Macdonalds then lived. Whether he intended the call for my brother or whether it had occurred to him that he would see how we all were, I do not know, but that which had been ordained was accomplished and we met again. He was then staying with Mrs. Catherwood, and it is curious to think of all that happened to him during this visit to London having for background her sober little Camberwell house. To its door the post brought the first letter Edward ever received from Ruskin—in answer, I believe, to one that had gone to him with the January number of the Magazine—and the excitement of this event is preserved in some words written to Cormell Price.

"I'm not Ted any longer, I'm not E. C. B. Jones now—I've dropped my personality—I'm a correspondent with RUSKIN, and my future title is 'the man who wrote to Ruskin and got an answer by return.' I can better draw my feelings than describe them, and better symbolise them than either." Beneath is a drawing of himself prostrate on the ground before an aureoled and nimbused presence intended for Ruskin.

On January 9th Miss Price's diary says very simply and truly: "Morris does not like being Editor of the O. and C. Magazine, so gives Fulford £100 a year to be Editor." This arrangement brought Fulford to live in London, where he and Heeley took a lodging together at 20, Montpelier Square, Brompton, that at once became a meeting-place for any of the Set who might be in town; it is referred to when, soon after his arrival in London, Edward writes to Cormell: "On Tuesday I dined at Brompton; Topsy and Macdonald were there, five of us altogether, like old times." About an article that Cormell was writing for the Magazine he goes on to say: "It is safe to be jolly, for you have worked well at it, and are in love with the subject, which is half the battle."

The same feeling that had impelled him to hunt for a portrait of Tennyson now made him eager to know what the man looked like who had drawn the Maids of Elfenmere and written the Blessed Damozel, and he cast about to find how he might be able to see the face of Rossetti. He has himself described so fully the way in which this was accomplished, that though the story has appeared elsewhere it must be repeated here. The quest also brought him and Vernon Lushington together for the first time. "I had no dream," he says, "of ever knowing Rossetti, but I wanted to look at him, and as I had heard that he taught in the Working Men's College in Great Ormond Street, a little University set up by Denison Maurice, where men skilled in science or history gave lectures and their services of evenings, I went to the College one day to find out how it would be possible that I should set eyes upon him. I was told that there was to be a monthly meeting that very evening in a room connected with the College, and that, for a modest payment, anyone could get admittance, including tea, and hear the addresses on the condition of the College and the advancement of studies which were delivered by the different professors—so without fail I was there, and sat at a table and had thick bread and butter, but knowing no one. But good fellowship was the rule there, that was clear, and a man sitting opposite to me spoke at once to me, introducing himself by the name of Furnivall, and I gave my name and college and my reason for coming. He reached across the table to a kindly-looking man whom he introduced to me as Vernon Lushington, to whom I repeated my reason for coming, and begged him to tell me when Rossetti entered the room. It seemed that it was doubtful if he would appear at all, that he was constant in his work of teaching drawing at the College, but had no great taste for the nights of addresses and speeches, and as I must have looked downcast at this, Lushington, with a kindness never to be forgotten by me, invited me to go to his rooms in Doctors Commons a few nights afterwards, where Rossetti had promised to come. So I waited a good hour, or more, listening to speeches about the progress of the College, and Maurice, who was president, spoke of Macaulay's new volume, just out, blaming much the attack on George Fox in a true Carlylese spirit, which was very pleasing—and then Lushington whispered to me that Rossetti had come in, and so I saw him for the first time, his face satisfying all my worship, and I listened to addresses no more, but had my fill of looking, only I would not be introduced to him. You may be sure I sent a long letter about all this to Morris at Walthamstow, and on the night appointed, about ten o'clock, I went to Lushington's rooms where was a company of men, some of whom have been friends ever since. I remember Saffi was there, and Rossetti's brother William, and by and bye Rossetti came, and I was taken up to him and had my first fearful talk with him. Browning's 'Men and Women' had just been published a few days before, and someone speaking disrespectfully of that book was rent in pieces at once for his pains, and was dumb for the rest of the evening—so that I saw my hero could be a tyrant and I thought it sat finely upon him. Also another unwary man professed an interest in metaphysics; he also was dealt with firmly.

"Before I left that night Rossetti bade me come to his studio the next day. It was in the last house by Blackfriars Bridge at the North West corner of the bridge, long ago pulled down to make way for the Embankment; and I found him painting at a water colour of a monk copying a mouse in an illumination. The picture was called 'Fra Pace' afterwards.

"He received me very courteously, and asked much

about Morris, one or two of whose poems he knew already, and I think that was our principal subject of talk, for he seemed much interested about him. He shewed me many designs for pictures: they tossed about everywhere in the room; the floor at one end was covered with them, and with books. No books were on the shelves, and I remember long afterwards he once said that books were no use to a painter except to prop up models in difficult positions, and that then they might be very useful. No one seemed to be in attendance upon him. I stayed long and watched him at work, not knowing till many a day afterwards that this was a thing he greatly hated—and when for shame I could stay no longer, I went away, having carefully concealed from him the desire I had to be a painter."

The passage in Edward's Essay on The Newcomes about the Maids of Elfenmere, the Blessed Damozel, and the Story of Chiaro was already known to Rossetti. In a letter to Allingham written shortly after this visit, he says: "That notice in the Oxford and Cambridge Magazine was the most gratifying thing by far that ever happened to me—being unmistakeably genuine. I thought it must be by your old acquaintance Fryer, of Cambridge, he having called on me once about those same things. But it turns out to be by a certain youthful Jones, who was in London the other day, and whom (being known to some of the Working Men's Coll: Council) I have now met. One of the nicest young fellows in—Dreamland. For there most of the writers in that miraculous piece of literature seem to be. Surely this cometh in some wise of the Germ, with which it might bind up." How the writers' hearts would have burned within them had they heard these words.

Edward remained in London till the second week in February, and then on his way home could do nothing less than stop for four or five days with his friends at Oxford. Mr. Price's diary says that on the evening he arrived, the whole set gathered at Morris' rooms in St. Giles's and there was a "delightful Babel." The next morning, Sunday, they all walked together to Summertown, and Edward and Morris called on MacLaren: a "glorious evening" at Dixon's, then a breakfast "gay, not to say noisy," and one night "Oakley and an Oriel man entranced us by music." Indeed they scarcely separated until, after missing one train, Edward was finally seen off for Birmingham by Cormell between ten and eleven in the evening of St. Valentine's Day. In the midst of all this it is not wonderful that poor little Mrs. Catherwood went short of her accustomed letter, and the national revenue was swelled by one more note of needless woman's anxiety which she posted to Cormell, enquiring whether Edward was ill.

The Easter term found him in Oxford again as he had intended, but the place had done all that it could for him, and he was now so restless that within the first week he gave up the idea of going in for honours and soon afterwards came to the conclusion that it was no use to think of taking even a pass degree until the October term. This decision arrived at, what was there to keep him away from London? His aunt's house was always open to him, and by the 6th of May he was there again. The Royal Academy that year had a wonderful show of pictures: five by Millais, Holman Hunt's "Scapegoat," Wallis' "Chatterton," Arthur Hughes' "April Love," and "Burd Helen," by Windus of Liverpool. Cormell was sent for to come up and see it as soon as possible, and was met by Edward at Paddington Station and rapt away to meet Morris at the Academy before going on to Camberwell. This was the last time that Edward and Cormell stayed there together; for though their affection for the mistress of the house was sincere, it was not possible for them any longer to breathe freely in its atmosphere of small restrictions, where to write a letter on Sunday was a marked thing, to sit on one chair rather than another was to arouse the anxiety of its owner, and Beresford Chapel was always in the background. So in the gentlest manner possible Edward slipped his neck out of the yoke and was very soon settled in rooms of his own.

Morris had been greatly delighted by the picture of

"April Love" and after brooding upon the subject for a few days made up his mind to possess it if possible, but as by that time he had gone back to his work at Oxford, he wrote up to Edward, asking him to see about its purchase. His note is dated Oxford, May 17th: "Will you do me a great favour, viz. go and nobble that picture called 'April Love,' as soon as possible lest anybody else should buy it." This reached Edward on a Saturday evening, and by half past nine on Monday morning he was off to the Academy, fortunately in time to "nobble" the picture, and make Morris happy with the news.

A letter from Edward to his father gives his new London address, 13, Sloane Terrace, Sloane Street, Chelsea, with great clearness, but for the date, May 18th, we are indebted to historical research. After the address the letter runs on: "That's where I live my dear little Pa! and where you'll please to write to me at least once a week. After Crom left I had to go every day to Chelsea to look after lodgings. We wandered, Fulford and I, over Brompton and Chelsea, calling at more houses than I should like to number, through countless, endless streets, and it was not till yesterday about two o'clock that we finally settled to come here. Our requirements were partly against us: first we wanted, and must have, two sitting-rooms, and should prefer two bedrooms—now, out of the 2845 houses we called at, 2374 had only one sitting-room, and of the remainder, 240 only one bedroom; and of the remaining 136 which had two bedrooms and two sitting-rooms, 130 had such dreadful landladies that we positively dared not go—such viragos some of them were, I didn't think womankind really was so appalling. Our present lodgings will do I fancy very well, they are not expensive and not beautiful, but my stay altogether in London will be such a torture as far as care for beautiful objects is concerned, that I am not very particular. Fulford does not join me just at present—he is away from London until to-morrow, and then I expect he leaves for Oxford for about 3 weeks: so I shall be all alone."

The figures, so readily given about the rooms looked at,

remind me that an audacious computation of numbers recklessly random and so fluently written or spoken as at first almost to deceive the elect, grew into a joke well known to Edward's intimate friends, but sometimes startling to others. This was brought home to us the only time I remember Mr. Gladstone coming to the Grange, when Edward told him, as they walked in the garden, that in the branches of a fine old hawthorn growing there, 801,926 birds nightly roosted, and was checked by the interest this statement aroused in his hearer, who courteously enquired, "How many birds did you say?"

To one so accustomed to live in constant exchange of friendly sympathy, solitude was irksome, and in Fulford's absence Edward complained of loneliness: "This is Sunday, and I have not yet seen a face I know, but a little desolation will be the making of one after being accustomed to the contrary for so long." Our door was within half a mile of him, but he never came to see us on Sundays, nor did we as a rule go anywhere on that day except to chapel: I remember thinking it a very bold measure when my brother in vacation time took a walk in the afternoon. This Sunday, May 18th, was probably the only one, however, that Edward spent by himself, for Morris began a pleasant custom of running up from Oxford on Saturdays, bringing with him whatever poems he had made during the week. Often on these Saturday evenings both the friends would go to some play or other with Rossetti, under whose guidance Edward had definitely placed himself and whom he now saw constantly. "But," Edward says, "this embarrassment sometimes happened; that Rossetti would grow sick of the play if it was a silly one, and propose that we should leave at once, which through worship of him we always assented to obediently, though much wanting to know how the story ended. And sometimes we roamed the streets, and sometimes went back to Blackfriars to Gabriel's rooms, and sat till three or four in the morning, reading and talking. Our Sundays were very peaceful days in Sloane Terrace, often spent by Morris in reading aloud the Morte d'Arthur while I worked, and often Rossetti would join us in the afternoon, and it became clear that he cared to be with us. Then by the first train to Oxford on the Monday morning Morris would go back, so as to reach the office by 10, and I would walk with him through the Park to Paddington."

The house in Sloane Terrace where Edward lodged was almost exactly opposite the chapel of which my father was a minister, and sometimes after service, as the congregation filed out, the eyes of a girl amongst the slowly moving crowd were lifted and saw for a moment his face watching at a window.

One day early in June my mother called me into her room and told me that Edward had been to see my father and herself; and then she went on with what seemed to me to have been written from the beginning of the world, and ended by saying that they left the answer they should give him entirely to my decision. There was no difficulty in her seeing what that was, and we knelt down together to ask for the blessing of God upon it. I was not quite sixteen then. Looking back I feel the deepest respect for my parents because they never discussed with me the "prospects" of my marriage; my father asked Edward no questions about his "position," but, so far as my judgment goes, acted as a minister of the Christian religion should do, seeking nothing but character and leaving the question of fortune altogether on one side. Neither he nor my mother had at this time any idea of Edward's genius, but they liked him very much and trusted him completely; by the young people of the house he was recognized more clearly, and the advent of "Mr. Edward," as the children called him, was of infinite importance to more than one of them. His sweetness of temper endeared him to them at once, and as they came to know him better his endless fun, and the treasures of knowledge that he was ready to share with them in ways proportioned to their understanding, made them adore him. One of the children, a girl of ten when he first entered the family, was very specially beloved by him in return, and to her he talked and wrote in a way

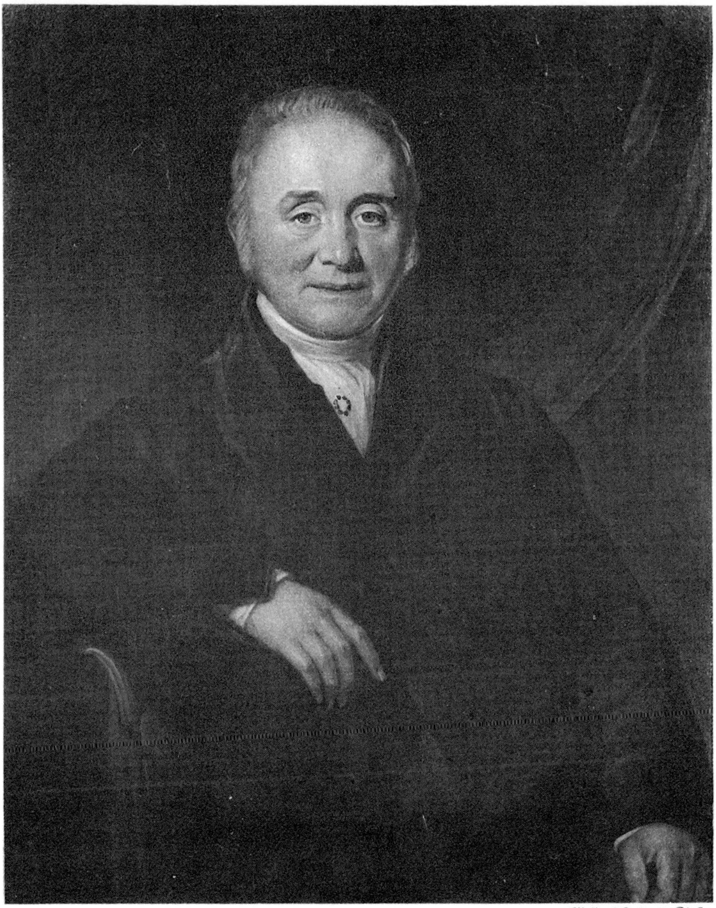

Walker & Cockerell Ph.Sc.

Mr. Benjamin Coley
from a painting.

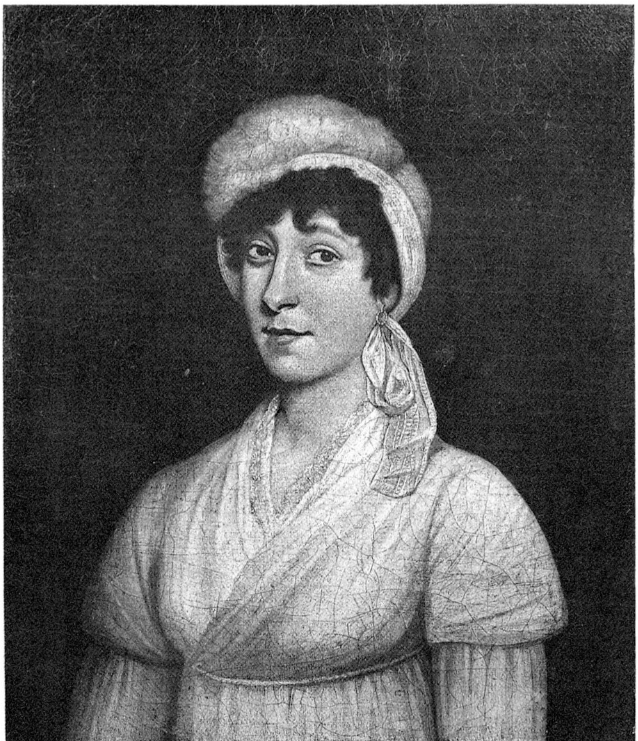

Walker & Cockerell Ph. Sc.

Mrs Edward Biven Jones
from a painting.

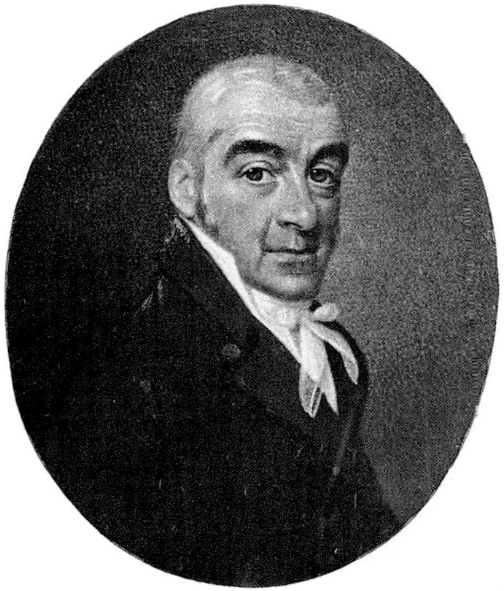

Mr. Thomas Burne
from a miniature.

Walker & Cockerell Ph. Sc.

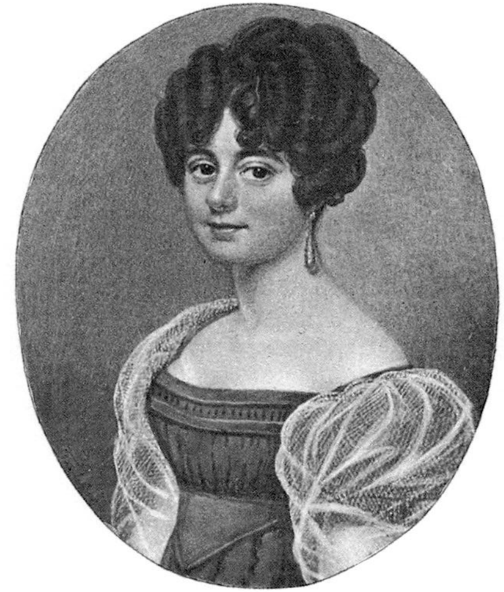

Mrs. Burne
from a miniature.

Walker & Cockerell Ph. Sc.

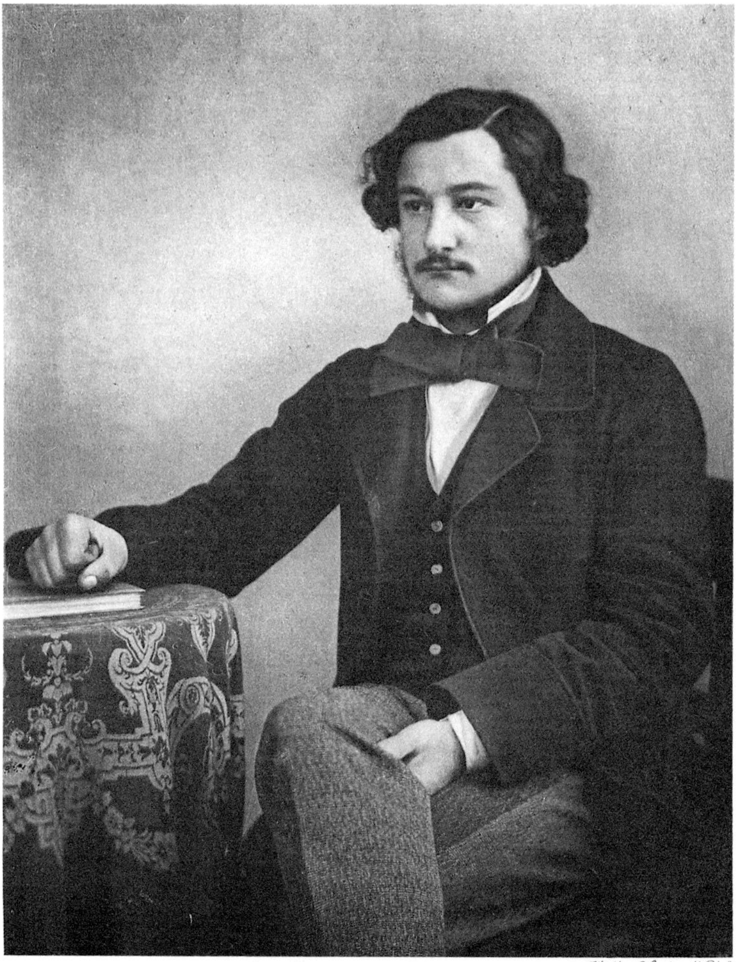

Walker & Cockerell Ph. Sc.

William Morris
aet 23.

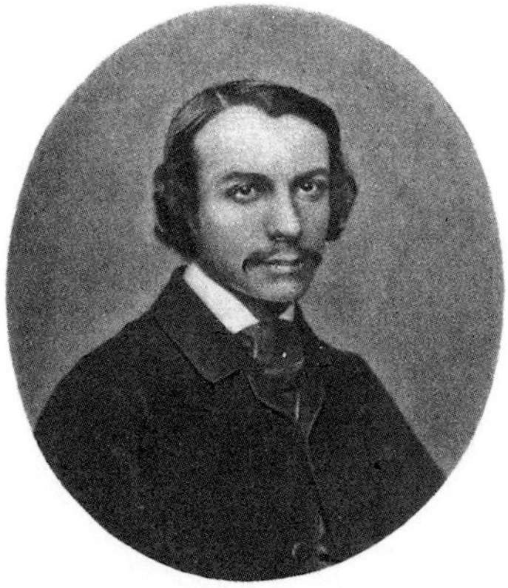

Cormell Price
aet 22.

Walker & Cockerell Ph. Sc.

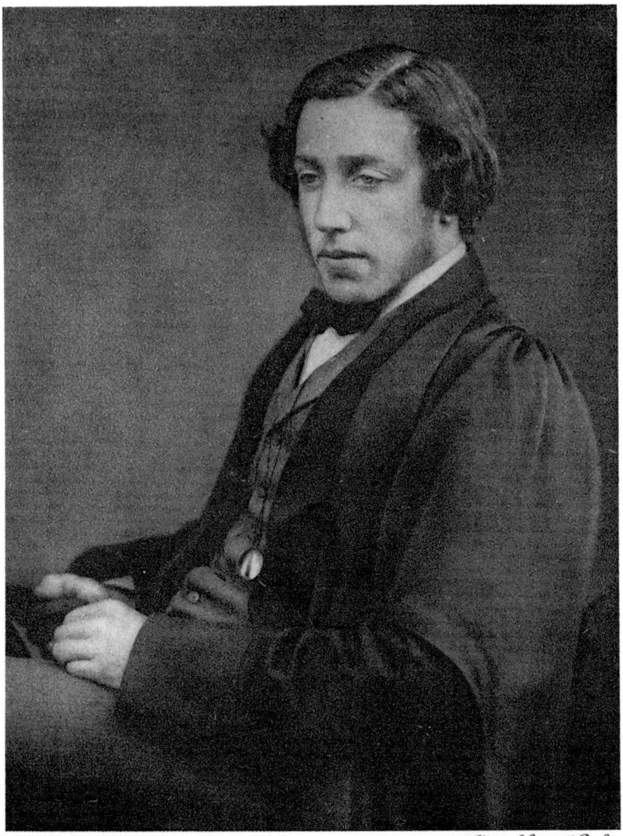
Walker & Cockerell Ph. Sc.

Charles J. Faulkner
aet 24.

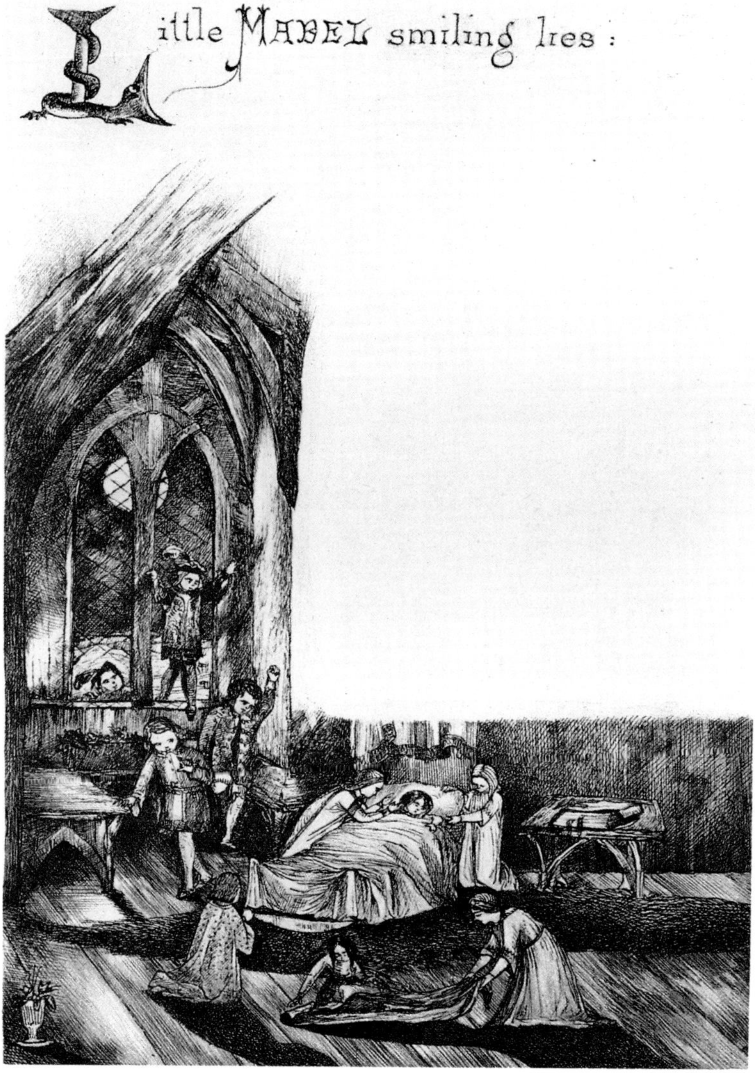

Edward Burne-Jones, Del. Walker & Cockerell Ph. Sc

Illustration to the Fairy Family by Archibald MacLaren.

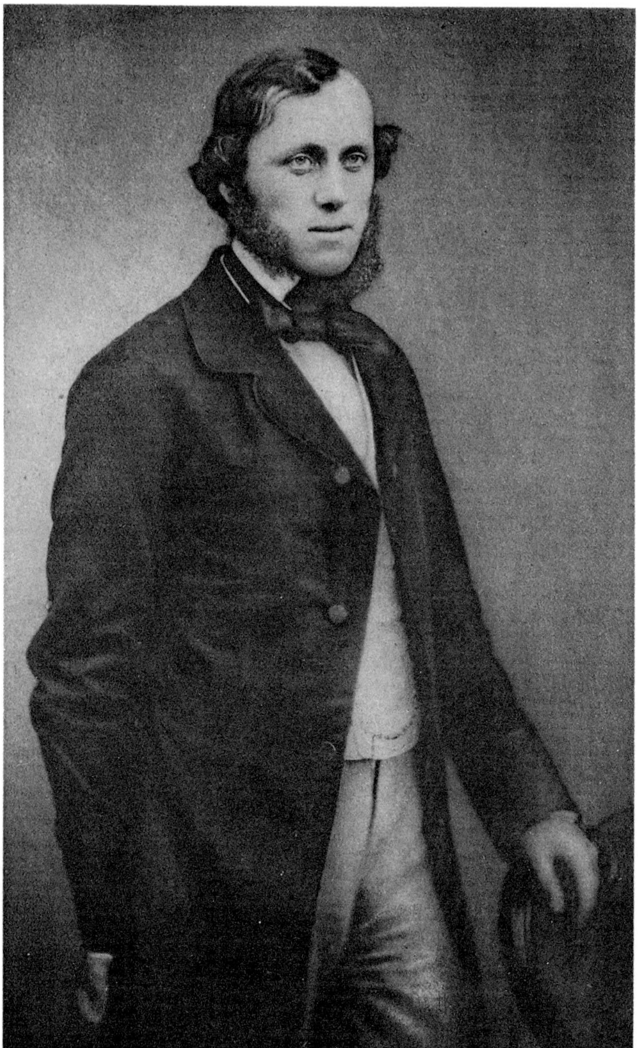

Walker & Cockerell Ph. Sc.

Vernon Lushington
aet. 26.

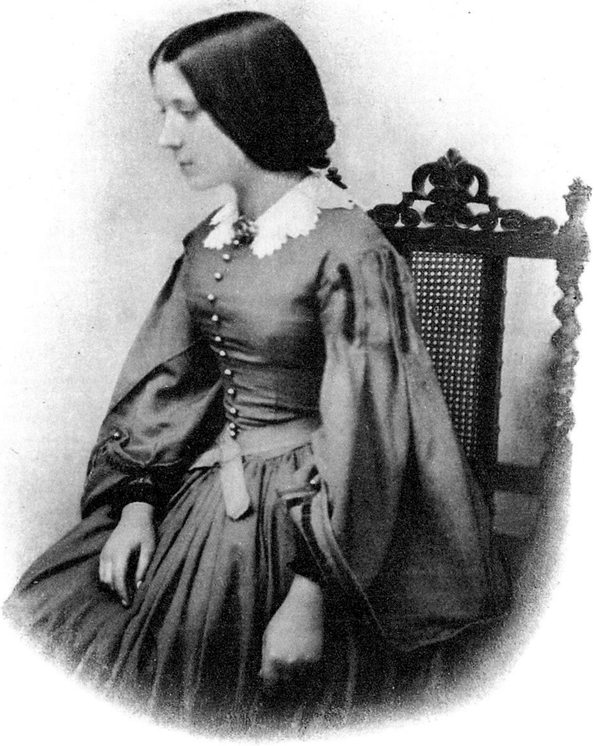

Georgiana Macdonald aet. 16
from a photograph.

Walker & Cockerell Ph. Sc.

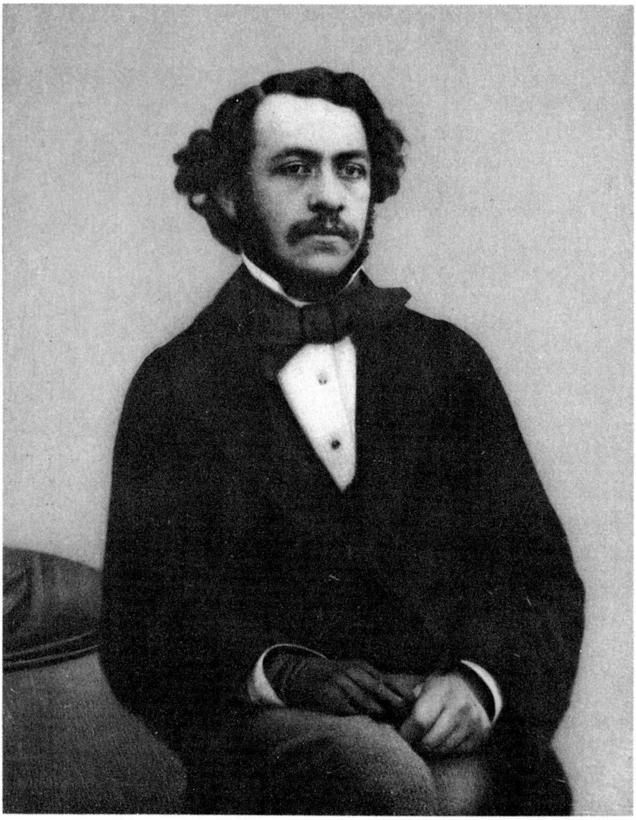

Walker & Cockerell, Ph. Sc.

Wilfred Heeley

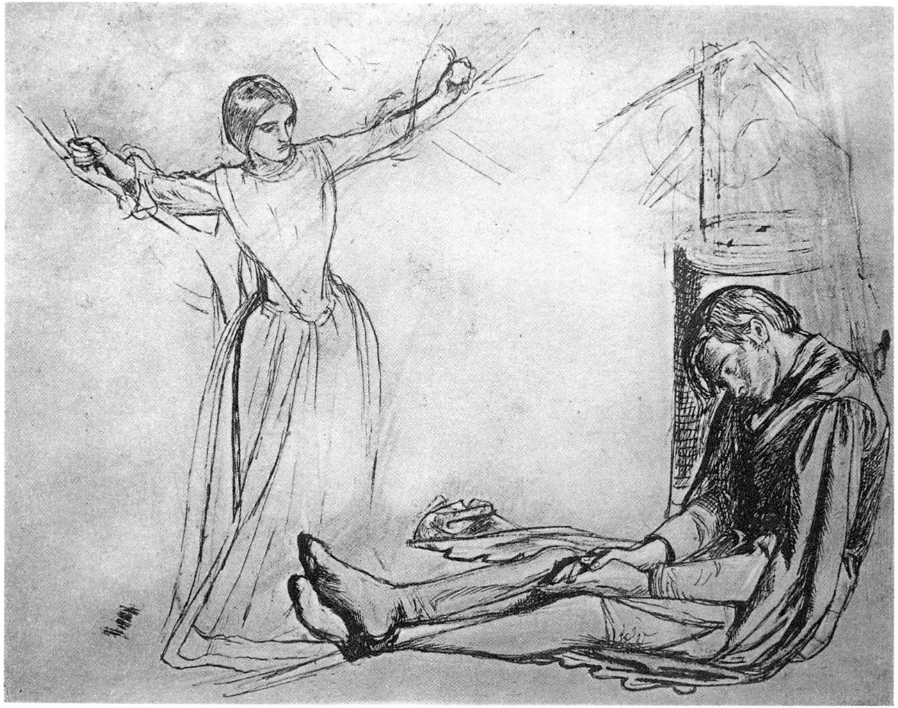

Walker & Cockerell Ph.Sc.

Lancelot's Dream of the San Graal:
sketch by D. G. Rossetti for a portion of his design
for the decoration of the Oxford Union.

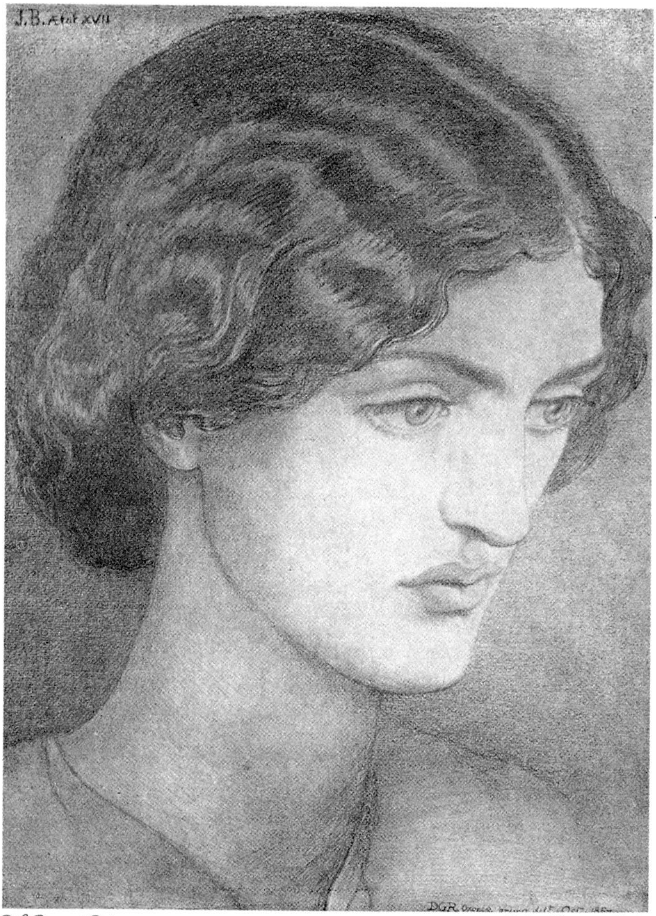

D.G. Rossetti. Del.

Walker & Cockerell Ph. Sc.

Miss Jane Burden.

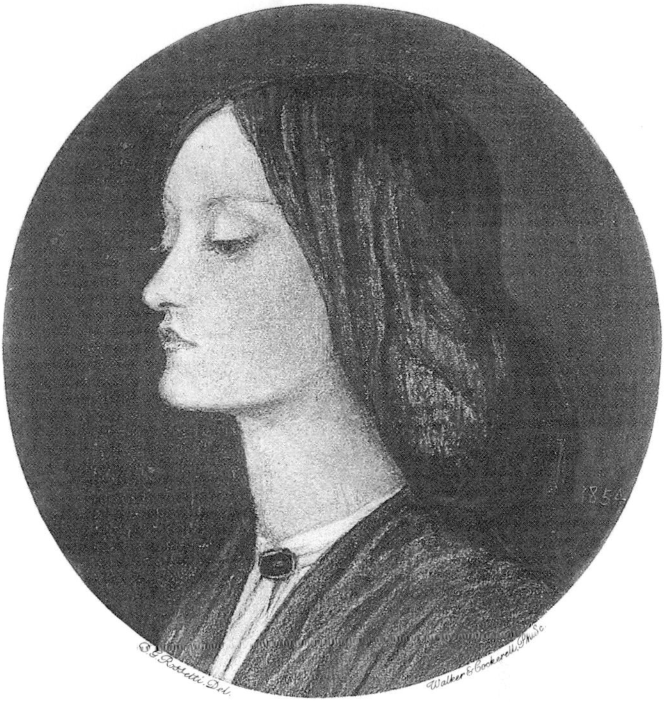

Miss Siddal.

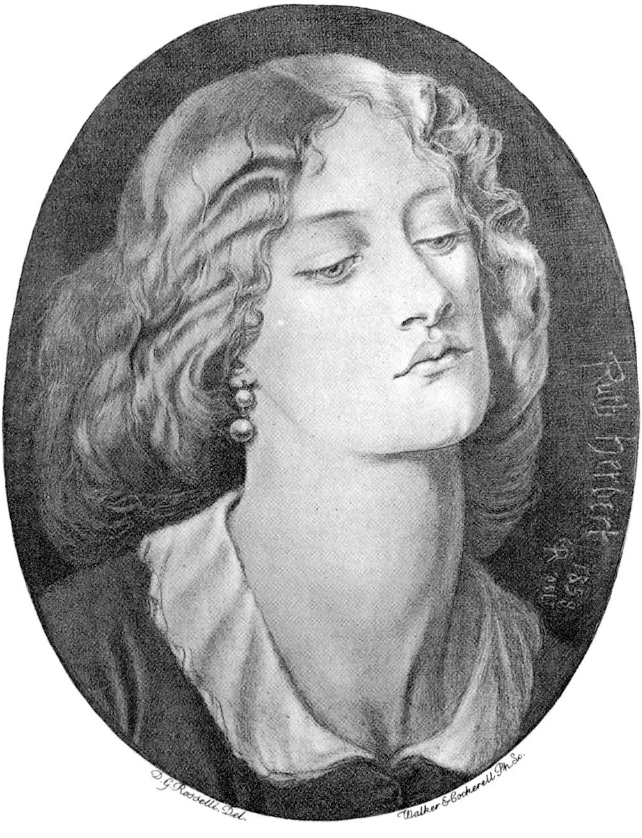

Miss Herbert.

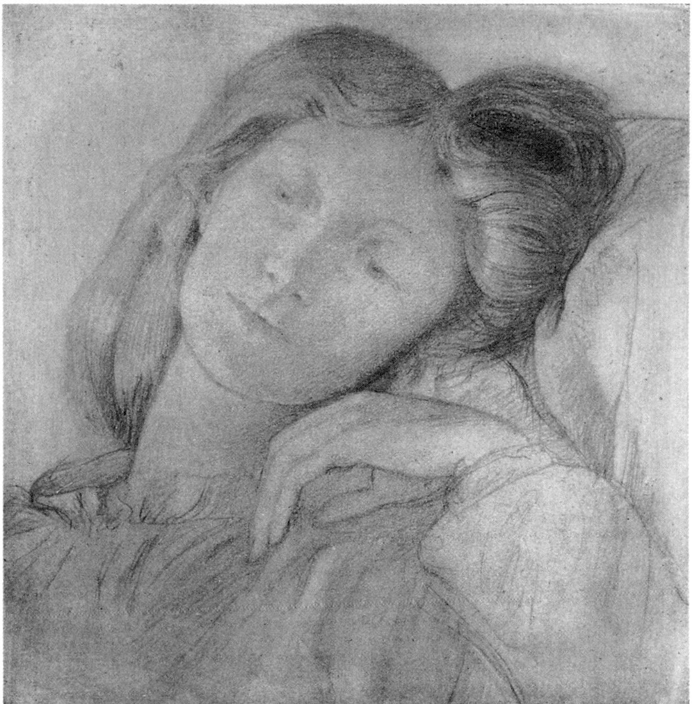

D. G. Rossetti, Del. | Walker & Cockerell Ph. Sc.

Mrs Dante Gabriel Rossetti.

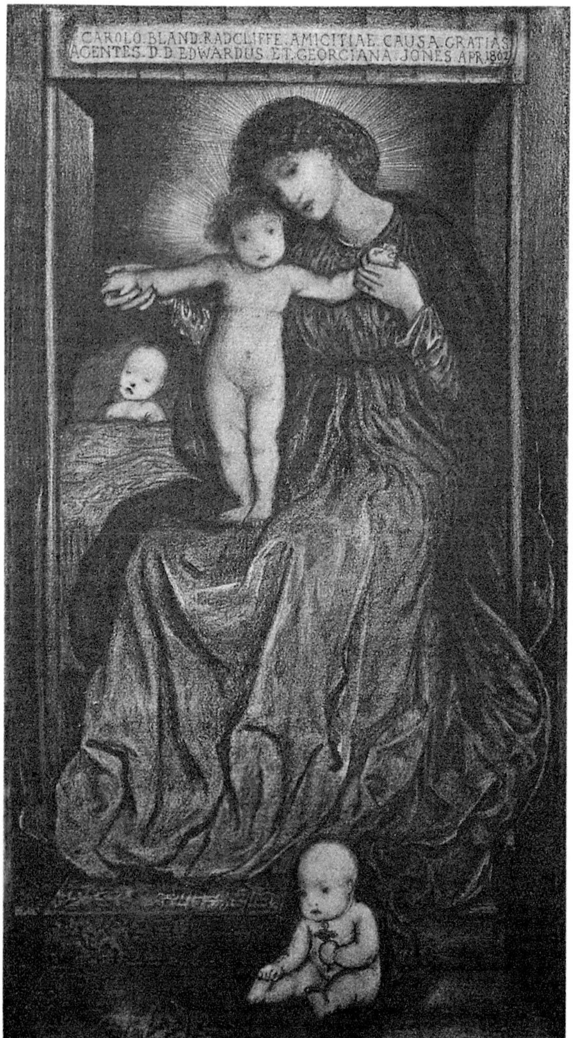

Edward Burne-Jones Del.   Walker & Cockerell Ph. Sc.

The Mother of Healing.

that the difference in their age would have seemed to make impossible.

Morris came up from Oxford to see Edward at this crisis, and in his usual generous way of accepting what a friend had done, called to see me. He brought Turner's Rivers of France in his hand, and I thanked him and he wrote my name in it, but we were not much the nearer for this meeting. The poet who wrote the poem of Guendolen seemed one person and the man I saw before me another—my eyes were holden that I could not yet see.

Mr. MacLaren also, who had waited vainly all through this year of surprises for the completion of the illustrations to his book, gave a fresh proof of friendship for Edward, by coming to our house with kindest messages from his wife and an opal ring for me as a sign that I was to be adopted into the friendship. Seldom, however, has the ring been worn, for superstition, which touched Edward here and there, made him think opals unlucky.

The drawings for the Fairy Family were never finished, but MacLaren's forbearance and generosity about the whole matter never gave way. For a long time Edward persuaded himself and promised his friend that he could go on with the designs, and then he would find it impossible, and disappoint both himself and MacLaren, while in another way the delay was harassing a business firm who were not particularly anxious to publish the illustrations at all, till at last a crisis came in which with dignified regret not untinged by rebuke MacLaren wrote to Edward saying that he had broken off the pending negotiations with Mr. Longman, and felt "simply grateful at being released from a transaction that was becoming altogether intolerable. The MS. is to be revised and returned," he adds, "as much of it was written with a view to pictorial designs accompanying the text, and the drawings I have collected in a portfolio and hold them at your disposal." A glance at these drawings explains everything, for they are the work of two separate people and nothing could have made them homogeneous. No harm, however, came to friendship from this failure of cherished plans, for MacLaren's frankness proved the truth of

> I was angry with my friend,
> I told my wrath, my wrath did end.

To the shrine of Rossetti at Blackfriars I was led for a short awestruck visit, of which I remember little except that he went on painting while we were there, and that I noticed the sensitive look of his hand as well as the beautiful olive colour of his skin, so different from that of a dark Englishman.

There was no more talk of Edward's going back to Oxford for his degree: Rossetti's encouragement and advice had decided him to give his whole life to Art. He was now close upon twenty-three years of age, a time when painters should have mastered the mechanical part of their craft, and he was only at its beginning: but Rossetti knew with whom he had to deal when he urged him against the Hill Difficulty, and Edward faced it with as few words as possible. His working materials henceforth seemed to become a part of himself, and my instinctive remembrance of him at this time is always with a drawing portfolio under his arm.

Meanwhile Rossetti set about finding some employment for him by which he might be able to live. The first idea that suggested itself was to get for him a commission to draw the wood block for an engraving that was to be made from Windus' picture of "Burd Helen," but before the plan was settled Morris one day shewed Gabriel some of Edward's own original designs, and he then refused to let him copy "Burd Helen." The drawings were probably some of those done for Mr. MacLaren, and were shewn without Edward's knowledge and in his absence, so that when he re-entered the room he was overwhelmed by Gabriel coming up to him and saying as he put his arm round his shoulder, "There are not three men in England, Ned, that could have done these things." Talking about

Rossetti, many a long year after this time, Edward said, "Towards other men's ideas he was decidedly the most generous man I ever knew. No one so threw himself into what other men did—it was part of his enormous imagination. The praises he at first lavished on me, if I had not had a few grains of inborn modesty, would have been enough to turn my head altogether."

Shortly after our engagement he went home to see his father instead of writing to tell him about it, and on a summer evening, at the side of his mother's grave, he opened his own heart and comforted that of the lonely man before bringing him up to see us all. I feel now the injustice which made me regard Mr. Jones at the age of fifty-four as an old man, but that was the impression I received. He was very different in appearance from his son. Edward was, as I have already mentioned, of ample size both in height and breadth, his head large and powerful, his complexion very fair, and his eyes light in colour. His father was short and slight, with a head small even in proportion to his figure, a dark skin, and hair and eyes both black. Still, between the two a subtle likeness in feature and expression occasionally showed itself, and in Edward Richard Jones there were hints of certain qualities which took larger form in his son. There was a romance in his nature which set him quite apart from most of his contemporaries, and an uncommonness that struck all who knew him, and made some dislike him because they saw nothing to excuse it; a kind of innocence, too, which kept him incapable of believing in the mass of the world's wickedness, together with hot prejudices for and against particular things and people. He was one whom no years could ever make really old, and the very last material for a successful tradesman. His disposition was affectionate, but his temper, I have heard, could be quick and fiery—to me he was always gentle. There was much of the old world in his extreme courtesy to women as a rule, but his horror of them if they were overfat or at all masculine was almost ludicrous. As Edward reached maturity his father seemed to abdicate his own position and to look up to his son in all things; which one of his grandchildren instantly fathomed when she saw a meeting between the two, saying afterwards, "I didn't know which was which, for papa said, 'Well, little chap, how are you?' and grandpapa said, 'Well, old boy!'" Imagination was strong in the father without any artistic power to use it, and both he and his sister, Mrs. Catherwood, were of the highly nervous physical organization which Edward inherited to the full. It must have been from his mother that he received a suavity of nature which laid to rest the irritability generally accompanying this temperament.

I was taken to make Mrs. Catherwood's acquaintance at a kind of half-way house between hers and ours, in the shape of a confectioner's somewhere near Trafalgar Square, where people went to lunch after seeing the Royal Academy—Farrance, I think, was the name—but the part of the meeting I liked best was the walk there through Eaton Square and St. James' Park with Edward, for though she was kind to me such times are always well over. At her own house afterwards I learnt to love her. In August of this year our term at Chelsea ended, but our father's new station was at no greater distance than Marylebone, whither we removed in time for him to be in the pulpit of Hinde Street Chapel on the first Sunday in September. The house prepared for us was No. 17, Beaumont Street, and dark and ugly it was, within and without: yet, as I remember it, I take hope in looking at such dwellings from the thought that they may perhaps shelter young hearts as ardent as ours were then. In August also Mr. Street came up to live in London, accompanied by Morris as his pupil, and his senior clerk, afterwards the architect Philip Webb, with whom Morris had already formed a close friendship. Of course Edward and Morris arranged to live together, and by the time we came to Marylebone they had found rooms at No. 1, Upper Gordon Street, and we all settled down more or less contentedly in our dingy surroundings. A ray of light fell on 17, Beaumont Street, when we found it was nearly *dos à dos* with a house in Devonshire Place where the Brownings stayed when in London. There Edward was taken by Rossetti one evening to see them, and met also Mr. Charles Eliot Norton of Harvard University, whose friendship was to mean so much for us in future years. A very small flagged backyard was the only playground belonging to our house, and there the youngest children pulled up one of the flags, and with the help of a little earth bought from a florist laboured the black soil until an occasional seed would germinate. The "Beast Gardens" in Regent's Park were within a mile or so from us, but we could not often go to them, and they chiefly remained a centre of imagined marvel, surrounded by the outer ring within whose palings was our country walk.

Edward now went to a Life Class (Lee's in Newman Street) on the evenings that he did not come to us, but he still continued to see a great deal of Rossetti at any hour of the day or night, and everything he saw increased his admiration. "I was sensitive enough," he once said, speaking of this time, "to have suffered a shock to my worship if any jar had come, but I heard and saw none, and felt him perfect."

A letter to his father describes his first seeing Holman Hunt. "A glorious day it has been—a glorious day," he exclaims, "one to be remembered by the side of the most notable ones in my life: for whilst I was painting and Topsy was making drawings in Rossetti's studio, there entered the greatest genius that is on earth alive, William Holman Hunt—such a grand-looking fellow, such a splendour of a man, with a great wiry golden beard, and faithful violet eyes—oh, such a man. And Rossetti sat by him and played with his golden beard passing his paint-brush through the hair of it. And all evening through Rossetti talked most gloriously, such talk as I do not believe any man could talk beside him."

And now Edward began the series of designs and pictures which never ceased as long as he lived. I shall not criticize what he did—I am not the right person to do that—but it is and always was impossible to think of him separately from the work, which was part of him.

The first design that I remember is the pen-and-ink drawing of "The Waxen Image," which he used to work at on the evenings that he came to our house. It was followed by "The Wise and Foolish Virgins," "Sir Galahad," "Kings' Daughters," "The Marriage of Buondelmonte," "Going to the Battle," and others. These are not named in order of time, but as I see them rise up in memory. He used to spin them out of his mind with unfailing certainty and swiftness, and with such apparent ease that at first I did not know how astonishing it was. Sometimes he would ask one of us to sit or stand to him for a few minutes, and if it was my sister Agnes, there were sure to be passages of fun between them. For a joke had grown up that she, whose features were certainly the most symmetrical in the family, was the plain, homely daughter who needed a little encouragement from time to time to keep her from being quite overwhelmed by a sense of her own deficiencies; and the task of reconciling this view with a request that she would just let him draw her profile, or please take such and such an action for a minute, was only to be achieved by the use of many words. It was a happy moment for us all when he begged her one evening to be good enough to sit for the Witch who tolls the bell in the second scene of "The Waxen Image," and her willingness to do it completed the jest. In those early years he worked constantly thus, in public, and looking back I cannot understand how it was possible, except by the power which I have noticed before as being so marked in him, that of withdrawing into the fastnesses of his own mind and there carrying on a second life. He never had a studio to himself until 1859, and even then he was still interrupted continually by friends whom it was impossible for him to do anything but welcome; indeed it was very long before the absolute necessity of being alone with his work forced itself upon him. In later years we used to know he was often really absent from us whilst pleasantly smiling and answering our questions, and when occasionally this was proved beyond all doubt by his gently uttering quite wrong words, we would tax him with it and laugh together as he confessed. He had told us of the word "Camels"; with us a passing jest furnished a convention of "The Tower of Babel" for the same purpose. An intelligent and favourite studio servant once brought home to his master a consciousness of this inattention to visible things by saying sympathetically, "Mind elsewhere, sir"—as indeed it often needed to be.

Every book by Ruskin that Edward possessed was brought round to me before breakfast the morning after we were engaged—a royal gift. That morning was the 10th June, 1856, so that the day which had meant so much to us had been the 9th—Dante's own day—and when we remembered this we said we would keep it for our own too, and however long it might be before we were married, our wedding-day should be the 9th of June—which came to pass.

On the eleventh birthday of the little sister of whom I have spoken, Edward took her, as a treat she could quite understand, to see Rossetti, who was very kind to her—talking with her and giving her a proof of Holman Hunt's beautiful etching for the first number of The Germ, with the date of her birth and his name and hers together written underneath it. Morris, too, came to love the child very much, and she used to spend whole days with him and Edward in their studio, furnished by them with pencils and paints, working after her own fashion and eagerly drinking in all they said to her and to each other. Edward in his encouraging way helped her to make two pen-and-ink drawings which he insisted on calling hers; one was of Christ receiving little children and one of the Prince waking the Sleeping Beauty: the figure of the Sleeping Princess is the same type that he used in 1890.

The first book that Edward gave me, even before our engagement, was Fouqué's Minstrel Love, and the next a translation of Rio's Poetry of Christian Art. There is a pencil list in his own handwriting, made since the death of Morris, where he has put down the names of a few amongst the books and stories that the Set especially liked when they were together—and it is this: "Heir of Redclyffe, Sintram, all Fouqué's books, Dickens, Ruskin, Kingsley (Alton Locke and Hypatia), Carlyle towards the last, and two stories in 'Household Words,' Alice and the Angel and Colonel Quagg's Conversion."

To Morris, soon after we knew him, we owed the priceless treasure of Lane's Arabian Nights, for he gave the one-volume edition of it to my sister Agnes, putting on the fly-leaf: "I write your name in pencil, in case you think it loathly." On the contrary, it entranced her and all of us, so that even the youngest sister would sit by the fireside on her little stool, reading it as long as ever she was allowed, whilst the outer world passed away and her sisters were looked at with dim eyes and addressed as "O daughters of my father." Ruskin's Lectures had reached us from Oxford through my brother Harry. The Seven Lamps was the next wonderful experience, and then on to The Stones of Venice and Modern Painters—much I fear that the common round and daily task were neglected by me in those days through the indulgence of my mother and elder sister.

While we lived in Chelsea I was sent to learn drawing at the Government School of Design, then carried on at Gore House, Kensington, for I had a certain deftness of hand, but I did not learn anything vital. Often on the way back Edward met me with flowers and we walked home together. I had no precise idea of what the profession of an artist meant, but felt that it was well to be amongst those who painted pictures and wrote poetry.

Edward went home for his birthday as usual this year, and whilst there found time to write to my little sister a letter of which this is part.

"Ah, Louie, my little pupil, best and dearest, I was so very glad you wrote to me, it would not have been quite my birthday without some memorial of you: even upon other days I can't get along so very well without you, and yesterday I should have been less happy certainly. By the bye, Louie, I am only twenty-three—a shocking old fellow I grant you, but not so hopelessly grey-haired as you thought me—no, I hope to be a very different kind of fellow when I am twenty-four, better and cleverer, and in every thing advanced beyond this present: up till now I seem not to have done anybody any good, but when I work hard and paint visions and dreams and symbols for the understanding of people, I shall hold my head up better.

"It is so strange, dear, that this time last year I did not know you. I spent the day with Topsy and Fulford, and I remember we laughed and enjoyed ourselves as well as possible, making all manner of fun out of everything and nothing, as occasion served: and all the time I never dreamed that the circling of another year would alter all my destinies so much: now I love you all more than life.

"I think it very kind of you to have begun Dante, you will not understand him fully yet—at least I cannot—but by and bye we will all learn Italian together, and follow him into the strange lands he visited as well as we may: he is the central poet of Art: for the most part I hate all translations, but I make one exception for Dante—no man dreams so fearfully and beautifully, or loves more intensely. I do so look forward, dear, to the years afterwards, when we shall learn things together (you and Georgie and I)—so much about Art there is to learn and live for. I want to teach you so many things at once—so much history, that your sympathy may grow continually wider, and you may be able to feel and realize past generations of men just as you do the present, sorrowing for them when they failed, and triumphing with them when they prevailed; for I find this one conviction never changing with me but always increasing, that one cannot live a life manfully or truthfully without a very wide world of sympathy and love to exercise it in. So long, I know, as I had no heroes, but all times and generations of the past and present years were as one dead level of interest or indifference, I then knew nothing truly, nor enjoyed deeply, nor loved strongly, but now that I have set aside my heroes for peculiar reverence—all such as have been highly blessed with Imagination, and have laboured nobly, and fought valiantly, hundreds of them up and down the great centuries—since then I have seen things more truly than ever before."

This same happy year Faulkner gained another distinction at Oxford, and the note that took the news to his widowed mother is so true a portrait of himself in its simplicity and modesty that it will tell more of our friend than anything I could hope to say. June 10, 1856, is its date.

"Contrary quite to my expectation, I have obtained a Fellowship at University College. I do not know anything about its value and so on yet; nor can I tell whether I shall be able to come home to-morrow now. Thank God I have succeeded at last. I cannot stay to write any more and methinks these few words are almost enough for a letter."

In October, when he entered his new College, he reviews the time when the Set used to be all together, and comments on it to his mother with affectionate regret: "The number of my old friends begins sadly to diminish up here, each succeeding term, and it does not seem as if I should meet with others of like character. They were men quite unlike the usual kind of University men. I shall never, I hope, lose their friendship."

At the end of the Long Vacation Heeley was married and went out to India. His wife lived in Birmingham and the wedding was made a rallying point for as many of his friends as possible; Edward, Morris, Fulford, Faulkner and Vernon Lushington all met there. Cormell was away, but a letter to him from his own home gives us a moment's glimpse of Morris, Edward and Fulford together again at Spon Lane, as they had been the year before.

"We spent a very happy day on Thursday," says Miss

Margaret Price, "but we always do when your friends are here. I had not seen Morris before; for I was out when he came down last year—I think he is the most splendid fellow! I don't at all wonder at your all loving him so, and his face is really beautiful. Fan thinks he has improved in looks very much lately. I never saw anything like his hair, it is much *greater* than ever it was before, in fact a mass of curls and waves that will soon sweep his shoulders. Edward doesn't look at all well, he is so thin and pale. Fulford was in the most noisy, quizzical humour imaginable, no one could get a word in edgeways for him, and whenever Topsy wanted to say anything he sprang into the middle of the room and flourished his fists till Fulford was silenced. Fulford talked for quite three hours without stopping excepting for Morris' flourishes."

A vision comes back to me now of the last time we saw Wilfred as quite a young man; a cab stopping at the door in Beaumont Street, with him and his bride in it and a mountain of luggage on the top, and all of us who were at home, including Edward, running out into the street to bid them good-bye and Godspeed. Then they drove straight to London Bridge, and so went on to India, and the Mutiny, and a life of happy marriage which lasted six years and then ended in a day with her death from cholera.

The close union of mind between Edward and Morris made Rossetti at this time equally a hero to them both, and their devotion, which was worth having, gave him pleasure. "Morris and Jones have now been some time settled in London," he writes to Allingham, "and are both, I find, wonders after their kind." Edward, at all events, was with him constantly; Morris had to spend part of each day in Mr. Street's office, but before long Gabriel persuaded him to give up architecture and take to painting, saying that if any man had poetry in him he should paint it, that the course of poetry had almost been run, but painting was still an unknown art in England, and that the next Keats ought to be a painter.

He knew that, in comparison with himself and Edward,

Morris was a rich man, and so had no scruples in urging him to take to what might be for some years an unprofitable profession; but for Edward, whose health was delicate and whose means were small, he felt responsibility, and with the true common sense of genius advised him to give up living in furnished rooms, an expensive form of bachelor life, and to seek for unfurnished ones as soon as possible.

He said that he thought some rooms at 17, Red Lion Square, in which he had lived with Walter Deverell in early P. R. B. times, were to be had; so next day they all went to look at them, and before evening they were taken. Gabriel wrote to Allingham that he had been to look at his old quarters and found them all dusty and unused, with an address that either he or Deverell had written on the wall of a bedroom still there after five years, the only sign of life left in the place, "so pale and watery had been all subsequent inmates, not a trace of whom remained." Red Lion Square was dark and dirty, but much more interesting than Upper Gordon Street, where the houses were so exactly like each other that Edward once entered the wrong door without noticing it, and had shouted for dinner and got halfway upstairs before finding his mistake. Morris and Edward had the first floor, on which there were three rooms; a large one in front with the middle window cut up to the ceiling for a painting light, a medium-size room behind this, which Edward had, and a further and smaller one, which was Morris'. Some French people named Fauconnier, who were feather-dressers, were the tenants of the house, and carried on their business below. Here Gabriel often came, and his influence with the two friends constantly increased. A trace of the removal to Red Lion Square at the end of November is found in a letter to a lady whom Edward had met at Heeley's wedding—Miss Charlotte Salt, of Birmingham. Her friendship, extended to me also, has been without shadow of turning from that time to this. He writes: "You see we have removed from Gordon Street—such a hideous nuisance this has been, for my notions of all domestic arrangements are of the most limited description. I think to see me in the midst of a removal is to behold the most abjectly pitiable sight in nature; books, boxes, boots, bedding, baskets, coats, pictures, armour, hats, easels—tumble and rumble and jumble. After all one must confess there is an unideal side to a painter's life—a remark which has received weight in the fact that the exceedingly respectable housekeeper we got has just turned in upon us in the most unequivocal state of intoxication." And the next day the story goes on in a letter to Miss Sampson: "We are quite settled here now. The rooms are so comfortable, not very furnished at present but they will be soon; when I have time I will make a rough drawing of the place and send it down. Topsy has had some furniture (chairs and table) made after his own design; they are as beautiful as mediaeval work, and when we have painted designs of knights and ladies upon them they will be perfect marvels."

In this same letter he says, "To-day we are to go and see Ruskin," and after their return, "Just come back from being with our hero for four hours—so happy we've been: he is so kind to us, calls us his dear boys and makes us feel like such old old friends. To-night he comes down to our rooms to carry off my drawing and shew it to lots of people; to-morrow night he comes again, and every Thursday night the same—isn't that like a dream? think of knowing Ruskin like an equal and being called his dear boys. Oh! he is so good and kind—better than his books, which are the best books in the world."

This strong personal feeling for Ruskin always lasted: I remember Edward's joy when some one said there was a likeness between them: and surely there must have been at that time, for when first Ruskin called at Red Lion Square he was shewn straight into the room where Edward was with no more introduction than "Your father, sir."

His promise to make a rough drawing of the place was fulfilled, and the half-sheet of notepaper on which it was done has survived the chances of destruction for these forty-eight years. It is a faithful record of the general aspect of

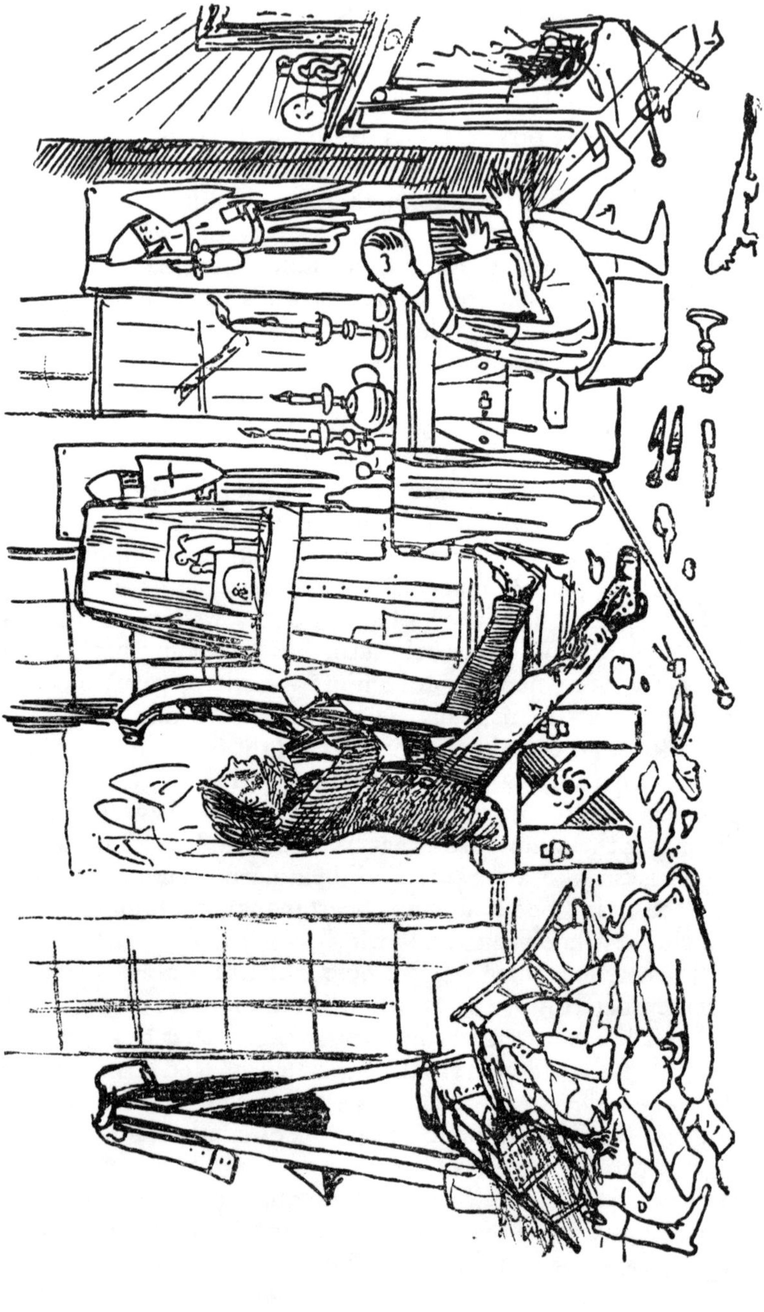

the room, with Edward himself, in caricature likeness, looking with devouring interest at a picture with which Rossetti had glorified one of the chairs that Morris designed. And not only chairs did Gabriel glorify for them, but everything else; for they first knew him when his splendid power was undimmed, so that he raised a lasting standard for them. As long as Edward lived he said that he never did anything without wondering what Gabriel would have thought of it, "whether he would approve it and be pleased with it, or whether he'd say it was rubbish."

All the actual study of painting that Edward did with Rossetti was a few mornings' work in his studio, but what he learnt from him was far more than painting. "He taught me to have no fear or shame of my own ideas, to design perpetually, to seek no popularity, to be altogether myself—and this not in any words I can remember, but in the tenor of his conversation always and in the spirit of everything he said. I remember that he discouraged me from study of the antique—the classical antique—giving as his reason that such study came too early in a man's life and was apt to crush out his individuality; adding that when a man had once found his own style and was much older and could front the fear of being crushed, a year or so given to such study would be an excellent thing. So what I chiefly gained from him was not to be afraid of myself, but to do the thing I liked most: but in those first years I never wanted to think but as he thought, and all he did and said fitted me through and through. He never harangued or persuaded, but had a gift of saying things authoritatively and not as the Scribes, such as I have never heard in any man. And mingled with this a humour that lightened his words of all heaviness so that I went from him cheerful and solemn. As I walked with him in the streets I wondered what the crowd were so busy about that it could not stop to look at him. In the miserable ending years I never forgot this image of him in his prime, and upbraided any fate that could change him." At another time Edward said: "I never knew anything that could encourage the superstition that some people have, that the gods are jealous of the possible achievements of great men, as much as in Rossetti's case. Everything was ready for the making of a glorious creature—the perfect hunger for romance that was spread abroad in the world at the time when he came into it, the mingling of blood in him, his own admiration and discrimination for all that was splendid; his surroundings and the things he was brought up among; the people of all sorts of cultivation that he must have known from his earliest days—never was any-one so started, so ready for a great career."

From this society, however, Edward and Morris used to tear themselves away sometimes on a Saturday afternoon, and run down to Oxford to spend a few hours with their friends, "carrying with them the banner of Art and Re-volt." They found the diminished Brotherhood hard at work reading for the Schools, but did not scruple to dis-turb them by urging them all to become painters, and for a short time Dixon, especially after he had seen Rossetti, declared that he was going to be one.

Mr. Price's diary of Saturday, October 25th, mentions one of these visits. "Ted and Topsy up. To Maclaren's; singlestick with Top. With them before and after hall at Dixon's—then on to Adams' who gave us music. What a difference their coming makes!"

At an early date in his friendship with them Gabriel took Morris and Edward to see Madox Brown, who then lived at 13, Fortess Terrace, Kentish Town, and they were much impressed by him; he, on his side, received them kindly, and his friendship was a great addition to their lives in those first years.

Morris took to wood-carving at intervals, and I can still see in my mind's eye the long, folded white evening tie which he nailed in loops against his bedroom wall in order to hold his tools. He and Edward were well settled in their new home by Christmas, but Edward went down to Birmingham then, according to faithful custom, and dined with his father at Spon Lane on Christmas Day. This is

Miss Price's verdict about his appearance: "Edward is much altered. He wears his hair so long and is not so neat as he used to be. He looks an artist."

The domestic troubles of Red Lion Square, mentioned to Miss Salt, disappeared together with the exceedingly respectable housekeeper who caused them. She was replaced by one who was known always amongst us as "Red Lion Mary."

The year of 1856 that looks so fair in memory seemed equally beautiful to us in reality. Recalling it long after youth was past, Edward deliberately wrote: "There was a year in which I think it never rained nor clouded, but was blue summer from Christmas to Christmas, and London streets glittered, and it was always morning, and the air sweet and full of bells."

CHAPTER IX

NEW LOVE, NEW LIFE

1857-1858

THE prelude year was over, but still Edward began the next one under his father's roof. Whilst there he wrote to my younger sisters a letter which has in it some of the lambent fun that brightened everyday life for all who had to do with him.

"I am sure you will both of you be very shocked and grieved to hear that the state of my health will compel me to leave home for a change of air almost immediately: I am recommended to try London, and accordingly on Tuesday I leave the bosom of my family. If I find London agree with me it is very probable that I shall stay some time there, in which case I shall most certainly do myself the pleasure of calling upon you, at least once during my stay. I understand the neighbourhood of Mary-le-bone is suitable to invalids in my condition; so on Wednesday morning you may expect me in a very emaciated state.

"Thank you for those two dear little letters you wrote me. One of them certainly wasn't sent, but then it was purposed, and we mustn't be hard upon each other, must we? I'm sure Heaven is paved in mosaics of good actions and good intentions together like serpentine and porphyry, and that the other place—unnameable in our company—has nothing whatever in the world to do with it. So, Agnes dear, I feel very thankful that you even intended to write to me."

In March Edward received his first commission, and a letter to Miss Salt soon afterwards says that it is for two pictures and gives a description of what he intended them to be.

"I have chosen The Blessed Damozel for my year's work. In the first picture I shall make a man walking in the street of a great city, full of all kinds of happy life; children, such as he will never have, and lovers walking, and ladies leaning from windows all down great lengths of street leading to the city walls; and there the gates are wide open, letting in a space of green field and cornfield in harvest; and all round his head a great rain of swirling Autumn leaves blowing from a little walled graveyard.

"And in the other picture I shall make lovely Heaven, where the lady stands at the edge of the garden and leans over, trying to count a thick flight of little souls in bright flames, and the garden of Heaven full of all flowers on every side of her and of lovers who have met again. Oh dear, I daresay it will turn out something awful."

He describes Browning's poetry to her also. "You won't at first like him much perhaps, he is too different from anyone else to be liked at first sight by most, but he is the deepest and intensest of all poets—writes lower down in the dark heart of things—rises up to the seemingly clear surface less often. Oh, how ten lines of him help one. 'Paracelsus' and 'The Soul's Tragedy,' and 'King Victor' and the 'Unknown Painter,' and the fifty men and women that follow, all sung out as if old Browning sat continually at the roots of human life and saw all things."

In this same letter there is a remarkable expression of self-confidence, where, after mentioning Ruskin with enthusiasm and saying "his noble words used to make me shake and tremble," he suddenly adds: "One seems to want no guide now, but to flow down with the course of great spirits new and old and understand them without an interpreter."

Of the two designs from the Blessed Damozel I know nothing further than that Edward was studying apple-blossom for one of them in the spring of this year and the next. Mr. Plint, a Leeds manufacturer, was the gentleman who had commissioned them, and he was kind and patient, always ready to agree that an artist should choose his own subject and carry it out in his own way, and, as far as possible, at his own time. "Please let me hear if you have any subjects in your mind and heart," he writes, "and what would be your ideas as to terms, and I will meet your views if possible. I have a fancy for a Scripture Subject, but you must have one you can delight in yourself. Let me have your best work and thoughts and the subject I leave to you." He was a business man, but had an unexpected habit of wishing to pay for pictures before they were begun, and sometimes used to send his payments in a way that hopelessly bewildered Edward—who had no banking account—namely by handing on to him numbers of small cheques for odd sums that he himself had received from various people, and in one instance I find that Edward returned them in despair: for his only idea of money was coin of the realm, and his notion of keeping it safely was to "put it into a box and sit upon it."

Rossetti had introduced Edward to Mr. Plint, who was one of his own not too numerous patrons. Madox Brown records an action of the same kind done to himself by Gabriel in the previous year: "Never," he says, "did fellow, I think, so bestir himself for a rival before." Besides pictures Edward now began making cartoons for stained glass, and has himself written down the names of five that he coloured and finished in 1857. Many designs too he made that were not carried out, and some pictures were begun that he never completed, but the habit of constant designing was formed and the quantity of work produced, finished and unfinished, was large.

A day of April in this year is fixed in memory by his taking me to Millais' studio in Langham Place to see the picture of "Sir Isumbras," and by an unexpected vision we had there of the painter himself. He was not supposed to be at home, but for some reason or other looked into the room—perhaps in search of a friend—and for a moment we saw his head at the door. His glance did not seem to recognize any one, but while it passed quickly over the people who were there I noticed the gleam of his clear eyes beneath a white forehead, his crest of curling hair, and the noble cast of his features.

Directly after this came two happy months when Edward went with my elder sister and me to Birmingham, where we stayed chiefly with our friends the Salts and he spent as much of the time as he could at his father's house, working on various designs.

The apple-blossom for the background of his picture of "The Blessed Damozel" he sought for in Warwickshire and Worcestershire orchards, but when found, the bitter wind of an English May blew it all to the ground before it could be painted.

He took us to his own home, where I made the acquaintance of Miss Sampson, and dimly perceived what became clearer to me afterwards, that an angel from heaven would have been unworthy in her eyes to occupy the position I then did. Her devotion to Edward, however, and the spirit of hospitality that reigned in the little house, controlled the flames of jealousy. In those days he used to make a little ceremony of always getting up from table to pour out the water that I drank, pretending that it must be done from a height so as to sparkle in the glass and be drunk with the foam on it. This was almost more than Miss Sampson could bear, and one day I heard "My patience!" ejaculated under her breath, as if the end of all things was at hand should such folly continue.

I recollect how destitute the house was of any visible thing that could appeal to imagination; chairs, carpets, tables and table furniture each duller and more commonplace than the other. The only objects I saw within those walls that had a touch of humanity in them were some framed pieces of needlework that looked like windows into another world, because it seemed as if some one had been interested and amused in their making. Amongst them were two animals—one a lion with a face like a man, with a handsome aquiline nose—the other, I believe, a tiger: also a smaller and finer piece, of a girl mourning at a tomb, with a pendant which I forget. Over the mantelpiece and above a hard-featured square clock was a picture of the church and churchyard of Snaith in Yorkshire which bristled with gravestones as if it had been a city cemetery. Miss Sampson told us that these were the tombs of her relatives, represented there as all together in order that the drawing might be kept within reasonable dimensions. Some pieces of old blue china, and the remnants of a Worcester dinner service copied from an Oriental pattern, together with a Sheffield-plated teapot and cream-jug of elegant design, were the only articles of household use that I remember as not actually ugly. Mr. Jones himself seemed to care nothing for outside things unless they were connected in some way with his "dear girl," as he named the wife who never grew old.

At breakfast, the first morning we were there, the door opened and Tom the cat came in; but, alas, his prime was over, for though he opened his mouth wide with the intention of mewing a salutation, there came no sound at all until it had almost closed again, and then merely a croak. Still, he lived on for some years more, and it was a sad day when news came to us that a strange dog had leapt over the fence and killed poor Tom when quietly walking in his own kitchen-garden.

I was taken to see the Caswells, but have only a dim recollection of a small house with a large garden and a kind little old lady's welcome; of Mr. Caswell nothing lingers in my mind. I learnt afterwards that he was deeply disappointed with Edward's view of art, had looked for him to be "a great historical painter," considered the influence of Ruskin fatal, and gave up all hope when he saw "The Merciful Knight."

It was arranged that on our way back from Birmingham to London we should stop at Oxford and pay a short visit to the MacLarens. We fixed our first anniversary of the 9th of June as the day on which we would go, and Edward should take us first to see "The Light of the World" at

Mr. Combe's house. Miss Charlotte Salt and her sister were persuaded to accompany us for the day, and Edward insisted at the last moment on kidnapping his father, who had met us at the railway station to say good-bye, so that the band of pilgrims counted six when they stood before the picture.

We found Morris painting a tree in MacLaren's beautiful garden with such energy that it was long before the grass grew again on the spot where his chair had stood. Most of the Set were in Oxford, but in spite of good company and summer weather on the river and fields Edward returned to his work in town, and our brother brought us up to London at the end of term.

This was the year of the beautiful little exhibition of Pre-Raphaelite pictures in Russell Place, Fitzroy Square, during the month of June, and to it Edward took me as soon as possible. The illustrated Tennyson was an excitement, but a very mixed pleasure, for he hated some of the pictures in it as much as he loved others, and the whole appearance of the book was far removed from his desire. One day in 1896, when talking of wood-engraving with reference to the Kelmscott Chaucer, he took out our old copy of the Tennyson and turned it about and mused over it. "As a book," he said, "it 's nothing. There was no command over the type and printing such as Mr. Morris has, and there were so many hands engaged on the pictures as to make it impossible as a book." When he came to Millais' "St. Agnes" he stopped, all his old admiration unchanged. "Look at her little breath," he said, "the snow and everything—that 's Millais at his best."

He told us what Rossetti suffered over the cutting of his designs, and the rage he fell into when a block about a sixteenth of an inch too short was sent him for his drawing of "St. Cecilia," in the Palace of Art, and how when some one who was by asked, could such a little space as that matter, he cried out, "Good God! what do you mean by that? I could get a whole city in there!"

Edward was now deep in his Paradise picture: "I have

been so busy all the week," he writes, "starting at half-past eight every morning, going ten miles, and painting till evening, when I get back so awfully knocked up." It was a cherry-tree in Mrs. Morris' garden at Leyton that he was painting.

Lilies for his picture he found much nearer home, namely, in the garden of Red Lion Square, wonderful as that sounds. These lilies are mentioned in a letter to Rossetti written at the end of June, where he also refers to an intended visit of Rossetti to Oxford, a visit that altered the disposition of Edward's time for months to come and that of Morris' whole life.

"I'm awfully sorry not to be able to go with you to-morrow to Oxford—on Sunday last I felt quite sure I should be able to leave town, but I could not now for two or three reasons. 1° Topsy comes from there to-morrow and I want to see him. 2° I have a friend staying with me, just arrived, and I can't well leave him. 3° I'm painting some lilies which are going, and keep me from doing the same, so I feel sure I ought not to go this week. I am very sorry, for it would have been most jolly—I could manage it well in a fortnight if that is not too late for you."

It was not Edward, however, but Morris who was at Oxford with Gabriel on the eventful visit when he conceived the idea of painting the walls of the Union. The Notes say: "When Rossetti and Morris came back they were full of a scheme, and I was to put everything aside and help it. Woodward had just built a new debating room for the University, and there were large bays above the gallery that ran round the room, hungry to be filled with pictures—Gabriel equally hungry to fill them, and the pictures were to be from the Morte d'Arthur, so willed our master."

This meant for Edward the putting aside of his picture of "The Blessed Damozel" and the giving up of an intended visit to the Art Treasures Exhibition at Manchester.

In the course of the Long Vacation, Rossetti enlisted also Arthur Hughes, Hungerford Pollen, Spencer Stanhope, Valentine Prinsep, and Alexander Munro the sculptor, to join in the scheme, and the time they all spent together was one never to be forgotten.

Mr. Prinsep clearly recalls the day that Gabriel came out to Little Holland House, and by the power of his personality made him promise to "join him and some other fellows in decorating the Union at Oxford." The young artist of course felt flattered by the invitation, but he says: "I had not studied with Watts without being well aware of my own deficiencies in drawing—so I told Rossetti that I did not feel strong enough to undertake such work. 'Nonsense,' answered Rossetti confidently, 'there 's a man I know who has never painted anything—his name is Morris—he has undertaken one of the panels and he will do something very good you may depend—so you had better come!' Rossetti was so friendly and confident that I consented and joined the band at Oxford."

In a letter written home one Sunday in July, Edward says how much he should have liked to be with his father at Spon Lane that day, "but instead of that I am going with Rossetti to be introduced to a lot of swells who'll frighten me to death and make me keep close to his side all the time." Long afterwards, in one of his moods of reminiscence, he wrote about this, his first visit to Little Holland House, and how Rossetti prepared him for it and for the sight of Watts, who then lived with the Prinseps.

"One day Gabriel took me out in a cab—it was a day he was rich and so we went in a hansom, and we drove and drove until I thought we should arrive at the setting sun—and he said, 'You must know these people, Ned; they are remarkable people: you will see a painter there, he paints a queer sort of pictures about God and Creation.' So it was he took me to Little Holland House."

Mr. Prinsep also remembers their visit and says: "This time Rossetti was accompanied by a younger man, who he declared was the greatest genius of the age—a shy, fair young man, with mild grey-blue eyes and straight light hair which was apt to straggle over his well-developed forehead—who spoke in an earnest impressive manner when he did speak, which was not often. On this, his first visit to my father's house, he did not impress me much; but then, as I said, he was almost painfully shy and my mind was filled with Rossetti. It was Burne-Jones, or as Rossetti and all of us called him, 'Ned Jones.'"

Edward never forgot the reception of Mrs. Prinsep, who, perceiving that he was in a strange world, both sheltered and took notice of him. Before he had seen her many times she was "Aunt Sara" to him, Mr. Prinsep, senior, was "Uncle Thoby," and he fell under the spell of the house as many another did.

By the middle of August the work at the Union was well begun, and the painters then hoped that it would be finished in about six weeks—that is, by the end of the Long Vacation—but it lasted till the spring of the following year. The difficulties they found were great, for the preparation of the surface to be decorated had not been considered, and each bay also was pierced by two windows which dazzled the sight and made anything painted on the wall-space between them almost invisible. The building is described in the Notes as being so new that the mortar was hardly dry, and the rough brickwork was only whitewashed over. "The walls were not quite flat and had a ridge in them over which we had to train a face, if a face happened to come there; but we began with enthusiasm, and repented, if we repented, afterwards. At any rate we had no misgivings, and when Gabriel willed a thing it had to be done."

At first Rossetti, Edward and Morris were alone, and they lodged together at 87, High Street, a pleasant old house opposite Queen's College, but later on, when the October term began, they moved to another house in George Street.

All the artists had promised to give their work, but the members of the Union were to pay the cost of their lodging and the materials used, both sides to this bargain being quite ignorant what this cost was likely to be; "and I am afraid," says Edward, "that as the task lasted so long, our gift did not turn out to be such a generous one as we meant: indeed natural complainings were made, and our gift underwent public criticism in the debating room, but Bowen was then Treasurer, and stood up for us and saved us from all inconvenience. He was much beloved by us—a courteous and delightful fellow and always regarded in the University as a man of exceptional promise—whom Rossetti loved at once.

"Morris began his picture first and finished it first, and then, his hands being free, he set to work upon the roof, making in a day a design for it which was a wonder to us for its originality and fitness, for he had never before designed anything of the kind, nor, I suppose, seen any ancient work to guide him. Indeed, all his life, he hated the copying of ancient work as unfair to the old and stupid for the present, only good for inspiration and hope. All the autumn through he worked upon the roof high above our heads, and Faulkner, in afternoons, when his work was over at University, would come to help, having always clever hands for drawing."

On Mr. Prinsep's first arrival at Oxford, there is a legend that he said to his cabman, "Drive me to the Union," and found himself quickly at the doors of the workhouse. His account of dining with Rossetti that first evening is very vivid.

"I was, of course, proud to accept the invitation," he says, "so at the hour mentioned I was punctually at the house. There I found Rossetti in a plum-coloured frock-coat, and a short square man with spectacles and a vast mop of dark hair. I was cordially received. 'Top,' cried Rossetti, 'let me introduce Val Prinsep.'

"'Glad, I'm sure,' answered the man in spectacles, nodding his head, and then he resumed his reading of a large quarto. This was William Morris. Soon after, the door opened, and before it was half opened in glided Burne-Jones. 'Ned,' said Rossetti, who had been absently humming to himself, 'I think you know Prinsep.' The shy figure darted forward, the shy face lit up, and I was received with the kindly effusion which was natural to him.

"When dinner was over, Rossetti, humming to himself as was his wont, rose from the table and proceeded to curl himself up on the sofa. 'Top,' he said, 'read us one of your grinds.' 'No, Gabriel,' answered Morris, 'you have heard them all.' 'Never mind,' said Rossetti, 'here's Prinsep who has never heard them, and besides, they are devilish good.' 'Very well, old chap,' growled Morris, and having got his book he began to read in a sing-song chant some of the poems afterwards published in his first volume. All the time, he was jiggling about nervously with his watch chain. I was then a very young man and my experience of life was therefore limited, but the effect produced on my mind was so strong that to this day, forty years after, I can still recall the scene: Rossetti on the sofa with large melancholy eyes fixed on Morris, the poet at the table reading and ever fidgetting with his watch chain, and Burne-Jones working at a pen-and-ink drawing.

Gold on her head, and gold on her feet,
And gold where the hems of her kirtle meet,
And a golden girdle round my sweet;
Ah! qu'elle est belle La Marguerite.

still seems to haunt me, and this other stanza:

Swerve to the left, son Roger, he said,
When you catch his eyes through the helmet slit,
Swerve to the left, then out at his head,
And the Lord God give you joy of it!

I confess I returned to the Mitre with my brain in a whirl."

Mr. Prinsep says that the windows in the spaces they were painting were whitened in order to tone the light, and that the whitened glass was covered all over with sketches, chiefly of wombats. "Do you know the wombat at the Zoo?" asked Rossetti; "a delightful creature—the most comical little beast." He was drawn by Edward in endless different positions and situations, and Rossetti's admiration led him years afterwards to buy a live one and try to make it happy at Cheyne Walk.

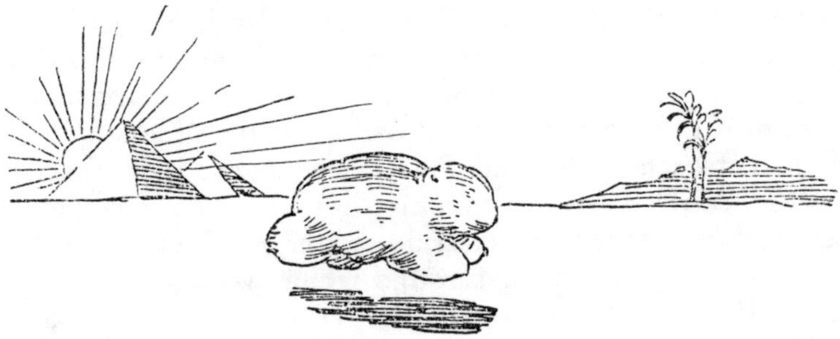

"What fun we had in that Union! What jokes! What roars of laughter!" writes Mr. Prinsep. His own splendid health and spirits contributed to this. Here is a portrait of him by a man who first saw him at that time: "Six foot one, 15 stone, not fat, well built—hair like finest wire, short, soft, fluffy, curly and seamless—age only 19." His strength was wonderful; Edward always liked to remember being picked up by him and quickly carried under one arm up a ladder to the gallery where they painted.

Round the artists who lived in the George Street house gathered what remained of the old set of 1855, as well as other men who had since joined it. Birkbeck Hill was one of these, and "Swinburne of Balliol," as Mr. Price's Diary calls him, having been introduced by Mr. Hatch, soon became such a devoted friend, and so worshipping a disciple of Rossetti's, that Edward says, "Now we were four in company and not three."

Gabriel's picture was "Launcelot's Dream of the San Graal," Edward's was "Nimuë luring Merlin," and Morris chose "Sir Palomides watching Tristram and Iseult." "If we needed models we sat to each other," say the Notes, "and Morris had a head always fit for Lancelot or Tristram." Gabriel drew the figure of the sleeping Launcelot from Edward. The picture was never completed, but the part that he did finish Edward always thought represented the highest character of Rossetti's work. Who else in the world could have designed the Guenevere who stands in the branches of the Tree of Temptation with the apple in her hand, hiding the vision of the Graal from her lover?

Rossetti had often to go back to London for a few days at a time because of the pressure of other work, and was also much distracted in mind owing to the illness of Miss Siddal, to whom he had long been engaged, so that his picture could not move quickly, but whilst he remained in Oxford he was the leader and inspirer of all his company. "Rossetti was the planet round which we revolved," says Mr. Prinsep; "we copied his very way of speaking. All beautiful women were 'stunners' with us. Wombats were the most delightful of God's creatures. Mediaevalism was our *beau idéal* and we sank our own individuality in the strong personality of our adored Gabriel." There is a letter of Edward's written at this time which distinctly reflects Gabriel's handwriting, but no one could reproduce the peculiar charm of his voice with its sonorous roll and beautiful cadences.

Mr. Spencer Stanhope, whose friendship with Edward says dates from these days, writes: "As time went on I found myself more and more attracted to Ned; the spaces we were decorating were next to each other, and this brought me closely into contact with him. In spite of his high spirits and fun he devoted himself more thoroughly to his work than any of the others with the exception of Morris; he appeared unable to leave his picture as long as he thought he could improve it, and as I was behindhand with mine we had the place all to ourselves for some weeks after the rest had gone. Another thing I noted about him was that, in spite of his love of fun and frolic, he seemed absolutely indifferent to everything in the way of athletic games or exercises."

A bear-fight was the nearest approach Edward ever made to these, and it was surprising how much muscular strength he shewed when it came to a steady, pushing, silent wrestle with a brother bear: practical jokes too never lost their charm for him, and they and their swift retribution made much of the day's fun. "Rossetti and Ned were for ever drawing caricatures of Morris, who most good-naturedly joined in the laugh," says Mr. Prinsep, and some of these caricatures found their way to us girls in London.

"The little tracings I have enclosed," Edward writes to my sister Agnes, "are accurately copied from designs which have created the greatest sensation in our limited circle. Others exist of the same subject variously treated, but of too colossal a size to trace comfortably and send you, but these I think you will enjoy (you will see them better if you lay them on white paper). The Topsy Cartoons. No. 1. Portrait of Topsy in usual attitude and expression. He is in the act of requesting Davis to put more size in the colour—his dearest friends alone can tell how truly this represents the forcible and energetic manner which characterises that unnaturally and unnecessarily curly being. The subject is broadly handled, especially about the chief figure—there is a world of satire about the sunflowers at the back. Davis is exact.

"No. 2. Topsy at the age of 24, in the act of suddenly noticing of his own accord what has long been patent to surrounding humanity, that he is growing fat—stout—corpulent. This design is called 'The Discovery' after the sentiment it expresses—your attention is drawn to the hands.

"No. 3 is the triumphant reply of the Great Master to the fallacious assertion on the part of Topsy that the sole resemblance of these and similar cartoons to himself lay in the hair—and that he would go to-morrow and get it cut. No. 3 is the answer. It represents Topsy in his usual action with watch-chain, and closely shorn. The other night Rossetti made a magnificent group—Ruskin, himself, Top and me, oh so exact—I screamed with delight."

In the same letter there is also the following description of a scene which makes one feel how young they all were together.

"I have from now till breakfast to write to you in, and I have no idea what *now* is, for after the most elaborate directions for being called early, which were strictly attended to, I turned over and dozed away like a pig, and now I expect every moment my usual morning tormentors, Rossetti and Pollen, who come at about 8 o'clock to insult me—laugh at me, my dear—point the finger of scorn at me, address me by opprobrious names and finally tear blankets and counterpanes and mattresses and all the other things that cover me, from my enfeebled grasp, and so leave me, to do the same to Topsy. I've done them this time; when they come in presently with no knocking at the door, they will see Virtue asserted in the form of a bold and upright figure at the dressing-table, who will slowly turn upon them a look of calm but significant defiance with one eye, while with the other he expresses similar feelings by a contumelious wink."

An occasional drawback to the happiness of the painters in this improvised Bohemia was the recognition of their presence in Oxford by various polite invitations to dinner, for after their day's work at the Union the men wanted nothing so much as to meet again at George Street in the evening, where they could smoke, talk altogether or not at all, read aloud or play whist, just as they chose.

Mr. Prinsep tells a story of an evening when they were honoured by an invitation to dine at Christ Church, which Edward, "being shy," declined, but Rossetti, Morris and Prinsep accepted. "The preparation for the dinner created some bustle. Morris found he had no dress clothes with him, at which Rossetti was indignant. 'You should always have dress clothes with you,' he said, 'Top, it's disgraceful of you.' However, Hughes had some, and although he was taller than Morris and rather thin, it was agreed that the clothes must do. But Morris was so long dressing that Rossetti having attired himself and having waited some time in his top coat declared he would wait no longer, and off we started. Before we reached Christ Church we heard the sound of Morris' footsteps and he overtook us.

"'What do you mean turning up like that?' cried Rossetti furiously, 'look at your hair!' There sure enough, on Morris' dark mop was a dab of blue paint, the relic of his day's work. 'Well, Gabriel,' answered Morris meekly, 'I'll go to Charley Faulkner's and get it off.' And so he did.

"When we arrived at Christ Church and took off our overcoats, I was amused to find that Gabriel, though he had been so particular about evening dress, had finished his own attire by absently putting on the old plum-coloured frock-coat he wore daily, which was itself not free from paint. I, however, discreetly said nothing, nor do I think he ever found out his mistake or I fancy we should have heard of it."

Edward's recollection of these disturbed evenings was not less vivid than Mr. Prinsep's:

"When we were happily together at meals a message would often come, and one of us was summoned, as if the lot of Death had fallen upon him, and he had to wash and dress and go to that house of Fate. If we had warning that such a thing was to be, we were all suddenly ill. Sometimes we had no warning, and we went—one or other of us—full of silent lamentation. One autumn evening Gabriel and I were alone, and our dinner was coming in and we were chatting together—and he to me was as Pope and Emperor—it was so nice, for when he loved man or woman they knew it and it was happy; and it was just then that a note came from —— to say that he would come in a few minutes to fetch us to dine to meet this and that.

"We never met this and that; we never dined at all that night; for an idea had come to Gabriel, and he rang the bell and asked the man when the next train started for London, and a cab was got and we were in the train for Euston when —— came. It was ten o'clock when we got to Euston Hotel, and we had tea or something and went to bed, and were called again at six, and were back in Oxford by nine and at work again—and it was all his idea, and I thought, 'this man could lead armies and destroy empires if he liked; how good it is to be with him.'"

Other interruptions the workers had of a more welcome kind, when Ruskin or Madox Brown came down from London to look at what they were doing. There is a reflection of Ruskin's visit in a letter of mine written to Miss Charlotte Salt at the beginning of November, where it says, "Edward is still at Oxford, painting away busily," and adds that Ruskin had been down there the week before and pronounced Rossetti's picture to be "the finest piece of colour in the world." Then—under seal of secrecy—I whisper that "he chooses Edward's next to Rossetti's." About ten days later another letter breathes in awe-stricken distress the fact that Miss Siddal is "ill again." The news had reached me through Edward, who had never even seen her, but so lived in Gabriel's life at that time as not only to share any trouble that Gabriel had, but also to impress real sadness for it upon another.

In Mr. Price's diary of November 14th, there is the following entry: "Rossetti unhappily called away through Miss Siddal's illness at Matlock"; and that was the end of the Oxford companionship, for he did not return.

By this date Morris had completed his work on the roof of the Union as well as his picture on the wall; "having," as the Notes say, "from first to last the faculty of carrying on his work and pushing it through, working his best and trying for no better than he could do at the time, leaving advance for the next work."

It was in the last days of the Long Vacation that Morris first saw Miss Jane Burden, who afterwards became his wife. She had been born and brought up in Oxford, and her beauty was of so rare and distinguished a type that one would have thought it impossible for Morris to have missed seeing her face during the time he was at College: but fate reserved the meeting until now, when, as it is said, "by chance" being at the theatre with Gabriel, Edward, and Hughes one evening, he saw her in a box above them, and so the story began. A pen-and-ink drawing of her by Rossetti (the one now in the Dublin National Gallery) was brought by Edward to Beaumont Street for us to marvel at, and future acquaintance with the original proved to us that it was a faithful portrait as well as a beautiful work of art. Morris' portrait of her also in his poem of Beata Mea Domina was equally true.

I wish it were possible to explain the impression made upon me as a young girl whose experience so far had been quite remote from art, by sudden and close intercourse with those to whom it was the breath of life. The only approach I can make to describing it is by saying that I felt in the presence of a new religion. Their love of beauty did not seem to me unbalanced, but as if it included the whole world and raised the point from which they regarded everything. Human beauty especially was in a way sacred to them, I thought; and of this I received confirmation quite lately from a lady whom I had not seen for many years, and who had been in her youth an object of wild enthusiasm and admiration to Rossetti, Morris and Edward. She and I sat and talked for an hour about them and the days when we were all young, and I found that she kept the same feeling that I do about that time—that the men were as good as they were gifted, and unlike any others that we knew. She had lost sight of them long ago and lived abroad and seen many people since then, but her regard for the young artists she remembered was still fresh and she loved to dwell on their memory. "I never saw such men," she said; "it was being in a new world to be with them. I sat to them and was there with them, and they were different to everyone else I ever saw. And I was a holy thing to them—I was a holy thing to them."

The life in Red Lion Square was a very happy one in its freedom. Red Lion Mary's originality all but equalled that of the young men, and she understood them and their ways thoroughly. Their rough and ready hospitality was seconded by her with unfailing good temper; she cheerfully spread mattresses on the floor for friends who stayed there, and when the mattresses came to an end it was said that she built up beds with boots and portmanteaus. Cleanliness, beyond the limits of the tub, was impossible in Red Lion

Square, and hers was not a nature to dash itself against impossibilities, so the subject was pretty much ignored, but she was ready to fulfil any mission or do anything for them at a moment's notice, which was much more important. Never did she dishonour their bills. "Mary!" cried Edward one evening when ordering breakfast overnight for Rossetti, who was staying with them, "let us have quarts of hot coffee, pyramids of toast, and multitudinous quantities of milk"; which to her meant all he intended. "Dear Mary," wrote Rossetti, "please go and smash a brute in Red Lion Passage to-morrow. He had to send a big book, a scrapbook, to Master Crabb, 34, Westbourne Place, Eaton Square, and he hasn't done it. I don't know his name but his shop is dirty and full of account books. This book was ordered ten days ago, and was to have been sent home the next day AND WAS PAID FOR—so sit on him hard to-morrow and dig a fork into his eye, as I can't come that way to murder him myself." From these hints she knew exactly what to say.

Her memory was excellent and sense of humour keen, so that some of the commissions on which she was sent gave her great enjoyment—as one day when Edward told her to take a cab and go to Mr. Watts at Little Holland House, and ask him for the loan of "whatever draperies and any other old things he could spare," and Mr. Watts, amused at the form of the request, sent her back with a parcel of draperies and an old pair of brown trousers, bidding her tell Mr. Jones those were the only "old things" he could spare. This delighted Edward, and he detained Mary while he took down his Vasari and read to her of the old Italian painter who had his breeches made of leather because they wore out so quickly; and then he professed to be grateful for Mr. Watts' gift, and said he would have the brown trousers made to fit him.

Mary wrote a good hand and spelled well, and would sit down and write with gravity such a note as the following dictated to her by Edward. "Mr. Bogie Jones compts: to Mr. Price and begs to inform him he expects to be down for

Commemoration and that he hopes to meet him, clean, well shaved, and with a contrite heart." Morris' quick temper annoyed her, but she once prettily said, "though he was so short-tempered, I seemed so necessary to him at all times, and felt myself his man Friday." There was a never-forgotten trick that she played him one day when relations were strained between them, which vastly amused Rossetti, Edward and Madox Brown, all present at the time. Morris was going to Oxford and had asked her before he did so to wind up his watch and set it right, on which the wily Mary put it forward nearly an hour, and he "remembered to mention it to her" on his return.

She could be trusted also like a good woman to shew kindness to another woman whose goodness was in abeyance, and could understand the honest kindness of a young man to such a one, and help him to feed and clothe her and get her back to her own people.

She was an excellent needlewoman and made models' draperies very cleverly—nay, would also have stood as model in them, had she been tall enough—for one day when Edward said to her, "Why were you made so short? I could do all I require while you are fetching Miss Joliffe, if you were only taller;" she, with pathetic goodwill, asked whether she "would be of any use if she stood on a stool?" When Gabriel heard of this he was so touched by it that he said "Mary shall go into a picture," and so she did, as one of the ladies accompanying Beatrice in the "Meeting of Dante and Beatrice in Florence." He also made a careful pencil drawing of her head and gave it to her upon her marriage.

Morris taught her to embroider his designs for hangings, and being in a fever to see how they looked, often made her bring her embroidery frame into the studio so that she might work under his direction—and many a funny conversation took place as she plied her needle and they painted. One day she being in the room, perfectly quiet, neither moving nor speaking, Morris, whose work presumably was going awry, said to her fiercely, "Mary, be quiet

—don't make that insufferable noise," and she answered, "No, sir; I won't, sir." Another day Gabriel, who was for ever humming a tune or crooning over lines of poetry, was haunted by a verse which had greatly amused him in a translation made by Mr. Thoby Prinsep from some Oriental legend, and as he painted he kept on chanting to himself in every intonation he could think of,

> Shall the hide of a fierce lion
> Be stretched on frame of wood
> For a daughter's foot to lie on,
> Stained with her father's blood?

Mary's coming into the room for something did not disturb him, but in his rich voice he trolled forth the words again, this time as a question addressed to her personally.

> Mary!—Shall the hide of a fierce lion
> Be stretched on frame of wood
> For a daughter's foot to lie on,
> Stained with her father's blood?

and she said briskly, "It shall if you like, sir." "That's a most remarkable girl, Ned," said Rossetti afterwards: "not one woman in ten would have given an intelligent answer like that to a question." Gabriel's humour was quite inimitable—pervading all he said, touched with the melancholy of his nature, and haughtily careless as to whether it was taken seriously or not.

Another office that Mary held was that of reader to Edward on Sunday mornings when he was alone, for then he generally worked till lunch time and enjoyed listening the while to her extracts from Reynolds' Newspaper. Also she took care of the key of a small Swiss musical box that he had, which played two tunes (one of them I remember was called on the label "the *Stelly* night") and wound it up and put it under his pillow. Some of the street organs too he liked very much. They were different in those days from the present ones—more mellow in tone, and with long-sustained notes, too, instead of staccato brilliance; their tunes varied of course, just as they do now, some of them being vulgar and some pathetic, but Edward never at any time joined in the cry against them. Only a few years ago, when one came and played outside the Garden Studio where he was working, he listened to it silently for some time and then said, "Pretty tunes those are; they quite melt my heart"; and turning to his friend Mr. Rooke, who was with him, "don't they melt your heart, little Rookie, and take the obduracy out of it? They soften my heart and make it less stubborn. Don't they soften yours?"

Edward's work at the Union lasted until the end of February, 1858, because he had to leave it occasionally, going home for Christmas and afterwards to London. "Rossetti is in London," he writes to his father on one of the first days of the New Year, "and it is so jolly looking at him again. My picture at Oxford is not quite finished yet, but very nearly—I shall not go on with it just at present, but work here." And then he proceeds to cheer up his father's spirits about the life he had chosen. "Did you see the notice in the Times the other day [of the Union painting]? There was one in the Times, one in the Saturday Review, one in the Morning Chronicle, one in the French Government paper the Moniteur, one in the Builder, and several more– I'm a famous man now!"

To Miss Sampson he writes about the same time: "To-day I have finished the Cartoon of Peter I began at home and have very greatly improved it. Hunt I have seen, who complimented me tremendously on my picture at Oxford—so I am getting on slowly, and a million times better than could ever have been expected: perhaps I shall be almost rich some day; that is, rich for me."

Edward took the opportunity of being away from London to let his beard and moustache grow, which altered his appearance considerably. Of course whilst his beard was growing he went through the usual misery of the process, and used to send caricatures in his letters of its appearance from the earliest stage, which he described in words as being "like the outside of the inside of a musical box."

By various unlucky accidents all the photographs of him taken before this change have been lost.

On the 2nd of January he had received a very welcome letter from Mr. Plint enclosing the balance of payment for the two "Blessed Damozel" pictures, and saying that he wished to have another of a more important size. Edward writes: "I am afraid he will stare at the price Rossetti says I must ask—I'm quite frightened to ask it, but I will, for I work hard enough. Isn't he a brick when I haven't done the first commission, indeed scarcely begun it?"

Mr. Plint's practice of paying beforehand for work was in one way very convenient and helpful, but in others not so good, for it was a cause of great anxiety unless both patron and painter lived and prospered. If Edward was well he had no doubt of being able to complete such commissions, but he felt burdened and depressed by the debt when his health broke down, as it did this year. Enthusiasm gave him strength until the end of his work at Oxford, and made him report himself during that time as "tremendously well," but it was clear to others that this was not the case. His lifelong tendency was to exhaustion from over-fatigue, followed by chills varying in their course from ordinary colds to serious illness, a constitution which made him peculiarly susceptible to every kind of malarial influence.

After his return to London the fictitious strength that had supported him through two years of mental and bodily strain suddenly failed, and, scarcely knowing how it had happened, he became so weak that for a few days he was unable to raise his hand to his head. A note written to Mr. Price just before he fell ill shews the dejection he felt at the end of the merry days and happy work at Oxford. "It is very dull. Oh, horribly dull—such a jolly time seems to have gone away so completely. I wake up miserably every morning." Then, a little later, "I've been very seedy and am only just up for a few minutes—to-morrow I am going to Camberwell to stay with our little Aunt till I get straight. Is Topsy in Oxford? love to him and everyone—tell him not to come up yet till I've done more to the wardrobe." Morris was staying on at Oxford almost permanently now, working at a picture of Tristram and Iseult for which Mr. Plint had given him a commission; so that, although the friends often met at the week's end, Edward was living a good deal alone in Red Lion Square. The wardrobe he speaks of was one painted with the story of Chaucer's Prioress' Tale, and the design was practically the same that, with another background, he used for the highly finished picture which was his last exhibited water-colour in the New Gallery forty years later.

Before March was over Edward proclaimed himself quite well, but we who had seen him laid so low were careful in receiving the assertion. However, he was out and about again on the 21st of the month, for he took me then to see Ruskin for the first time. We paid our visit to him in the basement of the National Gallery, where he was working at the classification and preservation of the Turner bequest of drawings. He received us very kindly, setting us to amuse ourselves as we liked with the drawings that lay about while he worked and then talked, or pointed out any special thing. He shewed us, too, some old pictures lately brought back from Italy by Sir Charles Eastlake, but not yet hung, and he praised Edward's work to me in the most unqualified terms—it was a golden hour. One more attempt was made to paint apple-blossom this spring when Edward carried his picture down to Maidstone, where Arthur Hughes was staying, but again the cold winds prevented it. A couple of letters to Madox Brown written at this time shew Edward's affectionate relations with him, and have reference also to a nebulous plan which pleased some of the friends—an idea of taking a large house where all the families should live together. "De-e-ear old Brown," he says, "have a card to see a house—20 rooms—2 acres ground—rent Gs: 100!!! Situation Kensington, close by Kensington Square—what do you think? Could you go and see it? Hughes would be ready to join any time." A postscript adds: "Little Huse sends his love, t'aint worth having, but as he is looking over me I must send it."

The place described here was, I believe, Cedar Villa, over whose fine old garden blocks of flats are now built. In the other letter he says: "By the bye, I must tell Gabriel about our plan, for he has been very pressing for me to join him at Blackfriars, and I cannot refuse except for the actual reason—all this when I return. I shall rush up to see you the moment I get back."

Madox Brown's kindness to me in these early days is one of the delightful recollections belonging to them which nothing can dim, and it is in allusion to his actually having allowed me to come and try whether I could handle a paint brush in his studio that Edward's letter goes on with a sudden outburst of gratitude: "God bless you, old fellow, how good you are to my Stunner—she does little else but talk about it. There never was any one in all this blessed world half so unselfish as you."

It makes one smile in the midst of the ghosts of this time to realize the standard of age by which we then measured each other, for in a letter that I wrote to my friend Charlotte Salt are these words, referring to the painters that I knew: "Have I ever mentioned Brown to you? He is the father of them all, a married man of, I should think, nearly forty." In reality he was just thirty-seven. "Rossetti," I tell her, "is still out of town, I saw him last at Christmas—did I tell you of it?—where I saw Hughes also, one of the most beautiful men in the world."

Where I saw them was at a party given by Morris and Edward in Red Lion Square, an invitation to which festivity, lightly scribbled to his "dear Bruno" by Edward, has found its way into my hands after all these years.

"Come to-night and see the chair, there's a dear old fellow—such a chair!!!!!! Gabriel and Top hook it to-morrow, so do come. Hughes will come, and a Stunner or two to make melody. Come soon, there's a nice old chap—victuals and squalor at all hours, but come at 6."

One part of the "melody" of the evening I remember

to have been some old French songs from Wekerlin's beautiful collection, *Echos du Temps Passé*, sung to a piano, itself a guest of the evening, which must have gone away next day with strange thoughts about "the chair" if, as I believe, it was the large one with a box overhead in which Gabriel suggested owls might be kept with advantage.

CHAPTER X

AD FONTES AQUARUM
1858-1859

WITHIN a short time after his return from Maidstone Edward was again alarming us by his condition of health. The early summer was intensely hot, and Red Lion Square was no fitting place for him when the thermometer stood at 90 in the shade, so one day Mrs. Prinsep in the kindness of her heart drove down there and took possession of him bodily, carrying him off with her to Little Holland House and putting him under the care of a fresh doctor. A letter of my mother's to my brother Harry at Oxford says: "We have had considerable anxiety lately about Edward, who is in a very delicate state of health. He is forbidden for the present to touch or smell oil paint, he is living quite by rule, and is as weak as you can imagine a man to be who is not confined to his room. Dr. Bright told Mrs. Prinsep that if he had gone on much longer working and paying no attention to himself, it would have been too late to do anything for him."

Besides ill-health and the anxiety he felt at the delay it caused in his work, Edward was troubled this year about his father's affairs. "Haven't heard from home for long," he writes to Mr. Price. "My father in business trouble a good deal—going to give up Poplar Place. Beastly being poor, isn't it, Crommie? I want to see you so badly—I would have come down to Oxford any Sunday if I could afford it, but till Sunday last I hadn't known £2 in my pockets together for months."

It was a bad time for several of the little circle. Miss Siddal continued wretchedly out of health, and a long illness of Mrs. Madox Brown's was weighing heavily on her husband. Edward writes to him: "I am so grieved to hear that your wife is so ill still—write me better news as soon as you can, I am very anxious for you. I don't go out yet —but I won't bother you about my little trouble when you are so unhappy. Wouldn't it be better to give up that little Academy for the present—it must jar on you." These last words refer to Madox Brown's incredible kindness in allowing me and Miss Seddon, sister to his dead friend Thomas Seddon the artist, to come and try to paint from a model in his studio. I remember how proud and pleased I was at the confidence Madox Brown placed in me when, during his wife's illness, he gave me leave to take his little three-year-old boy, "Nolly," back to my father's house with me for a few days.

Nolly was an enchanting child, and in his own home so bold and manly as he roved about in a rough pinafore, that I was unprepared for the infantine vision in white embroidered cambric which he presented when dressed for our journey: his manliness had been doffed with his holland overall, and as I lifted him in and out of the omnibus by which we travelled I felt an alarming sense of responsibility.

I shall linger a while with the memory of this child, whose death in earliest manhood frustrated the hope and expectation of his friends; for the things that he did and said whilst he was with us left a lasting image of him in our hearts.

The embroidered outdoor coat once got rid of, he became again the Nolly of Fortess Terrace, and justified all that I had said of him to my family. I remember that on one of his small fingers we found a neglected cut, which, though reckoned by himself as unworthy of notice, he courteously allowed us for our own satisfaction to have dressed and bound up at the chemist's, where his courage during the operation moved the chemist to fill a virgin pill-box with acid drops and present it to him afterwards. The acid drops were all given to dogs on his way home.

He was quite happy in the gloomy back-yard of our

house, where my little sisters kept a bad-tempered guinea-pig. Nolly feared neither tooth nor claw of any animal yet known to him, and had put his hand into the cage and been sharply bitten before there was time to say Don't. "O Nolly, has it hurt you?" some one cried. "No, dear," he answered gently, and a moment afterwards, with a benevolence that set all parties at their ease, he added thoughtfully, "It 's a very nice little pig."

Once, while he was with us, his father came to see him, and the interview astonished us all; for he did not kiss or caress the little fellow, but only perched him solemnly upon his knee and conversed with him for a minute or two before bidding him good-bye again. It was not possible to be angry with Nolly. He might plant his boot in the middle of a pie that was set in the window to cool, yet the cook bore him no grudge—or jump over the footboard into the middle of a new-made feather bed, and running up it sit grinning from the height of its downy pillows, but no one could do more than laugh. He tried to strike matches on the granulated tip of a dog's nose, and the dog itself did not mind, and he filled the eyes of a water-colour portrait of himself with drops of water, because "they were his own eyes, so he might do what he liked with them," without his father being seriously angry: the days of his childhood were happy ones. A flaxen-polled sister next above him in age was his home companion, with whom he played or fought as occasion prompted. Their antics seemed to perturb their father without his quite knowing what was the matter, and one used to see remonstrance slowly waking up in him long before it came to the utterance. Their mother was too amiable and indulgent to be any sort of terror to them, and Madox Brown's forehead would pucker helplessly at them all while he went on talking in his measured, serious way with friend or visitor. I have seen him carry on conversation for some time whilst one of the children wriggled backwards and forwards underneath the bars of the chair on which he sat. And now, farewell to the child Nolly—of whom we too soon lost sight.

By the middle of June Edward was well enough to take my sister and me to Summertown, where we had been invited for Commemoration by Mr. and Mrs. MacLaren, and he remained a week at Oxford before returning to Little Holland House. Even there, however, he soon flagged again, and presently rejoined us. We stayed together at Summertown until the pure air and country life helped him to gain strength, so that he was in good spirits and protested that he was perfectly well; but as one day he was found quietly fainting on the sofa in a room where he had been left alone, we judged him by that rather than by his protestations. An evening comes back to my mind when after a very hot day we had a terrific storm, and it was revealed to us for the first time that our host was afraid of thunder and lightning. He went upstairs, and taking his little Mabel out of her bed wrapped her in a blanket, and brought her down to the drawing-room, where, as he sat with her in his arms, his anxious face put an end to all talk. Our young spirits, awestruck though we were by the violence of the storm, objected to this ceremony of alarm, and Mr. Price good-naturedly took upon himself the task of reviving conversation. He always had a turn for statistics, and this time thought to cheer the company by announcing in a pleasant voice that it was a well-established fact that one ill-kept pig-sty did more harm than twenty thunderstorms; but, as a cannonade of thunder saluted the statement, MacLaren angrily exclaimed: "Price, you should be ashamed of yourself to speak so!" and the well-meant effort failed. Most of our stay was in beautiful weather, however. Edward read aloud to us a great deal from the Morte d'Arthur, and we had singing of old French and English songs, and we ate innumerable cherries, and told each other tales, and laughed a great deal with "Peggy" Talboys, a sister of Mrs. MacLaren's, whom we all loved. Edward, of course, had brought work with him, and the design he was then busy upon was the pen-and-ink drawing of "Sir Galahad." "I can't look at Galahad yet to finish it," he wrote afterwards; "every stroke in it reminds one of some dear little word or incident that happened as the pen was marking." He often spoke of these involuntary pictures within a picture which existed for him in all that he did.

Kind Mrs. Prinsep claimed him again on his return to London, and he had the pleasure of finding that Tennyson was then staying at Little Holland House. A reminiscence of Edward's about this meeting has been preserved. "It was there I got to know Tennyson first. It was in the days when he was fiercely attacked and reviled by people: afterwards when he wrote the Idylls of the King and gave them what they wanted, they were pleased and praised him—but in the days of the Poems and of Maud he was much abused by the English. Unfortunately he minded being abused and was very sensitive about it, and one evening at dinner he was in real distress about an anonymous letter he had received—which began "Abhorred Sir," and ended "Yours in aversion"—and one by one he took the guests apart and said "What would you do if you got a letter like this?" Lord Tennyson's Memoir of his father refers to this visit, and says, "here my father began 'The Fair Maid of Astolat.'"

Vivien had been written two years before, but was then called by its author Nimuë—the name of the Damsel of the Lake with whom, as she is represented in Malory's Morte d'Arthur, Edward's imagination had been dealing so closely in his Oxford picture—and Mr. Prinsep recalls his pained face and eager expostulation when he found that the poet in his Idyll had modernized and altered the character while preserving the ancient name. "Tennyson," says Mr. Prinsep, "good-naturedly changed it to 'Vivien.'" Ruskin also was to be seen at Little Holland House, and Lord Tennyson and Mr. Prinsep both relate a story which pleased and amused us so much at the time—of his being heard one day to exclaim, after looking at a design of Edward's, "Jones, you are gigantic!" This alliteration delighted the ear of Tennyson and was not allowed to drop, so that "Gigantic Jones" became a nickname until his friends tired of it.

Both Morris and Rossetti looked with some suspicion upon Edward's long stay at Little Holland House. Gabriel thought its situation too low, and was anxious as to its effect on one already so delicate, and Morris had, generally speaking, a defiant tone towards the fashionable life which existed there side by side with the literary and artistic. Edward, conscious of all this, certain of himself, yet eagerly breathing the new atmosphere, found in it as much excitement as rest; but rest was never the only thing he needed. I could not realize then as I do now what this visit to Little Holland House must have been to him. There, for the first time, he found himself surrounded without any effort of his own by beauty in ordinary life, and no day passed without awakening some admiration or enthusiasm. He had never gone short of love and loving care, but for visible beauty he had literally starved through all his early years. The lovely garden that surrounded the house was an enchanted circle separating it from other places: there in the summertime, and especially on Sundays, came most people of note in the different circles that made up the "world" of England—old and young, rich and poor, each welcome for some reason recognized by the hostess. Part of the great lawn was given up to croquet—the chief outdoor game of the time—and another to bowls, whilst elsewhere encampments could be seen of those who did not play; and all seemed happy. The very strawberries that stood in little crimson hills upon the tables were larger and riper than others. This was rather before the days in which Mrs. Prinsep's elder sister Mrs. Cameron was there with her photography, which became the mingled terror and delight of her friends. Her incalculable ways, brilliant words and kind actions had their fascination for everybody, but her lens, when levelled at them, was merciless. One story there was of Browning, the fiery and restless, brought to bay by her in the garden, and beguiled into sitting as she would have him, draped in strange wise, and left by her helpless in the folds of the drapery, forgotten for the time as she flew on some other quest.

Val Prinsep, who was living at home in his father's house during Edward's visit, was like a younger brother to him, and used his great strength tenderly for his help, sometimes carrying him upstairs in his arms when he saw him overwhelmed with fatigue, or if he were sleepless and light-headed through sheer weakness, as occasionally happened, bringing a companion mattress and spreading it on the floor by his friend's side, "to drive away the bogies." Sometimes there was pain as well as exhaustion, and Edward must have mentioned this to Rossetti, from whom I find an undated fragment of a letter that says he is "miserable" to hear it. "To think of you suffering so much and in such an unaccountable way! Of course I shall come to-morrow as early as I can—would come to-night also if possible but fear I cannot manage that. I know how much better cared-for you are at Kensington than elsewhere, but still cannot help fearing that the air may have to do with your illness as I know it is far from agreeing with every-one. You really *must* try something else immediately if you are not better in a few days—much as you will lose by sacrificing Mrs. Prinsep's care. There is nothing in the world I care for more than for your health, dear old fellow—hardly anything nearly so much. I know I must be fonder of you than you can possibly be of me—at any rate there is no man I love so well by half or who loves me so well. However, this letter begins to read rather flabby."

In the midst of the brilliance of Little Holland House Edward continued anxious about his father's affairs, and was looking forward to the time when he could go down to Birmingham. He writes to Miss Sampson: "I suppose you have been very busy removing and getting things straight. I want to know everything about you—how you are and my father, write and tell me, for he never tells me how he is. Do you like the new house better than the old one—does pussy like it better—is puss well? Are the Spozzis in town yet—write and tell me everything." And a little later, looking forward to his birthday: "We shall very soon meet now, in about 10 or 12 days I shall be down with you both, and stay a happy little fortnight. I shall bring my work down with me and be very snug and happy, shan't I?"

Poor Miss Sampson seems to have sent one letter to Edward this year which moved him to an unusually serious answer, for generally he wrote to her with a light pen and tried to make her smile.

"Cheer up," he begins, "don't be down-hearted—we shall have jollier days yet than we have had. Never mind, while I've got any tin you shall have some—and when I get on fast, as I shall soon, you shall be happy. Look upon it all as only a temporary thing, it won't last long, either my father will make head quickly against his difficulties or I shall be successful; don't talk about anything being difficult for your time of life, you are not old yet so don't fancy it—only be cheerful and don't repine as if you alone suffered. I see lots of misery in our station of life —lots of struggling to keep above water, privation, self-sacrifice, humiliation. If we had only known it we have been very happy these many years, only we weren't grateful; for nearly 25 years we have been together, and never wanted for much—we were a great deal happier than we knew at the time, and if we are good it will come back again. Don't let any person persuade you that you have been a fool for not looking after your own interest—God doesn't call such people fools—it's right to do it, but not wrong not to do it. I have worked very hard at art for two years and find it difficult to live—and I am thought a most successful beginner, and am spoken of in London a great deal—but there are so many things to be grateful for that it is not right to name anything as unfortunate."

It was natural that Mrs. Prinsep should wish to know something about the girl to whom the young friend in whom she had such an affectionate interest was engaged. One day she and her sister Lady Somers came by appointment to Beaumont Street, to call upon my mother. The two tall, handsome women brought with them a breath from a world that was strange to us, but its brilliance and kindness were familiar to our imagination, and love for Edward was our common meeting-ground. Nevertheless the visit was felt to be one of inspection as well as courtesy, and in spite of the gracefulness of the callers was something of an ordeal to pass through. An invitation sent afterwards to my elder sister and me took us one evening to dine at Little Holland House, and to this day the impression remains of its low, dimly lighted, richly coloured rooms, dark passages opening into lofty studios filled with the noble work of Watts, a vision of one beautiful human being after another, and the table spread with a sense of boundless welcome. The splendid growth of both the men and women of the family was more noticeable at that time than it would be now, and added an element of wonder to the place. I never saw Tennyson there, but heard from Edward of the added excitement that his presence always caused. Certainly in point of height and physical beauty he must have taken his place finely in that remarkable household.

It may have been in consequence of the weak sight of Mr. Prinsep that the custom began of having the living rooms of Little Holland House so dimly lit as they were; but it brought with it no feeling of depression and produced no silence. From the specially dark corner in which "Uncle Thoby's" couch was placed used to proceed much laughter, and visitors waited their turn for the pleasure of sitting by his side, while life never flagged in the circle where "Aunt Sara" lived and moved. One felt her guiding will through everything, and under all the ease and freedom of the house was a sense of her vigilance. When I learned that she was of mixed Irish and French descent, that seemed a clue to her wonderful vivacity.

Mrs. Prinsep's youngest sister, Mrs. (now Lady) Dalrymple, was a graceful and touching presence in the house, and memory of her always brings back the sound of soft, silken rustlings and the tinkling of silver bangles as she came and went. The exclamation of a child when he saw her for the first time pleased Edward, who often quoted it: "O what big eyes! O what wide hair!"

The beautiful Miss Herbert, then acting at the St. James's Theatre, used to come sometimes to sit to Watts, and the younger men, if they were there, would gather round her and make studies also. Echoes of their admiration reached us young people, to whom theatres were things unknown, and once we were shewn a small water-colour made by Gabriel of her, radiant in golden hair,—just the head and throat on an emerald-green background—and deeply did we feel the tribute rendered to her beauty when we read the names which he had written around the four sides of the little picture: "BEATRICE HELEN GUENEVERE HERBERT." I first saw this lady one evening in the early days of our marriage, at the house of her friends and ours, Mr. and Mrs. Street, and then after many years we met again in Rottingdean, when Miss Herbert drove out from Brighton and she and my husband shook hands across the gulf of time. Her grace and dignity of bearing remained very striking, and I do not think there could have been a shock on either side, for both still visibly carried the marks of their distinguishing gifts—of power and of beauty.

Red Lion Square was not very brilliant in 1858, as from one cause or another Morris and Edward were seldom there at the same time: a sense of change was in the air, and so early as Easter they began to consider whether it was worth while to keep the rooms on. Never from the time of their first meeting did the friends see so little of each other in any year as in this.

Mr. Price, who was reading for his degree, kept house at Red Lion Square most of the Long Vacation, and part of the time Rossetti was there with him, driven from his own studio at Blackfriars by the smell of the river below its windows. Mary looked after them both with a good will, for they were among her chief favourites. At the beginning of the summer Morris told Edward of his engagement to Miss Burden, and they both realized that the old ways were now at an end and that a new order of things had begun. I am surprised on employing the ruthless measure of weeks and months to find how short a time the brilliant days of Red Lion Square really lasted, for on looking back it seems so much longer. But I believe that it made the same impression upon many of us and that every minute then contained the life of an hour.

The fortnight that Edward promised to spend in Birmingham when he went down for his birthday grew into three weeks, but the only trace I have of it is in a note written whilst there to congratulate Madox Brown on his again receiving, as he had done the year before, the £50 prize from the Liverpool Academy. "Gabriel tells me you've got the prize at Liverpool: I'm jolly glad, and only wished it were 50 prizes instead, for you ought to have them all."

In mid September Morris, who had just come back from three weeks' boating on the Seine with Philip Webb and Charles Faulkner, was full of a scheme for building a house for himself, and the Red Lion Square days were practically over. Edward's health was now restored to its average state, thanks to the loving care of Mrs. Prinsep. "She was the nearest thing to a mother that I ever knew," he once said: and the whole time at Little Holland House had been refreshing, for he had enjoyed the new life revealed to him, yet had not been carried away by it from the old. He was more than eager for work, but first came the weary search for fresh rooms. "I have had such a week of fatigue as I never had before," he writes during the removal, "and am pretty well knocked up—the rooms are dear but very good, well-lighted, large and clean." They were on the first floor of a house at the corner of Russell Place and Howland Street: Russell Place is now numbered as part of Fitzroy Street, Fitzroy Square. In those days the existence of artists was scarcely recognized, and to find a window cut up to the ceiling in order to give a room some claim to the name of studio was good luck which Edward neither expected nor met with in this case.

When he was established in these new rooms he found

himself for the first time in his life quite alone, but friends followed him there, and to his great pleasure Val Prinsep became his near neighbour by taking the first floor of the house at the opposite corner of Howland Street. Mr. Price took his degree in October, but stayed on at Oxford reading medicine, for he in his turn had given up all thought of entering the Church and was now intending to become a doctor.

Mr. Spencer Stanhope tells me a story that belongs to Russell Place, of how one morning when he was going there he saw a small crowd coming along the street with Edward at the head of it, closely followed by a wretched, draggled-looking girl whom he had found, not quite sober, and the centre of a gang of boys and roughs who were jeering at and bullying her, so he had told her to come with him whilst he looked out for a policeman to protect her.

The Red Lion Square rooms were transferred to Mr. Swan, whose acquaintance Morris and Edward had made while painting the Union, and whose outward appearance may be gathered from Mary's exclamation when he first called on them, "Oh, sir, here 's a gentleman out of Byron come to see you!" The likeness did not alarm her, however, for she stayed on as housekeeper to him and working at embroidery for Morris until her marriage.

The latter months of this year are clouded over in my mind, and I only see things in it as if the sky opened for a moment to give light and then closed again. I remember that Fulford, whose engagement to my sister had been over for some time, but whom we always liked, became quite estranged from us and temporarily broke even with the Oxford Set, no one could tell why. I recall also one scene, of several of us young people at Euston Square Railway Station, on a miserable November evening, saying good-bye to my brother Harry as he started for America. He had passed the Indian Civil Service examination successfully, and we were preparing our minds to part with him in that way, when, with the sudden impetuosity which a reserved and seemingly self-controlled nature occasionally shews, he changed his whole plans in a few days and the rest of his life was passed in New York.

The first Hogarth Club—which dates from this year—ought to be mentioned here, for if in the end it proved something of a disappointment to its founders, still the discussions about it beforehand were a source of great pleasure to the inner circle of friends, and the club itself while it lasted was a gain to them as one more place of meeting.

In later years Edward referred to it as his "first experience in public life," and described his dismay on gradually finding that it involved rules and official meetings and the passing of resolutions, all of which was so opposite to what he had meant. "Stanhope and I thought it would be nice to have a club where we could chatter. But what a mistake I made. And then, to do him honour, we elected Carlyle—and after that we sent him all the rules and reports and notices of meetings and adjournments of meetings and changes of meetings—till one day, talking to a friend of his who knew us, he said the communications of the Hogarth Club had become an afflictive phenomenon. So his friend let us know of this, and we had another meeting about it. Full of uproarious laughter the meeting was—but though we saw the humour of it we had to propose and pass resolutions that Carlyle should be exempted from the affliction for the future. Then some one proposed that a copy of the resolution should be sent to him, and though others said that this was the very kind of thing that bothered him it had to be done."

The club died a natural death.

All through this unproductive year Mr. Plint, instead of shewing any anxiety as to the sums he had already paid for pictures yet unpainted, continued to send more cheques on account and accompanied them with the kindest expressions of sympathy about Edward's health. The impression of himself and his affairs which these notes give is that of simple goodness. He underlines his letters like any schoolgirl, and is not afraid to write, "It *is* happiness to look on a picture!"

It grieves me even now to think that he died before the work he so much looked for came into his possession, and my only comfort is a note dated "Xmas Day 1860" (he died six months afterwards), in which he says, "Thanks, my dear Sir, for the case and all the beautiful things of yours and Solomon's in it;" so that he had something —I do not remember what—to please him that last Christmas.

In February, 1859, Edward writes: "I am as busy as can be, and ought never to have any interruptions and never any idle hours, but I can't manage it so—I wish I could. People will call and must be attended to, and I often feel tired when I ought to be at work. My eyes have been very weak lately—I suppose from cold—to-day they are much better." The wonder is that his eyes and eyesight remained so strong as they did under the perpetual strain of work in the evening as well as the daytime, for now that the merry fellowship of Oxford and Red Lion Square evenings was at an end, he used the time it left him for the one purpose of work. Often he went first to Lee's life-school and then on to the Working Men's College, where he helped Madox Brown with a class for some time before he took one of his own. A pencil note scribbled to Mr. Brown brings these days before us. "Excuse foul paper—hands all over charcoal—don't like to wash them twice in the same day. As it is the first night of a new model won't you go to the W[orking] M[en]? I don't want to shirk work at all, but I should much sooner that you should have the entire rule of everything there—also as it is the first night of a new model at Lee's I should like to secure a good place for the next fortnight—so I would come on to W[orking] M[en] at 9 o'clock or 8½ rather."

Mr. J. P. Emslie, who was then a student and part of the time a pupil teacher in the drawing-class at the Working Men's College, has told me of things he remembers while there which clearly recall the individuality of Ruskin,

Rossetti and Edward. He says that Ruskin used to keep his pupils a long time drawing in black and white before he would allow them to begin colour, as he considered one great fault of modern art was that men began colour before they properly understood light and shade. However, to accustom his pupils to the use of the brush, he allowed them to make studies in Prussian blue. Rossetti, who was for having everybody learn to colour fully from the first, was filled with indignation when, walking round Mr. Ruskin's class-room one evening, he saw the system that was practised there. "How 's this?" he said; "nothing but blue studies —can't any of you see any colour but blue?" "It was by Mr. Ruskin's direction," one of the students answered. "Well, where do you get all this Prussian blue from?" asked Gabriel, going straight to the root of the matter; and being directed to a cupboard in the room he opened it and refreshed his indignation by the sight of the store which he saw there. "Well, I declare," he exclaimed, "here 's a packet with several dozen cakes of this fearful colour. Oh, I can't allow it; Mr. Ruskin will spoil everybody's eye for colour— I shall confiscate the whole lot: I must do it, in the interests of his and my pupils. You must tell him that I've taken them all away." When a few evenings later Mr. Ruskin found that his dear Prussian blues were all gone he inquired the cause, and, being told, "burst into one of those boisterous laughs in which he indulged whenever anything very much amused him."

Edward's name is on the prospectuses of the College from January, 1859, to March, 1861, and that means more than meets the eye, for he had an inmost dislike to teaching anything formally. Mr. Emslie says that he left with his pupils a feeling that he was their fellow-worker as well as their master, and was always trying to get them to think and see for themselves and gain self-reliance in their work; and another impression they received was a strong sense of his own delight in good works of art at every time of the world. He encouraged them to draw from the sculptures in the British Museum, and described to them with enthusiasm things that he had seen and they had not, but never spoke to them slightingly of the work of any brother artist. "The utmost I ever heard him say against any art-work," writes Mr. Emslie, was "Well, it doesn't interest me."

How often have I noticed this in him myself. "No one knows how difficult it is to paint even a bad picture," he used to say. This does not mean that he was not ready upon occasion to declare opinion plainly, but that it was never his habit lightly to condemn or disparage any one's work.

"February's half gone already," says a letter to Miss Sampson, "and I don't seem to have begun work yet, and yet every day I have been at work. I wish I could settle subjects for my pictures and then I should be all right; but at present I am full of anxiety and care, and feel quite worried about things. In six months the Macdonalds leave London, and then I shall be very dull—never mind, it is six months and I won't anticipate anything."

In as unaccountable a manner as he had estranged himself from the Set Fulford this year returned to it, and through a letter of his written in March to Miss Fanny Price we have almost the last glimpse of any number of them together at Oxford. He tells her that he had just spent a week there, "and of course I saw Crom and Faulkner. Crom seems to be taking to medicine famously, and I should think gets through a good deal of reading in it. He and Faulkner and another man were reading a French play. Of course old Charley is just the same as ever, glorious fellow, he never changes—in temper and disposition he couldn't well change for the better.

"Topsy turned up while I was there and the manner of his turning-up was highly characteristic—very, very Topsian. On Saturday all the Birmingham—or rather all the Set were invited by letter to dine with him on the Sunday at 5 or 5.30. Between 4 and 5 on Sunday he appeared at his lodgings and told them he wanted dinner. They were a little troubled at this, considering the day, but they were aghast when he said he wanted it for half a dozen people. However dinner did at length appear, at about 7 o'clock, and a very good dinner it was."

Fulford also mentions having seen Dixon and Edward in London, and his habit of criticism and comparison obliges him to measure the two men against each other. Both Fulford and Dixon had been ordained by this time.

"One hoped that Dixon would make a poet," he says. "I at one time felt quite confident of it, and I must say I regard any success in practical life (though the life and duties of a clergyman) as a poor substitute for this, perhaps the highest work allowed to human nature. I may be unfair in applying this to Dixon, for he not only reads but also writes poetry, and that I fancy in considerable quantity, but still I should like to see him living a definitely and manifestly poetical life, such as Edward's, whom one feels to be in the right path, pursuing the course which nature marked out for him."

In his correspondence with Miss Price, Fulford was accustomed to write at great length on literary subjects, and I remember his telling against himself with much amusement a story of how once on meeting her a few days after he had sent her a very long letter she told him frankly that it was in her pocket, but she "had not yet had time to read it."

In April, when Morris and Miss Jane Burden were married at Oxford, Edward and as many of the Set as possible were present. Dixon of course came down from London to marry them, and, to the satisfaction of his friends who had warned him against it until he could do nothing else, ended by pronouncing the young couple to be man and wife together under the names of "William and Mary."

It was a solitary time for Edward whilst Morris was away on his wedding journey; Val Prinsep was in Paris, and Cormell Price had not yet come to London. There was no Red Lion Mary now to bring her embroidery frame and sit behind him while he painted or cull the gems from "Reynolds" on a Sunday morning, and there is a breath of unusual depression about himself in a note that his little friend Louie Macdonald had from him while she was staying with Mrs. and Miss Talboys at Oxford this spring. "I am so worried and teased about things," he says, "because I am a big booby and can't paint or draw at all, that I behave shamefully to everybody, and never answer letters or reply to questions or do anything that a Christian man ought to do: that dear Mrs. Talboys wrote such a kind letter a whole month ago that makes me ashamed of myself for never answering. I want to see you, dear, so much and look at your work [wood-engraving] and calculate how long it is to come before we bring out a picture book together with little L.Ms and E.Js in the corners and make people say that Albert Dürer has come back again." Then he tells her that he is coming to Oxford "to meet the Dean of Christ Church"—an appointment that had to do with the commission for his Frideswide window in the Cathedral—but turns again to his first complaint: "I have been so busy and coming so many howlers and getting so unhappy that life is dear at 2d." The letter ends with "only three more months of you and then I lose my little three year pet. Shall you be very sorry to see me so seldom?" The time ran by all too quickly, and an evil fate caused me to be away for some weeks out of the few that remained, for a family council decided that I must accept an invitation to go with my mother to the seaside. May the shade of our kind host forgive me if I say how much my young self-consciousness suffered when, on the occasion of my birthday, he kindly invited Edward to join us, and addressed him in an after-dinner speech as "one of those happy men who would have a fortune *in* a wife instead of *with* her." But the next day made amends, for my mother and I accompanied Edward on his way home as far as to Canterbury, and he shewed us the Cathedral.

Meanwhile the Morrises returned from abroad and settled for a time in furnished rooms at 41, Great Ormond Street. There Edward took me one evening to see Mrs. Morris for the first time, and never shall I forget it—literally I dreamed of her again in the night.

Morris had already begun to occupy himself with carrying out his cherished scheme of building a house after his own heart with the help of his friend Philip Webb. Needs must it be in the country to please them both, and in the midst of apple-trees; and such a place was found at Upton, near Bexley Heath, Kent, a roadside orchard surrounded by meadows and with space where they could build in the orchard with scarcely any disturbance of the trees. It was not to be a large house, but so designed that additions could be made without difficulty, and to this idea it owed part of its form; indeed architect and client had but one mind about the whole work, and the result was happy. The plans of the house were complete before Morris' marriage, and there was nothing to do but to carry them out. Rossetti of course exulted when he learnt that a hollow close to the site Morris had bought was known in the neighbourhood as "Hog's Hole," and lost no opportunity of alluding to the house by this name, but his serious thought of it after its completion was expressed, in a letter to a friend, in these words: "I wish you could see the house that Morris has built for himself in Kent. It is a most noble work in every way, and more a poem than a house such as anything else could lead you to conceive, but an admirable place to live in too."

The time of separation anticipated in Edward's letters now drew near, and my father was appointed by Conference to go to a circuit in Manchester, whither, much against the will of the younger members of the family, we went in the first days of September. For Edward, however, the loss that this meant was fortunately lightened by its happening at the very time when it proved possible for him to join in a plan of going with Faulkner and Val Prinsep for a few weeks' travel in North Italy. He had worked extremely hard all the year in spite of dejection; his design for the large St. Frideswide window at Christ Church, Oxford, was finished, and nothing could have been more timely. Just as, when he needed it, the meetings with Morris and Rossetti had been brought about at the right day and hour for his help, so now the Ruler of his life led him on this journey; and the cities that he saw during it, and the pictures in them, were such a fulfilment of his desire and such a revelation of what man could achieve that he ceased to be afraid of failure for himself. Many a time I have heard him say that nothing disheartened or took the life out of him so much as looking at bad work, but that the best was always inspiriting and life-giving. He drew and made notes wherever he went, and through every sense absorbed what he found remaining unspoiled of the beauty of earth and the works of man. Before starting on his journey he went down to Birmingham to spend his birthday with his father and then joined his friends.

He was always a bad traveller, by land as well as by sea; change of hours and diet upset him at once, and the confinement of a railway carriage, with everything else that belonged to railway travelling, he particularly hated. Mr. Prinsep says of him that on this journey he was never completely happy except when visiting churches and seeing pictures, but that his energy in that way was wonderful. They went straight from Paris to Marseilles, and on by sea to Genoa and Leghorn, arriving at Pisa in time to hear Romagna's rejection of the Pope's temporal power proclaimed.

Thence, after two or three days, they went on to Florence, where they had hoped to meet the Brownings, for whom they had an introduction from Rossetti. In this, however, they were disappointed, as Mr. and Mrs. Browning had left for Siena, and it was here, when visiting the Cathedral later on, that the travellers found them, together with Mr. Walter Savage Landor. From Florence Edward wrote: "I have been quite well all the time through, and worked tremendously at the pictures, and shall go back quite an educated man. We have the most glorious weather here; in the country they are haymaking for the second time, all the vines are in full fruit, and roses are out everywhere; the climate too is just moderate with a quiet wind blowing always. All day long we work at the pictures and bathe about sunset—which gives us more rest than anything else—and then dine, and after that we are good for nothing but to lie down and go to bed about nine o'clock. I shall have got lots of good from this journey, and learnt very much, but I shall be glad when it is all over and I am back to work."

From Venice also there is a letter home which gives another surface view of how it was with him: "We are in the jolliest place in all the wide world at last—the queerest and jolliest a great way, and a million times the most beautiful—so you must say good-bye, for we mean to stay here always and never leave it again for a day. There never was such a city—all built in the sea you know, with the houses and palaces in the water and gondolas for Hansom cabs to take us everywhere: one comes every morning to take us from our hotel to breakfast in the great Square by the ducal palace and wonderful church—there every one breakfasts in the open air, and girls bring flowers to lay on your plates, and music plays and everything is so bright and stunning. All the day long we glide about the water streets in our boat, visiting palaces and churches—there are 100 islands all covered with churches and palaces, and all full of pictures, and bell-towers with big bells that ring all day long, and all the evening we sit out in the great square again and listen to music and see the sunset on the sea and the night come up over the Adriatic."

Wherever these three men went history was made, and I wish I could remember the tales we were told on their return. One there was about a spider, not to say a tarantula, of gigantic size, that was found in a bedroom and held it against them until it was caught in a wash-hand basin, where it terrified them by leaping high into the air whenever they tried to deal with it, and how after a council of war they hurled it out of the window and then suffered many things through imagining its fall upon a passer-by; and another story they had of a scene at the Douane when passports had to be examined, and Edward's and Faulkner's names were duly called out and responded to, but "Valentine Cameron Prinsep" was passed over until the last, when the officer, looking about in bewilderment, read "Valentine Comtesse Principessa," and the youth of six foot one answered to it amid a general roar of laughter.

At Venice they had to separate, as Faulkner was obliged to be at Oxford for the beginning of the October term, but Edward and Mr. Prinsep stayed on for a fortnight or so longer, taking Milan on their way back. Here Mr. Prinsep says that Edward was seized with such a longing to get home that nothing would content him but they must start at once. They had come very nearly to an end of the money they had with them, but Edward would not hear of waiting for any remittance, and Mr. Prinsep, who arranged all the business of the journey, calculated that with care they could manage to go straight through to England—so they started. Nothing was allowed for accidents though, and when at St. Jean de Maurienne they found the Mont Cenis pass blocked by an avalanche which delayed them for three days it made a serious difference to their expenses. The time was beguiled by the company of fellow-travellers, two most agreeable Frenchmen, with whom Mr. Prinsep had much conversation—Edward hardly spoke French at all—and these gentlemen proposed in their friendliness that when they joined the railway again at Culoz they should all four take a coupé together to Paris, a plan to which, without reflecting that it would mean extra charge, Mr. Prinsep readily agreed. Then the Frenchmen began saying how delightful it would be when they reached Dijon, the best buffet in France, after all their hardships, and what a meal they would have! An almost empty purse prevented the Englishmen from joining in this enthusiasm, and, pride coming to his aid, Mr. Prinsep suddenly made the startling assertion that he and his friend for their part never ate a meal when travelling by rail—could take nothing heavier than a cup of coffee and a roll. At Culoz they found a coupé: "Charming," said the Frenchmen; "so much more comfortable in this way—and only eighteen francs extra!" Then pride of another sort made the young Englishman confess that he and his friend had not the amount between them. "What does that matter?" cried the friendly strangers; "we will lend you what you need," and instantly produced £5, so that the trouble was at an end. But a fresh difficulty arose when they reached Dijon, hungry as hunters, and with means to command a dinner such as they had not seen for many a day, but with their new-found rule of abstinence "when travelling by rail" barring the buffet. They took counsel together and decided that for their own honour and that of their country they must stick to their word, and so while their companions turned the flying minutes to account by eating a wonderful dinner, they faithfully restricted themselves to "a cup of coffee and a roll."

On the night of the 25th-26th October they crossed from Dieppe to Newhaven in such a storm that they tossed for seven hours outside the bar, and Edward was so ill that the recollection of it remained always a black spot in his memory. The next day they knew that the wind which had beaten them back for so long from the shore they were seeking had been kinder to them than to the home-ward bound "Royal Charter," which with fearful loss of life had been dashed to pieces that same night upon the Welsh coast.

Only Edward himself, supposing he had ever sat down to reckon it, could have rendered full account of what was done for him by his first journey to Italy. Rossetti had taught him "not to be afraid of himself," that is to say, of the imagination that was in him, and now he had seen the way in which the great painters of a great time had painted what was in them, and had come away knowing that he was their own son. This I never heard him say, but I have felt sure that his strength under early opposition and discouragement lay in his certainty that he belonged to a race which had always handed down a tradition that had never finally missed acknowledgement; and by the devoutest labour he set about to establish this lineage.

Our marriage seemed no nearer at the end of three years

and a half than it had ever done, for his income had not yet allowed him more than a hand-to-mouth existence, and now that I lived in Manchester our chances of meeting were few: but he came down to see us in December, leaving for Birmingham before Christmas. The following sentence from a note written whilst he was with us, in answer to a suggestion of Madox Brown's that if I would like it his wife would invite me to pay them a visit in the following spring, is given here because our marriage was the direct result of that visit. "I am sure," Edward says, "Georgie would be glad beyond words to go and stay with you any time you ask her—it's immensely kind of you and Mrs. Brown—an invitation would be grabbed at by her I know."

He and his father spent Christmas Day with the Prices at Spon Lane, but Margaret Price, who had long been in failing health, was now dead, and the diary that records the meeting says: "It was not like a feast day, with all our attempts to make it one—dearest Madge had left us, and who could be gay?" A return visit from Spon Lane to Bristol Road went more brightly, however: "We enjoyed ourselves very much. Edward shewed us a picture he had nearly finished—'Buon del Monte's Wedding'—such a beautiful picture in ink." Affectionate praise for a "picture in ink" was ready for him, but he had passed the pleasant wayside places where the labourer rests with his friends after a day's work, and had begun the world-long day of those who seek no rest or reward but that of contenting the rigour of the Judge Invisible.

CHAPTER XI

THREE HOUSEHOLDS
1860

MRS. MADOX BROWN did not fail in due time to send the invitation, which it will be believed was eagerly "grabbed at," and in April, 1860, I went up to London for a happy month in Fortess Terrace, seeing Edward constantly and making and renewing pleasant acquaintances. The unselfishness of Mr. and Mrs. Madox Brown in this matter is clearer to me now than it was at the time, for I realize on reflection that, besides their risking the proverbial irksomeness of the society of betrothed people, it must have needed the best will in the world to accommodate in their house even one person beyond their own family; but a small house and slender means were made spacious and sufficient by their generous hearts, and my recollection is of one continuous stream of hospitality. Who that was present at it could ever forget one of their dinners, with Madox Brown and his wife seated at either end of a long table, and every guest a welcome friend who had come to talk and to laugh and to listen? for listening was the attitude into which people naturally fell when in his company. He had so much to say and was so happy in saying it that sometimes he would pause, carving-knife in hand, to go on with his story, until Mrs. Brown's soft voice could be heard breathing his name from her distant place and reminding him of his duties. At their table the standard of the common English willow-pattern plate was boldly raised, in spite of Gabriel's enquiries for it at a china shop having been met with insult by the proprietress: it was before the days of real Chinese ware for any of us, but

Rossetti's fine collection in later days may be traced back to his first quest after these despised "kitchen plates."

It would be hard to say when Madox Brown found time for painting the pictures that we know, for he was the very sport of distraction, letting people come up to chat in his studio, which was not large enough for himself, and being lured downstairs, palette on thumb, by the sound of the piano if it played a tune that he liked, to the oblivion of everything else. His manner of talking was characteristic—very slow and distinct. Though he recollected facts well and held the attention of his hearers by endless tales of his own experience or original reflections upon life, he had an incapacity for remembering names which, while endearing him to us all, made havoc of some of his remarks. At other times, if the word itself was not wrong, he would vary its accent, but in either case it would be uttered with such deliberation that there was no doubt as to the change which had been wrought. "Have you heard," he asked in measured tones one evening, "of a novel called The Mill on the Floss, by Miss Atkinson?" "Miss Atkinson, my dear fellow—it's Miss Evans!" rose from the listening circle. His brow clouded, and more slowly than before he answered, "Well, Atkinson or Evans, it's the same thing!" And we agreed that it was, and that if Michael himself were to weigh the names in a balance the poise would be found equal. Another time, talk falling upon Mary Queen of Scots, his listeners could hardly trust their delighted ears when Madox Brown, after reviewing the character of the lovers of the luckless lady that are known to history, summed up the matter by saying deliberately, "There's no doubt that she had a real feeling for Boswell."

Before my visit came to an end Madox Brown had decided that Edward had better be married without further delay, and since his character as counsellor stood high and we had no arguments to oppose to the suggestion, it was suddenly settled. I wrote to my mother to the effect that so much of me had already left her kind hands that I prayed her now to set the rest free, and she and my father consented, asking Edward no questions, but committing us both to the care of God.

Since the time that Rossetti was called away from Oxford, in October, 1857, by the illness of Miss Siddal, he and Edward had been less together, but there had been no decrease of affection between them, and so it was of the most vital interest to us when we learnt that Gabriel was to be married about the same time as ourselves. He and Edward at once built up a plan for our all four meeting in Paris as soon as possible afterwards; I went home to Manchester to make my preparations, and it was decided that the fourth anniversary of our engagement, the 9th of June, should be our wedding-day. The conditions on which we started life were, practically no debts, except of work to Mr. Plint, and the possession of about £30 in ready money; and I brought with me a small deal table with a drawer in it that held my wood-engraving tools. Three days before our marriage, however, came a note from the unfailing Mr. Plint: "The two pen-and-ink drawings are to hand to-day. I enclose order for £25 which you may need just now." So here was riches.

The 9th of June fell on a Saturday, and we decided to go no further that day than to Chester, where we should see its curious streets and attend service at the Cathedral on Sunday; Gabriel and his wife were by this time in Paris, and we hoped to join them a few days later. But this was not in store for us, for unhappily Edward had been caught in a rain-storm a day or two before and already had a slight sore-throat, which now so quickly grew worse that by noon on Sunday he was almost speechless from it and in the hands of a strange doctor. This illness was a sharp check, and we found ourselves shut up for some days in a dreary hotel in an unknown place; but a gleam of satisfaction reached us when the doctor spoke of me to Edward as "your good lady," and gave me directions about what was to be done for the patient, with no apparent suspicion that I had not often nursed him before. Trusting in this and in some half-used reels of sewing cotton ostentatiously left about, as well as a display of boots which had already been worn, we felt great confidence that no one would guess how ignominiously newly-married we were.

It was quite clear that we must give up Paris and get to our own home as soon as the doctor gave Edward leave to travel; so ruefully enough I wrote to Gabriel and told him how things were; and his answer was a comfort to us, for he reported that they were both tired of "dragging about," and looked forward with pleasure to sitting down again with their friends in London as soon as possible. "Lizzie and I are likely to come back with two dogs," he continues, "a big one and a little one. We have called the latter Punch in memory partly of a passage in Pepys's Diary, 'But in the street, Lord, how I did laugh to hear poor common persons call their fat child Punch, which name I do perceive to be good for all that is short and thick.' We have got the book with us from Mudie's, and meant to have yelled over it in company if you had come to Paris. We are now reading Boswell's Johnson, which is almost as rich in some parts." This reading of Boswell resulted in the water-colour drawing of "Dr. Johnson at the Mitre" which Rossetti brought back with him from Paris.

Our own home coming was informal, for Russell Place had not expected us so soon and was unprepared to receive us; there were no chairs in our dining-room, nor any other furniture that had been ordered except a table. But what did that matter? if there were no chairs there was the table, a good, firm one of oak, sitting upon which the bride received her first visitors, and as the studio was in its usual condition there was a home at once. The boys at the Boys' Home in Euston Road had made the table from the design of Philip Webb, and were busy with chairs and a sofa, which presently arrived. The chairs were high-backed black ones with rush seats, and the companion sofa was of panelled wood painted black. The chairs have disappeared, for they were smaller articles, vigorously used and much moved about, but the table and sofa have always shared the fortunes of their owners and were never superseded: we ate our last meal together at that table and our grandchildren laugh round it now. How modest the scale of our housekeeping was it would be hard to say, and also how rich we felt: "we live in great happiness and thankfulness" was the clue given my friend Charlotte as to our estate.

William Allingham came over from Ireland this summer, and was, I believe, the first friend I made in my new life. How well I remember his visit, even to where he stood in the room and the way the light fell upon him. He was a distinguished-looking man, though not tall; dark, with a fine cast of face and most Irish eyes—light in the darkness; his thick black hair was brushed close to his head and parted in the middle, but rippled in smooth, close lines that no brush could straighten. He was disposed to convince me that I was a sister of George MacDonald the novelist, for the *dramatis personae* of his life were of importance to him and this arrangement fitted in well with his conception of their order. His conversation was extremely interesting; serious in manner, with an attractive reserve which yet gave the impression that he cared for sympathy, and an evident minute interest in all that passed before him; a good companion, ready to talk and easily amused. He did not stay long in London, having to return to Ballyshannon, his native place, where at that time he had an appointment in the Customs, but the threefold friendship then begun never ceased.

In the unsettled week before his marriage Edward had amused himself by painting some figures upon a plain deal sideboard which he possessed, and this in its new state was a delightful surprise to find. "Ladies and animals" he called the subjects illustrated, and there were seven pictures, three on the cupboard doors in front and two at each end, which shewed them in various relations to each other. Three kind and attentive ladies were feeding pigs, parrots and fishes; two cruel ones were tormenting an owl by forcing him to look at himself in a round mirror, and gold fish by draining them dry in a net; while two more were expiating such sins in terror at a hideous newt upon the garden path and the assault of a swarm of angry bees. Mrs. Catherwood gave us a piano, made by Priestly of Berners Street, who had patented a small one of inoffensive shape that we had seen and admired at Madox Brown's house; we had ours made of unpolished American walnut, a perfectly plain wood of pleasing colour, so that Edward could paint upon it. The little instrument when opened shows inside the lid a very early design for the "Chant d'Amour," and on the panel beneath the keyboard there is a gilded and lacquered picture of Death, veiled and crowned, standing outside the gate of a garden where a number of girls, unconscious of his approach, are resting and listening to music. The lacquering of this panel was an exciting process, for its colour had to be be deepened by heat while still liquid, and Edward used a red-hot poker for the work.

Rossetti and his wife, after their return from Paris, took a lodging at Hampstead, but she was so ill at first that we never saw her till near the end of July, when to our great delight a day was fixed for the deferred meeting, and Gabriel suggested that it should take place at the Zoological Gardens. "The Wombat's Lair" was the assignation that he gave to the Madox Browns and to us. A mention of this meeting in a letter that I wrote next day gives the impression of the actual time: "She was well enough to see us, and I find her as beautiful as imagination, poor thing."

I wish I could recall more details of that day—of the wombat's reception of us, and of the other beasts we visited—but can only remember a passing call on the owls, between one of whom and Gabriel there was a feud. The moment their eyes met they seemed to rush at each other, Gabriel rattling his stick between the cage bars furiously and the owl almost barking with rage. Lizzie's slender, elegant figure—tall for those days, but I never knew her actual height—comes back to me, in a graceful and simple dress, the incarnate opposite of the "tailor-made" young lady. We went home with them to their rooms at Hampstead, and I know that I then received an impression which never wore away, of romance and tragedy between her and her husband. I see her in the little upstairs bedroom with its lattice window, to which she carried me when we arrived, and the mass of her beautiful deep-red hair as she took off her bonnet: she wore her hair very loosely fastened up, so that it fell in soft, heavy wings. Her complexion looked as if a rose tint lay beneath the white skin, producing a most soft and delicate pink for the darkest flesh-tone. Her eyes were of a kind of golden brown—agate-colour is the only word I can think of to describe them—and wonderfully luminous: in all Gabriel's drawings of her and in the type she created in his mind this is to be seen. The eyelids were deep, but without any languor or drowsiness, and had the peculiarity of seeming scarcely to veil the light in her eyes when she was looking down.

Whilst we were in her room she shewed me a design she had just made, called "The Woeful Victory"—then the vision passes.

A little later and we were with the Morrises in their new house at Upton, and the time we spent together there was one to swear by, if human happiness were doubted.

First was the arrival at Abbey Wood Station, a country place in those days, where a thin fresh air full of sweet smells met us as we walked down the platform, and outside was the wagonette sent from Red House to meet us; then a pull up the hill and a swinging drive of three miles of winding road on the higher land until, passing "Hog's Hole" on the left, we stopped at our friends' gate. I think Morris must have brought us down from town himself, for I can see the tall figure of a girl standing alone in the porch to receive us.

It was not a large house, as I have said, but purpose and proportion had been so skilfully observed in its design as to arrange for all reasonable demands and leave an impression of ample space everywhere. It stood facing a little west of north, but the longest line of the building had a sunny frontage of west by south, and beneath its windows stretched a green bowling alley where the men used to play when work was over. For it was by no means on a holiday that Edward had come down, nor only to enjoy the company of his friend again, but that they might consult together about the decoration of the house, of which much is said in the Notes from which I have so often quoted.

"The house was strongly built of red brick, and red tiled: the porches were deep and the plan of the house was two sides of a quadrangle. In the angle was a covered well. As we talked of decorating it plans grew apace. We fixed upon a romance for the drawing-room, a great favourite of ours called Sir Degrevaunt. I designed seven pictures from that poem, of which I painted three that summer and autumn in tempera. We schemed also subjects from Troy for the hall, and a great ship carrying Greek heroes for a larger space in the hall, but these remained only as schemes, none were designed except the ship. The great settle from Red Lion Square, with the three painted shutters above the seat, was put up at the end of the drawing-room, and there was a ladder to its top and a parapet round it, and a little door above, in the wall behind it, that led into the roof. There at Christmas time it was intended that minstrels should play and sing. I began a picture from the Niebelungen Lied on the inside of one of the shutters of this settle, and Morris painted in tempera a hanging below the Degrevaunt pictures, of bushy trees and parrots and labels on which he wrote the motto he adopted for his life, 'If I can.' He worked hard at this and the room began to look very beautiful."

On one of his visits to Red House Rossetti found many of these labels still blank, waiting for the words "If I can," and in his reckless way instantly filled them with another motto, "As I can't." When Morris saw this pleasantry, Edward said, "it would have puzzled the discriminator of words to know which of those two was most eloquent in violent English."

Charles Faulkner came down a couple of days after we did, and helped to paint patterns on walls and ceilings, and played bowls in the alley, and in intervals between work joined in triangular bear-fights in the drawing-room. Once, in the middle of a scrimmage that had surged up the steps into the "Minstrels' Gallery" he suddenly leapt clear over the parapet into the middle of the floor with an astounding noise; another time he stored windfallen apples in the gallery and defended himself with them against all comers until a too well-delivered apple gave Morris a black eye; and then, remembering that Morris had promised to give away one of his sisters at her marriage a day or two afterwards, Edward and Faulkner left him no peace from their anticipations of the discredit his appearance would bring upon the ceremony.

A few days before this we had been telling each other riddles, and one of us asked, "Who killed his brother Cain?" Morris instantly fell into the trap and shouted, "Abel, of course!" amidst a peal of laughter from us all. Afterwards he thought it very funny himself, so on his return from the wedding we were not surprised to learn that he had amused the company at breakfast by trying the trick on some one else. "I asked the parson"—he told us triumphantly—"I asked him 'Who killed his brother Abel?' and when of course he said 'Cain,' I said 'Hah! I knew you'd say that—every one says it.'" And we laughed again, more than before.

Oh, how happy we were, Janey and I, busy in the morning with needlework or wood-engraving, and in the afternoon driving to explore the country round by the help of a map of Kent; we went to the Crays one day and to Chislehurst Common another, finding some fresh pleasure everywhere and bringing back tales of our adventures to amuse the men we had left working at home. Sometimes, but not often, they would go with us, for Edward always hated "expeditions," and was only supported in them by good fellowship; nor did he at any time seek the country for its own sake. At this I have often wondered, for the backgrounds of his pictures shew how deeply it touched his imagination and feeling: and I came to the conclusion that one reason why he found so little peace and rest in it might be that he did not, and perhaps could not, submit himself passively to its influence, but was for ever dealing with it as an instrument. In a note written to his father during this very visit to Red House he says, "I hate the country—apples only keep me in good spirits—Topsy's garden is perfectly laden with them." I remember his dread of anything that appealed to the sadness which he shared with all imaginative natures, who "don't need to be *made* to feel," he said, and I believe that this "hatred" was partly an instinct of self-preservation from the melancholy of autumn in the country.

The Niebelungen Lied design of which Edward speaks was never finished, and if it was begun upon the back of either of the beautiful "Salutations of Beatrice" which Rossetti painted on the outside of the doors of the big settle, it may perhaps still remain there.

It will be taken for granted that the two men visitors had endless jokes together at the expense of their beloved host. The dinner hour, at middle day, was a great time for them because Mrs. Morris and I were there, either as eager onlookers at the fun or to take sides for and against. The dining-room was not yet finished, and the drawing-room upstairs, whose beautiful ceiling had been painted by Mr. and Mrs. Morris, was being decorated in different ways, so Morris' studio, which was on the same floor, was used for living in, and a most cheerful place it was, with windows looking three ways and a little horizontal slip of a window over the door, giving upon the red-tiled roof of the house where we could see birds hopping about all unconscious of our gaze.

Perhaps the joke which made two out of the three men happiest at dinner-time was that of sending Morris to Coventry for some slight cause and refusing to exchange a word with him at his own table: it was carried on with an unflinching audacity that I cannot hope to describe, and occasionally reached the height of their asking Mrs. Morris if she would be good enough to communicate with her husband for them and tell him anything they wished to say—but a stranger coming in upon our merriment would never have guessed from the faces of the company who were the teasers and who the teased.

After work, when it was dark, sometimes there was a game of hide-and-seek all over the house. A fragment of one of these games remains in my memory, and I see that Edward, leaving the door open behind him, has slipped into an unlighted room and disappeared into its black depths for so long that Mrs. Morris, who is the seeker, grows almost terrified. I see her tall figure and her beautiful face as she creeps slowly nearer and nearer to the room where she feels sure he must be, and at last I hear her startled cry and his peal of laughter as he bursts from his hiding-place. There was a piano in the sitting-room, and in the evenings we had music of a simple kind—chiefly the old English songs published by Chappell and the inexhaustible *Echos du Temps Passé*.

Many flowering creepers had been planted against the walls of the house from the earliest possible time, so that there was no look of raw newness about it; and the garden, beautified beforehand by the apple-trees, quickly took shape. In front of the house it was spaced formally into four little square gardens making a big square together; each of the smaller squares had a wattled fence round it with an opening by which one entered, and all over the fence roses grew thickly. The stable, with stalls for two horses, stood in one corner of the garden, end on to the road, and had a kind of younger-brother look with regard to the house. The deep porches that Edward mentions were at the front and the back of the house; the one at the back was practically a small garden-room. There was a solid table in it, painted red, and fixed to the wall was a bench where we sat and talked or looked out into the well-court, of which two sides were formed by the house and the other two by a tall rose-trellis. This little court with its beautiful high-roofed brick well in the centre summed up the feeling of the whole place.

One morning as Janey and I sat sewing (she was an exquisite needlewoman) I saw in her basket a strange garment, fine, small, and shapeless—a little shirt for him or her—and looking at my friend's face I knew that she had been happy when she made it; but it was a sign of change, and the thought of any change made me sigh. We paid other visits to the Morrises after this, but none quite like it—how could they be?

Speaking of Red House in the Notes Edward says: "It was from the necessity of furnishing this house that the firm, Morris, Marshall, Faulkner and Co., took its rise. There were the painted chairs and the great settle of which mention has been made already, but these went only a little way. The walls were bare and the floors; nor could Morris have endured any chair, table, sofa or bed, nor any hangings such as were then in existence. I think about this time Morris' income that was derived from copper mines began to diminish fast, and the idea came to him of beginning a manufactory of all things necessary for the decoration of a house. Webb had already designed some beautiful table-glass, made by Powell of Whitefriars, metal candlesticks, and tables for Red House, and I had already designed several windows for churches, so the idea grew of putting our experiences together for the service of the public. For the fireplaces at Red House I designed painted tiles, but the floors were covered with Eastern carpets, for it was some years afterwards when Morris added that industry to his many others. For the walls of other rooms than the drawing-room at Red House Morris designed flower-patterns, which his wife worked in wool on a dark ground, and it was a beautiful house."

Before we left in October Edward had finished his three pictures, but unfortunately the walls were new and not properly prepared for painting, and, as in the case of the Union, the colour soon faded in patches. For him, whose work was so interwoven with his life, what memories must have risen up when thirty-seven years later he made for the Kelmscott Press another design from this same Romance of Sir Degrevaunt. He was often a little hard upon his own early pictures, and did not wish to see them again, but I never remember hearing him quarrel with their subjects—also he said, "The first stammerings I knew had all the imagination that is in me to feel, only I can say it better as time goes on."

In the winter of 1892-3, when the New Gallery exhibited as complete a collection of his work as was possible, he was for a time really disturbed, and a letter that he wrote about it recalls so clearly the spirit of the years with which we are now dealing, and ends with so beautiful a vision of the friendship between himself and Morris in later life, that it may well be given here.

"Why did I dread Wednesday? Only because I had to go to the New Gallery to look at ancient work of mine—and I dreaded it and came back deeply disheartened about myself and feeling to the chilled marrow of me that it had been a poor futile life. Perhaps it will cheer one or two young fellows to see how poor and faint my beginnings were—a little twitter at dawn—but I am far away from noontide yet; I wonder if I shall live to do the thing that I want—there isn't much time left. I think I had no equipment but longing—that I had, but nothing else. I want to forget it. Is all this a phase of vanity? I don't think that. I want a perfect thing and can't forgive imperfection at all, and my faults and sins, which are many, scream at me, and drown the praise. Can't help it, made like that. And I won't think of this show or look at it, or talk of it—if a young thing or two, some such fantastical creature as I was at twenty, goes and gets help, that is enough. And now no more of it. This morning Morris brought fresh life to me—for all the week my head had been low in the dust—and he talked of the high things till I forgot my abasement."

"I am home again now for the next two months," Edward writes to his father in October, 1860. "I want to work and not stir out if possible at all. How soon can I have those frames? I am waiting for two of them now to sell the drawings they belong to—it makes such a difference having them in frames, that I don't care to shew them without." I think the drawings referred to were the little water-colours of "Sidonia" and "Clara Von Bork" which he had made before we went to Upton, and the father was very happy in framing his son's pictures, but, alas, any original design which must be exactly carried out baffled the skill of his small workshop, and Edward had gently and by degrees to let the arrangement drop through. A mirror still exists, made by Mr. Jones with his own hands, and intended to be a ring of small round mirrors placed at equal distances from each other, and encircling a larger one. The measurement of the spaces, however, was faulty, and destroyed the effect of the design. It is painted in the little water-colour of "Rosamond's Bower," with the fierce face of Queen Eleanor reflected in each separate disc.

Swinburne was the next remarkable personality I remember in these days; he had rooms very near us and we saw a great deal of him; sometimes twice or three times in a day he would come in, bringing his poems hot from his heart and certain of welcome and a hearing at any hour. His appearance was very unusual and in some ways beautiful, for his hair was glorious in abundance and colour and his eyes indescribably fine. When repeating poetry he had a perfectly natural way of lifting them in a rapt, unconscious gaze, and their clear green colour softened by thick brown eyelashes was unforgettable: "Looks commercing with the skies" expresses it without exaggeration. He was restless beyond words, scarcely standing still at all and almost dancing as he walked, while even in sitting he moved continually, seeming to keep time, by a swift movement of the hands at the wrists, and sometimes of the feet also, with some inner rhythm of excitement. He was courteous and affectionate and unsuspicious, and faithful beyond most people to those he really loved. The biting wit which filled his talk so as at times to leave his hearers dumb with amazement always spared one thing, and that was an absent friend.

There was one subject which in these days he raised our

hopes that he might deal with; but the time passed, and now we shall never see his proposed Diary of Mrs. Samuel Pepys, kept concurrently with that of her husband.

Dear Lizzie Rossetti laughed to find that she and Swinburne had such shocks of the same coloured hair, and one night when we went in our thousands to see "Colleen Bawn," she declared that as she sat at one end of the row we filled and he at the other, a boy who was selling books of the play looked at Swinburne and took fright, and then, when he came round to where she was, started again with terror, muttering to himself "There's another of 'em!" Gabriel commemorated one view of her appearance in his rhyme beginning "There is a poor creature named Lizzie, Whose aspect is meagre and frizzy," and there, so far as I remember, his muse halted; but he completed another verse on her to her great satisfaction, thus:

There is a poor creature named Lizzie,
Whose pictures are dear at a tizzy;
And of this the great proof
Is that all stand aloof
From paying that sum unto Lizzie.

He almost blamed me personally for the difficulty he had in finding any rhyme for my name except the classical "Porgie," and never rested until one day he called for sympathy, and received it, on rolling forth in his majestic voice, "There is a poor creature named Georgie, Whose life is one profligate orgy," after which his course was clear. Mr. Price came to London this summer and took a lodging opposite to us, which allowed of our meeting continually, and we hoped to keep near each other all through his hospital course; but not long after our return from Upton we found to our dismay that this fair prospect was changed, for he had resolved to give up the profession he had chosen and to accept a private tutorship in Russia, which would give him an immediate income. The engagement, if satisfactory, was to last for seven years, and we had hardly realized the thought before our friend was gone. I do not think Cormell personally regretted his change of profession very much, for the experience of the dissecting-room was a terrible one to his nature, but the difference between daily intercourse and an occasional letter written and received on either side was a sad one both to him and to us. Of his brief apprenticeship to medicine a trace remains in one of Gabriel's verses, which ran (in allusion to a legend cherished, if not created, by his friends):

> There is a young Doctor named Crom,
> Whom you get very little good from.
> If his pockets you jog,
> The inside of a dog
> Is certain to trickle from Crom.

Rossetti's descriptions of his friends, usually uttered in their presence, would be a collection of vivid interest and give, in the reading, no faint portrait of himself. Artistic vanity was a subject quite open to his piercing insight, and one day it occurred to him to distribute his friends into various classes of it, beginning with himself and Swinburne and Edward in the first class; Morris, he said, should go into one all by himself. Then Edward wanted to know why he, who was always in trouble about his pictures, should be put in the forefront of the list, and Gabriel said, "Oh, Ned thinks even *his* pictures aren't good enough for him to have painted." He also said that Edward was the laziest man he knew, and, when called upon to explain this in the face of facts, answered unabashed, "Well, when once you sit down to work you are too lazy even to get up again."

A five or six months' experience of housekeeping in Russell Place did not teach me much, though a couple of small drawings by Edward on the back of my first account-book shew his impression that I practised housewifery as well as music. Light-hearted indifference, however, to many things generally regarded as essential lent boldness to domestic arrangements, and I remember thinking it quite natural that in the middle of the morning I should ask our only maid—a pretty one—to stand for me that I might try to draw her; to which she, being good-tempered as well as pretty, cheerfully consented. This poor little drawing was to have been one of several illustrations that Mrs. Rossetti and I were to make for Fairy Tales written by ourselves. I made one, and Lizzie began another, I believe, but nothing came of it. It is pathetic to think how we women longed to keep pace with the men, and how gladly they kept us by them until their pace quickened and we had to fall behind. It was the same a few years later with the Du Mauriers, I remember: he brought his handsome *fiancée*, Miss Wightwick, to see us, and she and I took counsel together about practising wood-engraving in order to reproduce the drawings of the men we loved. I had begun it already, but she, though eagerly interested, had scarcely seen the tools required for the art, and I do not know how far she went in it. I can recall Du Maurier's distress though, when she drove a sharp graver into her hand one day. I stopped, as so many women do, well on this side of tolerable skill, daunted by the path which has to be followed absolutely alone if the end is to be reached. Morris was a pleased man when he found that his wife could embroider any design that he made, and did not allow her talent to remain idle. With Mrs. Rossetti it was a different matter, for I think she had original power,

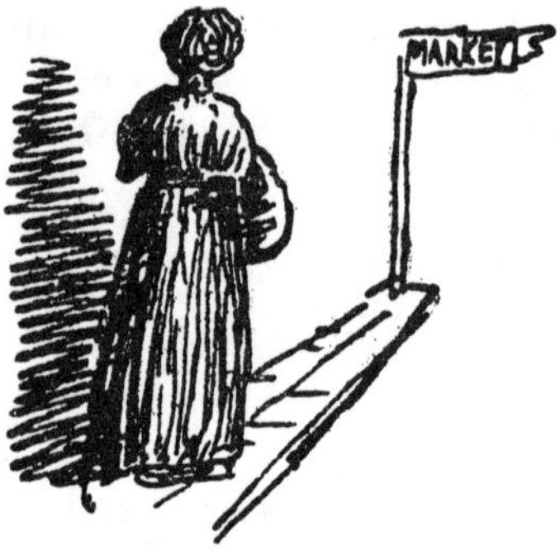

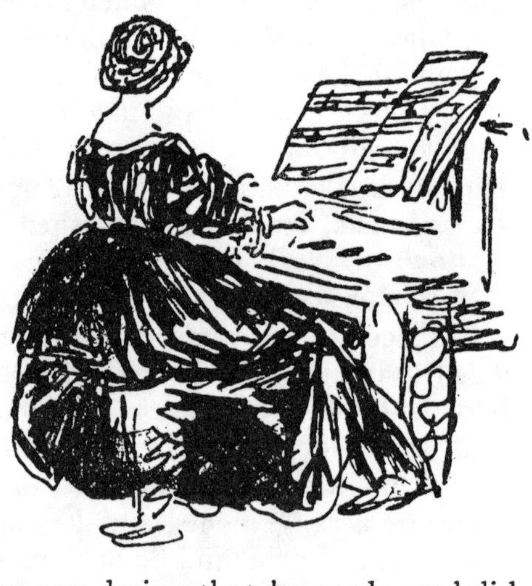

but with her, too, art was a plant that grew in the garden of love, and strong personal feeling was at the root of it; one sees in her black-and-white designs and beautiful little water-colours Gabriel always looking over her shoulder, and sometimes taking pencil or brush from her hand to complete the thing she had begun.

The question of her long years of ill-health has often puzzled me; as to how it was possible for her to suffer so much without ever developing a specific disease; and after putting together what I knew of her and what I have learnt in passing through life, it seems to me that Dr. Acland's diagnosis of her condition in 1855 must have been shrewd, sympathetic, and true. He is reported by Gabriel as saying, after careful examination and many professional visits, that her lungs, if at all affected, were only slightly so, and that he thought the leading cause of her illness lay in "mental power long pent up and lately overtaxed"; which words seem to me a clue to the whole matter. This delicately organized creature, who had spent the first sixteen years of her life in circumstances that practically forbade the unfolding of her powers, had been suddenly brought into the warmth and light of Gabriel's genius and love, under which her whole inner nature had quickened and expanded until her bodily strength gave way; but Rossetti himself did not realize this so as to spare her the forcing influence, or restrict his demands upon her imagination and sympathy. It is a tragic enough thought, but one is driven to believe that if such a simple remedy as what is now called a "rest-cure" had been known of and sought for her then, her life might have been preserved. However, let us follow what we know.

Gabriel dreaded bringing her to live in London, where she was so often ill, but after vainly seeking for a house that would suit them at Hampstead or Highgate they resolved, as she seemed to have gained a little strength since her marriage, to try the experiment of wintering at Blackfriars. The landlord of Chatham Place offered them the second floor of the next house in addition to the one that

Rossetti already had, and by making a communication between the two houses they gained an excellent set of rooms. All seemed to promise well, and for a brief time I think it was so. We received a note from Gabriel telling us they had "hung up their Japanese brooms,"—a kind of yard-long whisk of peacock's feathers—and made a home for themselves. He was happy and proud in putting his wife's drawings round one of the rooms, and in a letter to Allingham says: "Her last designs would I am sure surprise and delight you, and I hope she is going to do better now—if she can only add a little more of the precision in carrying out which it so much needs health and strength to attain, she will, I am sure, paint such pictures as no woman has painted yet."

We used to go and see them occasionally in the evenings, when the two men would spend much of the time in Gabriel's studio, and Lizzie and I began to make friends. She did not talk happily when we were alone, but was excited and melancholy, though with much humour and tenderness as well; and Gabriel's presence seemed needed to set her jarring nerves straight, for her whole manner changed when he came into the room. I see them now as he took his place by her on the sofa and her excitement sank back into peace.

One evening our errand to Chatham Place was to borrow a lay-figure, and we gaily carried it off without any wrapper in a four-wheeled cab, whose driver soon drew up at a brilliantly lighted public-house, saying that he could go no further, and under the glare of the gas lamps we had to decant our strange companion into a fresh cab.

I never had but one note from Lizzie, and I kept it for love of her even then. Let it stand here in its whole short length as a memento of one of the Blackfriars evenings, and in the hope that some one beside myself may feel the pathos of its tender playfulness.

"My dear little Georgie,

"I hope you intend coming over with Ned to-morrow evening like a sweetmeat, it seems so long since I saw you dear. Janey will be here I hope to meet you.

"With a willow-pattern dish full of love to you and Ned,

"LIZZIE."

Both Edward and I had promised to return to our respective families for Christmas, so when the time came we bade each other an eternal adieu, and whilst I was at Manchester he went to Birmingham. He was at Spon Lane with his father both on Christmas Day and the day following, when it is recorded in the journal of the young girl there who watched her friends so closely and sympathetically, "Edward seems to have got very quiet since his new responsibilities." On the last day of the year I rejoined him at his father's house.

CHAPTER XII

HOSTAGES TO FORTUNE
1861-1862

THIS was a year of wonders quite different from those of 1856, for all its marvels were visible to others beside ourselves. Let who will smile, but to most people the sight of a first child is one of the miracles of life, and it is noteworthy that Morris, Rossetti, and Edward now went through this experience within a few months of each other. First came the owner of the little garment that was being fashioned for her when we were at Red House the summer before, and then, just as we were taking it for granted that all would go as well in one household as another, there was illness and anxiety and suspense at Chatham Place, and poor Lizzie was only given back to us with empty arms. This was not a light thing to Gabriel, and though he wrote about it, "She herself is so far the most important that I can feel nothing but thankfulness," the dead child certainly lived in its father's heart. "I ought to have had a little girl older than she is," he once said wistfully as he looked at a friend's young daughter of seven years.

When we went to see Lizzie for the first time after her recovery, we found her sitting in a low chair with the childless cradle on the floor beside her, and she looked like Gabriel's "Ophelia" when she cried with a kind of soft wildness as we came in, "Hush, Ned, you'll waken it!" How often has it seemed to us that if that little baby had lived she, too, might have done so, and Gabriel's terrible melancholy would never have mastered him.

Lizzie's nurse was a delightful old country woman, whose

words and ways we quoted for years afterwards; her native wit and simple wisdom endeared her to both Gabriel and Lizzie, and were the best possible medicine for their overstrained feelings. Naturally, after meeting her at Blackfriars, we invited her to come to us.

On the day little Jane Alice Morris was christened many friends went down to Red House for the christening feast, and beds were made up for their accommodation at night in the true Red Lion Square spirit of hospitality, the drawing-room being turned into a big dormitory for the men. At dinner I sat next to Rossetti, and noticed that even amidst such merry company he fell silent occasionally and seemed absent in mind. He drank water only, and, after he had helped himself, I asked him if he would give me some, which he did with an instant return to the scene before him, saying at the same time with grave humour in his sonorous voice, "I beg your pardon, Georgie: I had forgotten that you, like myself, are a temperate person."

At this time Faulkner was thinking seriously about leaving Oxford, for he longed to share the struggle which he saw his old companions beginning in a wider world: they, of course, encouraged this desire, and Edward, for one, says distinctly, "I'm doing all I can to persuade him to leave Oxford and settle in London at some profession." This happened a few months later, when Faulkner came up to town and entered the office of a civil engineer, where he patiently sat and drew rivets by the thousand in plans for iron bridges—or at least that was the impression we had of his occupation. Out of office hours he kept the books of the firm of Morris, Marshall, Faulkner and Co., now legally registered partners in business.

The list of work done by Edward this year is a long one, but I shall only refer to those things which, as I think of them, especially recall his personality. To begin with, there were two large triptychs that he painted in oil, each with an Adoration in the centre, and the Angel and Virgin of the Annunciation on the wings. These side figures were the same in both cases, but the treatment of the middle subject was different. The origin of these pictures was a commission for an altarpiece in St. Paul's Church, Brighton, but when Edward had painted his first design he found that the composition of the centre panel was too elaborate to tell its story clearly from a distance. Just about this time Mr. Plint's death occurred, and finding that it was important for his estate to be realized as soon as possible, Edward took counsel with his friends and decided to offer the executors this, by far the most important work he had done, and to make another and simpler design for the church. He proposed that in it the kings should be standing instead of kneeling, with their figures more detached from each other, and, for clearness' sake, that the whole should be painted upon a gold background. The arrangement was agreed to by every one concerned, and the second triptych has remained in St. Paul's Church ever since. In both pictures there are portraits of Morris as one of the kings, and of Swinburne and Edward amongst the shepherds. The commission came through our friend Mr. G. F. Bodley, who unselfishly suggested that the church should have a painted altarpiece instead of a reredos, which he himself had been asked to design, and that Edward should be the artist employed. It was by a curious chance that, some ten years afterwards, Mr. Bodley, hearing of an "old Venetian picture" somewhere in London, went to see it, and under that name recognized and bought the first of the two triptychs. It had been sold at Mr. Plint's sale and then disappeared. Mr. Bodley says that the man from whom he bought it had no idea but that it was an old Italian picture, and adds, "It was, for me, a curious and happy thing that I should see it."

Edward painted also in this year a water-colour of "Clerk Saunders," which embodies his passionate sympathy with the Border Ballads. Mr. Marshall, a big, handsome Scotchman, the least prominent member of the Firm, made us very happy with the traditional tune of the poem, and we started a manuscript music-book to preserve it and a few other treasures. "The Three Ravens" was a song for which Rossetti used to ask.

There was a small water-colour "Laus Veneris" too, which contained the germ of one of Edward's most elaborate pictures, and I remember that in it was the only cat ever allowed a place in his serious work. It was not reproduced in the large "Laus Veneris." Perhaps it was a silent tribute to the memory of his own friend and companion "Tom," who had lately met with a sudden death: chance words now and then taught me that such a thing was possible.

There were special flowers—the lily, the sunflower, and the rose, for instance—which at various times Edward studied profoundly and finally knew by heart. We have seen him painting lilies in Red Lion Square garden, and nearly ten years afterwards he finished his apprenticeship by the masterly pencil drawing, familiar to many, of a group in his own garden at Kensington Square. Roses he was still looking at with uncritical love—the time for grappling with them had not arrived—but that he was already far on in his knowledge of sunflowers is shown by a pen-and-ink design begun this year of "Childe Roland," in which they fill up the whole background: he knew them from their roots to the tips of their petals before he had done, and never lost interest in them.

"Did you ever draw a sunflower?" he writes: "it is a whole school of drawing and an education in itself." And again: "Do you know what faces they have—how they peep and peer, and look arch and winning, or bold and a little insolent sometimes? Have you ever noticed their back-hair, how beautifully curled it is?" The sunflower affectation, which was a fashion at one time amongst hangers-on of Art, filled him with disgust. "As to those sunflower-worshippers," he says, "I do renounce them—I will not stand godfather to that feeble folly without crying out. What have I done ever to deserve such a fate? I do renounce and denounce, and will have none of them. Was I not at work happily and peacefully years before their rubbish began—and shall I not survive them happily and peacefully? Away with them, the feeblings."

Poppies also had their fascination for him: Mr. Bodley

remembers him, at Red House, coming in to breakfast one day with a beautiful drawing of a poppy that he had done in the early morning.

We continued the excellent habit of going to Red House very often from Saturday afternoon to Monday morning, when we would return to town with Morris, who came up every day to the works at 8, Red Lion Square. This place become a fresh centre for friendly as well as business meetings of the members of the firm, and here they laid plans for the future, discussed work going on at the moment, and in the intervals told anecdotes and played each other tricks which prolonged the youth that seemed as if it would never fail.

On one of these evenings Madox Brown surpassed himself in a display of his peculiarity of forgetting names. He wanted something brought upstairs, but, in order to make sure of calling the right person, first turned round and carefully asked: "What is the name of your housekeeper, Morris?" "Button," answered Morris. Whereupon it took no longer than his stepping to the head of the stairs before Madox Brown was heard shouting in his slow, clear voice, "Mrs. Penny, will you——" but applause drowned the rest. Another time Morris being called away during a meeting, the devil suggested to Faulkner that it were well in his absence to make an elaborate "booby-trap" to await his return; so the London Directory and two large copper candlesticks were swiftly balanced by his clever fingers upon the top of the half-open door, and of course at Morris's entrance fell like "Goddes grame" "right amiddlewards of his crown." Bumping and rebounding they rolled to the ground, while Morris yelled with the enraged surprise of startled nerves, and was very near to serious anger, when Faulkner changed everything by holding him up to opprobrium and exclaiming loudly in an injured voice, "What a bad-tempered fellow you are!" The "bad-tempered" one stopped his torrent of rage—looked at Faulkner for a second, and then burst into a fit of laughter, which disposed of the matter.

"The Co. gets on," Edward wrote to Cormell Price in Russia; "have you heard of the Co.? It 's made of Topsy, Marshall, Faulkner, Brown, Webb, Rossetti and me—we are partners and have a manufactory and make stained glass, furniture, jewellery, decoration and pictures; we have many commissions, and shall probably roll in yellow carriages by the time you come back."

Under the general pressure of the time Edward had joined the Artists' Corps of Volunteers when it was first formed, but his attendance was not regular, and of this episode in his life I remember little except a very tired man in a grey uniform.

Another unlikely recruit was Rossetti, who I believe presented himself on the drill-ground, although his name does not appear in the Muster Roll Book of the Corps: but Major Horsley suggests that, as Volunteer economy was doubtless imperfect at the beginning of the movement, it is quite possible that he may have tried the work, found it distasteful, and never really joined. At any rate we clung to the legend of Gabriel's unmistakeable voice having been heard to ask quite politely "Why?" in response to the sergeant's fiercely shouted "Right about face": and Madox Brown is quoted by his grandson, Mr. Ford Hueffer, as relating that Gabriel's first shot was a wonderful one, hitting the centre of the bull's-eye.

Morris figured far better as a defender of his country, for he attended drill regularly, and I distinctly remember that he was camping out at Wimbledon on the night of the great Tooley Street fire. This was on a Saturday, and Edward and I were going down to Red House as usual, though Morris would not be back till next day. As we got near London Bridge Station we saw something was the matter, for crowds were running in one direction, and presently we knew that it was a big fire, and were so much excited that when on reaching the station we found it was close to us, we decided to go to Upton by a later train and stopped where we were to see how things might turn out. The sight was appalling, and the heat so great that we had to turn away from time to time to cool our faces. We did not hear of any danger to life, though there was evidently great destruction of property, but in spite of this, as it was burning, we felt a kind of fearful satisfaction in being there to see. This form of excitement gave way to another before long, for as we were watching the fire, a woman near us suddenly covered her face and then we heard a shout and saw a wall of the burning building totter and fall with a splash of fire, while a groan went through the crowd and every one knew that life had been lost. We turned away, but could learn no details, and it was not until we saw the newspapers on Monday morning that we knew it had been the death of James Braidwood, the head of the Fire Brigade, and two of his devoted men. When we got to Woolwich the sky was so red there that people were running out from their cottages to see what the fire was, and Morris saw it also from his tent at Wimbledon. On Monday morning when we returned to London the flames were not yet got under, nor were they for many days.

Before the birth of our first child we removed from Russell Place into a larger set of rooms just left by Mr. Henry Wallis, at No. 62, Great Russell Street. Here Edward's studio was again only the front room on the first floor, but as the house was opposite to the British Museum the large open space before it gave a better painting light than usual. Behind the studio and communicating with it by a door was our sitting-room, and beyond that a very small third one. The outlook of the sitting-room was upon a little back-yard entirely built over and covered with a skylight; beyond this was the high blank wall of the back of a house. This had once been coloured and was now blotched in a leprous way. Our own walls inside were beautified with some old tapestry left there by Mr. Wallis while he was travelling abroad.

To these early days in Great Russell Street belongs a note I received from Gabriel, one part of which I can never read unmoved: "By the bye, Lizzie has been talking to me of parting with a certain small wardrobe to you. But don't let her, please. It looks such a bad omen for us." Seldom did I come so near the real Gabriel as this. More often he seemed to wear a surcoat of jesting; as when he wrote, "Lizzie to-day enters on the adventure of Hog's Hole," by which I understood her to be gone to Red House—or sent the message, "My qualified love to the Pang of your Life," a form of remembrance to Edward suggested by one of the many nonsense verses he had made:

There is a poor painter named Jones,
For whose conduct no genius atones.
The course of his life
Is a pang to the wife,
And a plague to the neighbours of Jones.

The rhyme he found for his own name was most skilful:

There was a poor chap called Rossetti;
As a painter with many kicks met he.

And that on Gambart, the picture-dealer, must surely have won the admiration even of its subject had he ever been privileged to hear it:

There is an old he-wolf named Gambart,
Beware of him if thou a lamb art.
Else thy tail and thy toes
And thine innocent nose
Will be ground by the grinders of Gambart.

Writing to Cormell Price in Russia towards the end of September, Edward tells him that he thinks in about a month "either a little Ned or a little Georgie will appear," and just adding "don't tell, I keep it quiet for fear it should be a monster," passes to other subjects. But the reflex of the idea of having a child of his own appears on the next page, where he writes of his father: "I want my dad to come and live near me: business doesn't answer and he grows old [he was fifty-nine] and a little cottage 12 miles out of London seems a good idea. Next year I hope it can be managed—by then I shall be out of debt and getting on a bit. Dads ought to have their whack sometimes; it 's very dull to be a dad and have a son cutting about and enjoying himself and still be working on drearily—I shall hate it when I'm a dad." I cannot remember when it was that Mr. Jones decided to give up the struggle of business, in order to avoid the possibility of failure, but I know that when he did so, with his usual ill-luck, he sold the house in Bennett's Hill just before property in that neighbourhood increased so much in value that its rental would have made him comfortable for the rest of his days.

The arrival of our child, though not a "monster," brought us face to face with strange experiences. No one had told us any details connected with it essential for our guidance, the doctor and the wise woman were to arrange everything—but as neither of them happened to be at hand when wanted I doubt whether Edward or I had the more perturbed day. By his own energy, however, he guided the disjointed time and set it straight, for with him intellect was a manageable force applicable to everything, but good dame Wheeler, who soon arrived to supersede the strange nurse of the moment, saw at once how great a demand had been made upon his physical power, and was almost as anxious about him as about either of her recognized charges. I can remember, in the reaction that followed, a day on which the small stranger within our gates was the most valiant member of the family. Those who have gone through such times as these know them to be amongst the testing times of humanity.

I do not think that Edward was a man with whom parental feeling was very great in the abstract, but from the moment he had a child of his own, strong natural love for it awoke in his heart. This new love was accompanied, however, by a fearful capacity for anxiety which was a fresh drain upon his strength. "A painter ought not to be married," he once said; "children and pictures are too important to be produced by one man."

I must not forget to mention the transporting satisfaction

of Miss Sampson, who happened to be staying for a few days with us and had the unexpected bliss of receiving Edward's son in her arms and then going back to Birmingham with the story. To this time belongs a clear recollection of the appearance of Janey and Lizzie as they sat side by side one day when in a good hour it had occurred to them to come together to see the mother and child. They were as unlike as possible and quite perfect as a contrast to each other; also, at the moment neither of them was under the cloud of ill-health, so that, as an Oriental might say, the purpose of the Creator was manifest in them. The difference between the two women may be typified broadly as that between sculpture and painting, Mrs. Morris being the statue and Mrs. Rossetti the picture: the grave nobility and colourless perfection of feature in the one was made human by kindness that looked from "her great eyes standing far apart," while a wistfulness that often accompanied the brilliant loveliness and grace of the other gave an unearthly character to her beauty. "Was there ever two such beautiful ladies!" said dame Wheeler, with a distinct sense of ownership in one of them, as soon as they were gone.

A few weeks after this, whilst I was in Manchester, showing their first nephew to my sisters and younger brother, Edward wrote to me of having been with Rossetti to Chelsea, to see Alexander Gilchrist, in whose forthcoming life of Blake they were both keenly interested. They were told that one of the children of the house had scarlet fever, but that the case had taken a favourable turn, and people in those days did not dread infection as they have learned to do now, so the two friends stayed on, spending the evening in conversation with Mr. Gilchrist, and the news of his death from the fever within a fortnight afterwards was a great shock to them. Edward joined me in Manchester and we took our child to be baptized at the Cathedral, Ruskin and Rossetti being his godfathers by proxy. After stopping at Birmingham to present the little one to his grandfather there, we returned to London and were settled again in our own home early in December.

Our friendship with Mr. Ruskin was one of the happiest things of these early days, for we loved him profoundly and he drew us very near to himself. When he was in England we often saw him, and when abroad he wrote to us, at first as "My dear Edward and Georgie" and afterwards as "My dearest Children," which name was never quite dropped. It was his custom to write freely if he wrote at all; his notes and letters must lie thick as leaves in autumn in many a desk and drawer, and we received our share of this golden shower. A letter of his from Boulogne in July mentions a death that all England was lamenting: "There's Mrs. Browning gone, who *was* a friend, and such a one, but one must not think about oneself in talking of her—it is all the Earth's loss. I get horribly sad whenever I give myself time to think: and can only keep up by help of those things [fishing boats] which you think so sad when you see them going out. I was on the deck of one all Wednesday night, it blowing hard; and the sea ablaze with phosphoric foam, one perpetual torrent of white fire rushing over the lower side of the deck, for we were going fast—and when the moon went down at one the night was nearly black, all but the fire of the waves. We began mackerel fishing off Hastings at five in the morning. No—there's no real sadness, though much solemnity in the life." And speaking of the fishermen, he says: "They were as merry when they began fishing as if they had been in an alehouse—nay, what say I—immeasurably more; they came out of their oily, tarry, salt, black hole, in perfect peace of mind, to meet the face of Dawn, and do their daily work: would they have come in the same peace of mind out of the alehouse? And then their sense! One of the pilots I've been sailing with—I was out with him all day on Monday when it was calm enough for talking—is precisely of my way of thinking on all points of Theology, morality, politics, and economy. He kept saying, in good French, just the very thing I meant to have tried to say in bad. There's wisdom for you!"

There came a most characteristic answer to something

we told him of a scheme for my engraving Edward's designs: "I'm delighted to hear of the woodcutting. It will not I believe interfere with any motherly care or duty, and is far more useful and noble work than any other of which feminine fingers are capable without too much disturbance of feminine thought and nature. I can't imagine anything prettier or more wifely than cutting one's husband's drawings on the woodblock: there is just the proper quantity of echo in it, and you may put the spirit and affection and fidelity into it which *no* other person could. Only never work hard at it. Keep your rooms tidy, and baby happy—and then after that as much woodwork as you've time and liking for."

Alas, time and liking never came together and the pretty scheme dropped through, finding a place, let us hope, among the pieces of porphyry or serpentine with which Edward claimed that good intentions pave the floor of Heaven.

As December went on, Edward's health failed. A sore throat, a cough, and general weakness were always with him the symptoms of exhaustion, and this time he was very much exhausted. On Christmas Eve he went to bed early, quite worn out, and as he lay there, coughing frequently, he put his handkerchief to his mouth and took it away marked with a large stain of blood. We looked at each other and the same thought passed through both our minds—that this was his death-warrant. We took and gave what comfort we could, trying to persuade ourselves in a flash of time that it was a thing of the commonest occurrence, that it happened to most people at some time in their lives, but—we had better see the doctor. Our dear physician-friend, Dr. Charles Bland Radcliffe, lived then in Henrietta Street, Cavendish Square, a place easily reached, and soon I was on the way there. Who does not know that threading of the streets in a hastily-summoned jolting cab, with the one haunting fear for companion? In this case when the cab stopped at the door after an endless-short journey it was evident at a glance that the doctor's house was given up to festivity, and that a Christmas Eve party was going on. His consulting-room was filled with hats and coats, and for a moment the master of the house was hoping to be free from the haunting calls of his profession, but I knew that Edward's name would bring him to me and waited till he came. He looked very grave when in my distress I silently laid before him the terrible crimson sign that told more than I could do, but hope revived with the kind light that came into his eyes as he said quietly, "I'll see him to-night." Then the cab jolted back again, and we waited together until he came with his never-failing steadiness and help. After examination he was able to assure us that the hemorrhage was from the throat, not the lungs, and it never returned, but for a few years after this there was a delicacy of the chest which needed care.

Somewhere about this time—whether before or after the New Year I cannot say—belongs the story of the happy discovery of FitzGerald's Omar Khayyám, which Swinburne brought one day to Edward in triumph, having just purchased it for the sum of twopence, and marvelling who the anonymous translator could be. From Swinburne I have an account of how he first heard through Rossetti that this treasure had been discovered on a bookstall near Leicester Square—I believe outside Quaritch's shop in Castle Street. It had been published by Quaritch in 1859, but, proving a dead failure, the greater part of the edition was turned out of doors and anybody might have it for a penny a copy. "Thither we repaired," says Mr. Swinburne, "and expended a few pence on a few copies. Next day, when we were returned for more, the price was raised to the iniquitous and exorbitant sum of twopence. You should have heard, but you can imagine, the eloquent and impressive severity of Gabriel's humorous expostulations with the stall-keeper on behalf of a defrauded if limited public. But we were extravagant enough to invest in a few more copies even at that scandalous price. I think it was within the month that Quaritch was selling copies at a guinea—so at least we heard and read."

It is curious to think that in January of 1858 the manuscript of this now famous work had been sent to Fraser's Magazine, whose editor expressed some faint wish to have it, but that in November of the same year FitzGerald had heard nothing from him about it, and wrote to a friend, "I suppose they don't want it, I really think I shall take it back; add some Stanzas which I kept out for fear of being too strong; print fifty copies and give away." And now, though poets such as Rossetti, Swinburne and Morris were eager to know who had done the marvellous thing, they had no clue to its author, nor could even learn his name for many a year.

The copy of the first edition that Swinburne gave to Edward has always been one of our precious possessions, and before the book was reprinted became worn with frequent reading and transcribing.

Edward's convalescence was slow, but fortunately for him his work was of a kind that could be carried on indoors, and he did a great deal in spite of cold and dark days; for nothing short of acute illness ever prevented his painting. Our wants were few in these days, and it came quite naturally to us both to be what is called "poor"—indeed I never remember our having any hopes that depended upon the possession of money or feeling that it would make us much happier. One day we had a delightful treasure-trove in the shape of an envelope containing small cheques to the value of between twenty and thirty pounds, which Edward had put by in his dressing-case because they were crossed and had then forgotten. I think they were Mr. Plint's, and I know that, to our great satisfaction, they got cashed somehow. Another time a half-sovereign lurking in the pocket of a waistcoat was found and brought forth in triumph—but that was the last windfall of this description, and the mere fact that such things could happen shows how many meanings there are to the word "poor."

The difference in our life made by the presence of a child was very great, for I had been used to be much with Edward—reading aloud to him while he worked, and in many ways sharing the life of the studio—and I remember the feeling of exile with which I now heard through its closed door the well-known voices of friends together with Edward's familiar laugh, while I sat with my little son on my knee and dropped selfish tears upon him as "the separator of companions and the terminator of delights."

The first time the child ailed anything was an anxious experience for two people who shared the almost universal ignorance of men and women about the young of their own species. The infant being unable to describe his sufferings, of whom should we ask help? Swiftly it occurred to us that kind Mrs. Rossetti, Gabriel's mother, loved and revered by us all, must be a mine of wisdom as to the management of children. Had she not brought up the most precious of all boys to maturity? If only she could come and say to us that she had often seen Gabriel like that, we should take comfort. A messenger was despatched, begging her to come to us: nor did her kindness fail, for she came at once, and we shewed her the tiny invalid whose cries still pierced our hearts, while we hung upon her lips for advice. Judge then of our dismay when, after looking on him gravely for a few seconds, her only words were—slowly and distinctly uttered—"It is certain that the child is suffering great agony"; nor had she the least cheer to give or anything to suggest.

On the other hand whilst Edward himself was still unwell a lady came to see us one day for the first time, and looking at him took the situation in at a glance. Husband gifted and attractive, young and probably incapable wife—a case for prescription and advice if ever there were one. Had we heard of the wonderfully strengthening remedy now given in cases where there was weakness of the chest? No; would she tell us? Yes, indeed, gladly. And it was so simple, so easily procured; the only thing was to prepare it rightly, and she herself fortunately knew exactly how it should be done. "Iceland Moss, my dear. You take two pounds of it and put it to soak in water. A most life-giving gelatinous liquid is the result—but the healing qualities are much increased by the addition of a little brandy, if liked by the patient." Two pounds of Iceland Moss were forthwith got, and put to soak in water. It swelled and it swelled till no jug or basin would hold it; a libation of brandy little short of a bottleful was poured upon it, but it only became a slippery and unmanageable mass which had finally to be thrown away, leaving a sense of guilt upon my mind for a long time.

Mr. Ruskin's return to England at the end of the year was a great comfort to us, and as Edward slowly gathered strength we began to let our hearts dwell on the thought of carrying out a hope long cherished of going with him to Italy. But first deep waters had to be passed through. One morning in February—a dark and cold one—Edward had settled as usual to such work as the light permitted, when there came a tap at the door, and to our surprise Red Lion Mary entered. How she told her tale I do not know, but first we heard the words "Mrs. Rossetti," and then we found that she had come to bring us the dreadful news that our poor, lovely Lizzie was dead, from an overdose of laudanum. There was nothing we could do—all was over—so, begging Edward not to risk going out on such a day, I hastened to Blackfriars to bring him any word I could learn about the unhappy Gabriel.

The story can never lose its sadness. To try to tell it afresh now, with a knowledge of its disastrous effect upon one of the greatest of men, would be for me impossible. I will simply transcribe something I wrote about it the next day to one of my sisters: "I am sure you will feel for Gabriel and all of us when I tell you poor Lizzie died yesterday morning. I scarcely believe the words as I write them, but yesterday I saw her dead. The evening before she was in good health (for her) and very good spirits—she dined with her husband and Swinburne and made very merry with them—Gabriel took her home, saw her prepare for bed, went out to the Working Men's College, and on his return found her insensible from the effects of an overdose of laudanum which she was used to take medicinally.

She never knew him or anyone else for a second—four physicians and a surgeon did everything human skill could devise, but in spite of them all she died, poor darling, soon after seven in the morning. The shock was so great and sudden that we are only beginning to believe it to-day—I wonder at myself for writing about it so coolly. I went down directly I heard it and saw her poor body laid in the very bed where I have seen her lie and laugh in the midst of illness, but even though I did this I keep thinking it is all a dreadful dream. Brown was with Gabriel and is exactly the man to see to all the sad business arrangements, for of course under such circumstances an inquest has to be held. Of course I did not see Gabriel. Edward is greatly troubled as you will believe, and all the men. I leave you to imagine the awful feeling there is upon us all. Pray God to comfort Gabriel."

The Chatham Place days were ended now, and Rossetti in his sorrow turned to his mother, whose grave tenderness must have been a refuge for his wounded heart, and went for a time to live in Albany Street with her and his sisters and brother. Poor Lizzie's bullfinch went there too, and sang as sweetly and looked as sleek and cheerful as ever.

It must have been in April of this year that we paid a Saturday to Monday visit to the Marshalls at Tottenham. A cheery, reckless household it was, with big Peter Paul ("Poll" was the sound his little wife gave to the name she called him) at the head of it: I remember a small cup of gunpowder being given to the boys to keep them quiet in the morning. Marshall sang the Scotch songs for which we always asked, and besides "Clerk Saunders" we got from him the beautiful tunes of "Sir Patrick Spens" and "Busk ye, busk ye, my bonny, bonny bride!"

Our hapless child, however, occupied the time of our visit in taking, all unknown to us, a severe cold, which soon after our return developed into congestion of the lungs that brought him quickly to death's door. Then again our friend Dr. Radcliffe came to the rescue, and one afternoon there was a fight between him and death, when the invisible enemy all but revealed himself to our eyes, so sharp was the struggle and so clearly delivered both blow and counter-blow over the child's senseless body. A recovery without check followed, however, and then we addressed ourselves to preparations for the Italian journey, which seemed almost too happy an idea ever to come true.

Just before the baby's illness my two younger sisters, Agnes and Louisa, had come up to stay with us according to an old promise, and so began a series of visits from them which provided many a happy memory. These two young girls were very dear to Edward, and to them he was a brother whose care and affection fostered their native gifts and stimulated them, mind and soul. Devoted to each other, next in age and always making a life of their own together in the midst of our large family, when they came to us they were no drain on our powers of entertainment, but gave us joy whilst eagerly enjoying themselves. They were good to look at also; our friends loved and admired them, and their whole lives were affected by the times they spent with us.

After the recovery of our child the sisters shared in our thanksgiving and then helped us to get ready for our journey as quickly as possible. It was arranged that the baby should be left with his grandmother and aunts in Manchester, and after the anxieties and trouble of winter and early spring it was sweet to us to become children again, and to rest upon one so much older and stronger than ourselves as Mr. Ruskin. He did everything *en prince*, and had invited us as his guests for the whole time, but again in his courtesy agreed to ease our mind by promising to accept the studies that Edward should make while in Italy, and all was arranged and done by him as kindly and thoughtfully as if we had indeed been really his "children," as he called us.

Before we went Edward made and presented a thank-offering to Dr. Radcliffe, who had, humanly speaking, saved the life of his little son. It was a pencil drawing of the sick child in a bed, on the foot of which sits the Virgin Mother, who has brought her Child of Healing and holds him standing on her lap, with his little arms spread out in the form of a Cross; while upon the floor, seated upon a corner of her robe, is the healed child, happily playing.

CHAPTER XIII

FRUITFUL REST
1862

ON the morning of May 15th we started with Mr. Ruskin for Italy, crossing the Channel by Folkestone and Boulogne. We had no anxiety in leaving our little son in the house of his grandparents, but nevertheless felt parting with the unconscious creature extremely, and solaced ourselves with photographs of him and a drawing that Edward had made. A photograph was opened in the railway carriage before we reached Folkestone and shewn to Ruskin, who greeted it with wholesome chaff. At Boulogne we stayed the night, at the Hôtel des Bains, and in the afternoon he took us a walk down to the shore, where the tide was far out and only a great stretch of wet sand lay before us. Here a mood of melancholy came over him and he left us, striding away by himself towards the sea; his solitary figure looked the very emblem of loneliness as he went, and we never forgot it. Later in time this loneliness and melancholy become still more impressive, when it was realized that a few days before starting he had signed his preface to the first edition of Unto this Last. In this book he had reprinted the essays which had been despised and rejected as they appeared separately in the Cornhill Magazine. The thoughts expressed in these prophetic pages had not found acceptance even in the heart of his own father—no wonder that to us he was silent.

In Paris we went to Meurice's Hotel, and there we stayed two days, from Saturday till Monday, during which time of course we visited the Louvre. In the evening we were at a theatre and saw I know not what upon the stage, but something of the talk in the box comes back to me—about the Doré illustrations to Balzac's Contes Drolatiques, and the passionate horror with which Ruskin spoke of them, saying that on first seeing them he had literally been made physically ill with disgust. The next day, Sunday, finding that I had a friend who lived in Paris, he insisted on sending me in the afternoon to see her. She was an English girl, the wife of a French Methodist preacher, whose Christian name was *Jean Wesley*, and I found her at a little square chapel that was own brother to such fanes in England. Mr. Ruskin dined out that evening, and on his return told us where he had been. It was to the house of "Adèle," his first love, long since married in France. He had met there, perhaps a sister of hers, at all events some two or three people who had known him as a boy, and he seemed in a dream of the past as he threw himself down on a couch and talked to us. "They called me John," he said; and we felt how few people could ever do that, and how sweet it must have been to him. Then he went on to tell us how good a wife Adèle was, and the image of the lady was stamped on the minds of his hearers as he told them that in her country-home she used to amuse her husband, who was a sportsman, by translating Punch to him.

From Paris we went on to Dijon and then to Bâle, where I remember the balcony of the "Three Kings" over the rushing river, and *truite au bleu* for dinner (always served in a private room), and next morning a walk with Mr. Ruskin, to look at pictures somewhere, before we started again for Lucerne. We stopped there for a few days, and saw the green water of the lake through the floor of the painted bridges, and looked around us and felt ourselves *in montibus sanctis*. One afternoon we rowed out on the lake, and the two men talked all the time of scientific discoveries about the formation of the earth and the gradual development upon it of animal life; Edward contributing a description, I remember, of an era when "huge white cockroaches" reigned supreme.

We left by the steamer that took us up the Lake to

Fluelen, where our thoughtful friend and guide had arranged that we should spend the night, so as to be ready in the morning to begin at once the glorious drive over the pass of St. Gothard. I have a vision of us all three sitting together that evening, in a room with an exquisitely clean bare-boarded floor, and Mr. Ruskin reading Keats to us.

In the morning we went on up the pass. Towards evening we came suddenly, as if through a gateway, upon the wonderful uplifted plain of the Valley of Hôpital, with its swift, wide river rushing through it and the mountain tops around doing duty as mere hills. Next morning we started again in unfailing sunshine and went over to the Italian side; our road at first cut through the eternal snows, but those were left behind, and then began the descent into the promised land. The beautifully-engineered road waved before us, our leader was unfastened and went to the rear, and the two other horses flew along with the carriage; sometimes the zigzag of the road was so sharp that the horse who followed would look down upon us from the turn above as if he needed but a sign to jump into our laps. By the early evening we had reached Bellinzona with thankful hearts. And, next day, still driving, by Lugano and Como, past gardens whose roses were bubbling over the tops of their high walls, seeing as we went many beautiful women whom Edward called "spoiled studies for Janey," and on till it grew dark and the fire-flies came out before we reached Milan. How frightened we were there next morning, when the spirit of the mountaineer shewed itself in our beloved companion and made him skip about on steep slopes of the Cathedral roof until each moment we thought to see him fall into the piazza below, where the omnibuses crawled no bigger than flies. And to San Ambrogio he took us, and had treasures unlocked and brought out from behind its altar—and two of the little company knew and felt and understood all they saw, but the third looked chiefly at them.

From Milan we went to Parma for two days, and Correggio's name is associated with the daytime and the opera of Rigoletto with both evenings. We all three went, through moonlit streets, to hear it the first night, and Mr. Ruskin took me again the second time, at his own suggestion—but Edward would not go—and the only difference in the entertainment this time was that we saw it from a different side of the house.

The scheme of our journey made us part company on returning to Milan, where we two left Mr. Ruskin, and went by ourselves to Verona, Padua, and Venice. The sense of our friend's great loneliness of spirit came over us again at parting, when he said, without leaving us room to doubt his affection, that he never minded the going away of any one. But this spiritual loneliness did not relax the visible tie between him and his parents, to whom he either wrote or telegraphed every day.

At Verona the church of San Zeno and the Adige with its bridge and the Amphitheatre and the Market-place all rise up in memory—also a sign of the Austrian occupation in the presence of Austrian officers at *déjeûner* in the hotel—but I do not think we stayed there more than a day, for we were pushing on to Venice. First, however, came a Sunday at Padua, when we spent the morning alone in the Arena chapel, standing in a kind of rough grassy orchard, its beauty unutterably touching even to the ignorant; and there Edward made drawings from the Virtues and Vices in the lower belt of pictures.

At Venice our very first evening in a gondola revealed Edward's susceptibility to malarial influences, for he was feverish and ill in the night; so that afterwards we went about almost entirely on foot. He had a strong sense of topography, and soon found his way everywhere as if he had been born in the place, and thus, perhaps, we saw more of the city than if we had gone by the canals. To row out to the Lido, however, or to Torcello and Murano, was another matter, and our expeditions there were very happy. A sunset that we saw one evening from the Piazzetta was of awe-striking beauty, when the façade of the Ducal Palace was flooded with pink golden light reflected again from the upturned faces of the silent crowd.

"We are already enjoying ourselves intensely," Edward wrote to Mr. Ruskin soon after we were settled; "the weather is glorious, by no means too hot, and we happen to be in the best of health these two days. I am at work on a little head of Paolo in the Ducal Palace. How little I shall be able to do for you—even a slight pencil-sketch takes so long—but I know now so well how entirely you wish us to enjoy ourselves and me to get strong, that I shall not be anxious about the quantity I do (nor about the quality, for it is bad, it is, it is), and you must let me give you all kinds of drawings for years to come when they happen to be pretty, and so I shall feel comforted. We have arranged to stay at the hotel for three weeks.

"Georgie is growing an eye for a picture, she darts at a little indistinct thing hung away somewhere, and says timidly 'Isn't that a very nice picture?' and it generally ends in being a Bellini or Bonifacio, whom she calls Bonnieface—and O what pictures of his there are here! We get on very well by our little selves, but what may be termed the domestic pleasure of the trip is gone now we have left you. We are alone in this big hotel, at dinner there is a table for forty or more, and we alone sit there; that is a dull time I own, for the rest we are very happy, and take great care not to see too many pictures in a day at first. The look of the pictures has done me good: I feel that I could paint so much better already. I never knew quite what a memorial of old St. Mark's that picture of Gentile Bellini's is. We followed it carefully bit by bit to-day, and it is as exact down to the least item as it can be; it will be absolutely invaluable presently, for it is quite as exact as a photograph, with colour besides. We know the front of St. Mark's so well that we could have detected a slip I really believe. And do you know, they are hard at work restoring St. Mark's; all the north side is covered up and peeled off; it is so miserable. I hung quite affectionately about that Bellini, and thought how soon it might be the only record of that seventh heaven."

It was not long though before he was restless to be back

in his own studio, for the ancient pictures set him on fire, and yet so long as he was amongst them he could do no original work. "I should never paint another picture if I lived in Italy," he said. So he wrote to Ruskin: "Georgie begins to grow pining for her kid and I long to be at work, for I don't work here, and I have cheated and defrauded you into bringing me out to do nothing, and if I thought of it much I should be miserable—only I set my teeth and swear inwardly that you shall have drawing after drawing when I get home from time to time, original drawings, not copies—ha! don't scold me and call me unfriendly and mean for bothering about the tin, I should be a pig if I had no feeling about business, you must confess. At the most I can only bring you back four rotten little sketches; one of a head in the Veronese Triumph at the Ducal Palace, one of the Bacchus head of Tintoret (as nearly original size as I could guess), one of St. Catherine, and one of the Harem or Marriage of Cana. They really are so far more faithful than those I did under your eye, for you frightened me, you did. A sketch is a slight name, but how long it takes—one could do a dozen designs for one little worthless copy, but O it does one good. Directly my eyes close a canvas appears and I scrawl away with brown and white—yes, dark figures on a white ground, that's the secret: you have done me so much good by giving me this chance of seeing the old miracles." Then follows a complaint about the irregularity of the post, which shows that it was not one person only who was homesick. "The post here is horrible, we get no letters from home, and are in utter darkness about our families—shall you be ready to return then when we said? If you could return and we might go straight back through the quick way of Cenis it would comfort our fretful homesick hearts." A day at Torcello he also writes about. "We went early to Torcello and confided much poetic sentiment to each other on the occasion—it was lovely beyond words. To-day we went out to the Lido, and dabbled at the edge of the sea. The sea was glorious and it was pleasant to look out towards

Ithaca, and think that only sea divided us from it. Altogether we are bubbling over with poetry here and dreadfully need you to put in a judicious No."

We celebrated the day when Edward finished his first sketch in the Ducal Palace by going to Murano. The place looked very sad and the church was shut up; when we got in at last we found it filled to the roof with ladders and scaffolding poles. There was no need to ask what was going on; but the pavement and the great solemn figure of the Virgin in the apse were untouched, and so we worshipped and came away. On Corpus Christi Day, from one of the galleries of St. Mark's, we watched a great procession form in the church below and afterwards go round the piazza; and on the last morning of our stay, when we went to bid the hallowed place good-bye, we found there the only funeral we saw whilst we were in Venice, and followed it with its many candles out of the darkness of the church into the sunlight and down to the water's edge, until the red-covered coffin was put upon a gondola and swiftly rowed away to the island of the dead.

Mr. Ruskin's reply to Edward's letter shewed that our homesick cry raised no echo in his heart. He wrote: "Harry the 8th 's a good king [this was a name he had given the child] but the notion of his interfering with the Venetian Senate in this way is too bad. If Ned 's well, (and of course I assume Harry the 8th to be well too—if he 's ill, I've nothing to say) and bettering in health and painting, you ought not to leave so soon. And don't make such mighty grand sketches. I want a very slight one of the Sebastian in St. Rocco (Scuola) and a rough sketch, in colour, of the High Priest in the Circumcision—in Scuola, by the stair foot. And I want you a week *here* [Milan]. I will have ever so many cwts. of candles lighted in the Monasterio, and you must sketch the two [Luini] Christs for me please. This is more important than anything in Venice to *me*. I don't care about the Salute Cana one, but finish it as is best for your own work."

To which Edward answered: "We have heard at last of

Harry VIII., who stands fair for 6 wives at least, so all is well there: I have done the sketch of St. Sebastian with some difficulty for it is so dark. The water-colour of High Priest turns out very badly for I worked much in the dark at it, and the picture is itself very black and covered with chill in the deep shadows; to-day I make a sketch of the St. Catherine. Perhaps I shall do better at the Luinis—yet why should I?"

Where was the "Monasterio" to which we went in Milan, with Mr. Ruskin, to see Luini's pictures? Probably this question would be easily answered by reference to any guide-book, but I shall speak only of what remains in memory. It was a large church that had been used as a military hospital during the Franco-Sardinian War with Austria, and still bore marks of rough usage: the pictures were in an extremely dark place, where it was almost impossible to light them up sufficiently for Edward to work. In a letter to my sisters there is his own account of this.

"I am drawing from a fresco," he begins boldly, "that has never been seen since the day it was painted, in jet darkness, in a chapel where candlesticks, paper flowers and wooden dolls abound freely. Ruskin, by treacherous smiles and winning courtesies and delicate tips, has wheedled the very candlesticks off the altar for my use, and the saint's table and his everything that was his, and I draw every day now by the light of eight altar candles; also a fat man stands at the door and says the church is shut if anybody comes, and when the priest himself put his head in, the fat man said 'hush-sh-sh-sh!' and frightened poor priest away!"

Then follows a fresh expression of anxiety for home news. "We left Heaven, which is Venice, last Saturday—on which day a letter—but no letter at all waiting for us here!! And now it appears too plain no letter at all, so please cause a long and sufficient one to be waiting for us at 62, so that on leaping from the cab we may as it were be in possession of its contents—so very ready as that, please. How we long to see you, but these are days never to be repeated and I cannot break through them. As for that same Ruskin, what a dear he is; of his sweetness, his talk, his look, how debonnaire to everyone, of the nimbus round his head and the wings to match, consult some future occasions of talk. Now good night, you pretties."

As soon as the week in Milan was over we bade farewell to the friend who had done so much for us, and hastened back to England, while Mr. Ruskin remained to finish a full-size copy of a beautiful St. Catherine in the dark Luini chapel. We had been ten weeks abroad.

On our return we found Rossetti well in health and settled at work in Lincoln's Inn Fields, where he had taken chambers whilst arrangements were being made for his removal to a beautiful old house at Chelsea: he had never gone back to live in Chatham Place after his wife's death. The firm was in great activity; had received two medals for what it shewed at the International Exhibition, and many commissions from it were waiting for Edward; amongst them one for coloured tiles which proved a welcome outlet for his abounding humour, and in this form the stories of Beauty and the Beast and Cinderella took at his hands as quaint a shape as they wear in the pages of the Brothers Grimm of blessed memory. Some "lay" stained glass also was demanded, for which he designed a scene in the story of King Mark and La Belle Iseult. His regular habit now and for years afterwards was to design and draw such things in the evening—the presence of friends making no difference—and men returned to the habit of dropping in after dinner almost as freely as before his marriage. Of Charles Faulkner we saw a great deal, as he and his family had left Birmingham and were settled in Queen Square, Bloomsbury, near and welcome neighbours. He was the eldest surviving son of a widowed mother; two sisters and a young brother completed the household. Both sisters shared Faulkner's own skill of hand, and one of them, as it proved, was but waiting time and opportunity to develop a power of beautiful ornamental design: friendship with them was a foregone conclusion, and between Kate Faulkner and me there grew up a lifelong intimacy: both Morris and

Edward loved her also. Gabriel came to us at rare intervals—once it was to see his godson, to whom his manner was very tender—and another evening he wrote down for us a song which he said was the first he had written for an age. It was now that we learned of his having by a passionate impulse put into the coffin of his poor Lizzie the manuscript volume which contained almost all the poems he had written, and we feared they were lost for ever; so those who loved him began to compare notes and write out what they could remember. Swinburne of course was chief at this, and dictated some to us out of his marvellous memory; amongst others Sister Helen, of which we sent out a copy to Mr. Ruskin, who had asked for any that we could lay hands on. From him we heard in due course of the completion of his copy of Luini's "St. Catherine," which, when it had been put together and framed in England, he asked us to go out and see at Denmark Hill; and who so willing as we? It was a happy day, for, beside the unusual pleasure of going out together in the daytime, it was beautifully fine, and it was also my first visit to Mr. Ruskin's home. That fact alone, that it was his home, gilded it within and without; otherwise it had no charm, but was a house of the dullest and most commonplace type; a huge cedar in front of it was the only thing that redeemed the approach from bald ugliness.

I do not know whether his parents were in town, for we saw nothing of them, but in the vestibule of his mother's drawing-room we found the Luini facsimile, looking so beautiful as to make one forget its incongruous surroundings. We were taken afterwards into another room, where Edward shewed me the portraits of Mr. and Mrs. Ruskin senior, but I had no idea, until he told me, that a fair-haired little child with a landscape background through which he was represented as running, in white dress, blue shoes and fluttering sash, was the author of The Stones of Venice.

The arrival of Allingham in London this autumn was a great addition to our circle, for he liked and was liked by so many different people. And he brought with him a breath of the wild Irish loughs and mountains when he told us that he had been wandering amongst them quite lately, with a barelegged little goat-herdess of fourteen or fifteen years for his guide, who was very intelligent and chatty in two languages, English and Irish, but had never heard of London.

Edward, rejoicing in the companionship of friends, and knowing Mr. Ruskin to be alone and sad, wrote out to urge him to come back to us all. "Wouldn't cheery company do you a little good? How I wish you were here in London. I feel so certain that you would be better for a little sympathetic circle of men to see you sometimes. Gabriel sends much love to you; I know how glad he would be if you were amongst us; a little 3 or 4 of us this winter might be so quiet and happy if you would but come."

In October Rossetti removed to 16, Cheyne Walk, Chelsea, and whilst furnishing and arranging it found amusement and distraction for some time. His old rooms at Blackfriars had been taken by his friend Mr. G. P. Boyce, the water-colour painter, whose love for collecting "blue pots" equalled Rossetti's own, and many a story was told of their rivalry in the search. One I remember was about a struggle of will on the subject of a "pot" that Mr. Boyce had actually bought and Gabriel openly and loudly coveted; but neither money nor fair words had the slightest effect upon its gentle, determined owner; argument also availed nothing and exchange was scouted. One evening Gabriel went to Blackfriars and tried again to get it, but after vainly using every kind of persuasion the subject was dropped, and finally Mr. Boyce walked back with him to Chelsea, talking of other things. On reaching Cheyne Walk they went into the house together, and then Gabriel, throwing back his Inverness cape, drew the dish carefully from beneath his arm where it had been all the time, and placed it upon the table in the fond hope that its owner's heart would be melted when he saw it actually there: but Mr. Boyce quietly took back his property, and after a friendly good-night returned home with it under *his* arm.

The happiness may be imagined with which, after Mr.

Ruskin's return to England, we accepted an invitation to dine at Denmark Hill, and the respect with which we looked upon those "without whose life he had not been." The appearance of old Mr. Ruskin was striking; his dignity and simplicity, together with a latent tenderness of manner, made our hearts expand with confidence. He was of fair height and size altogether, neither so tall nor so thin as his son, and a dark plum-coloured evening coat which he wore impressed us by its individuality and as being a link with the past. The little old lady who ruled the house from her low seat by the fireside was less easy to understand. She had had an accident not long before we saw her—a fall, in which what she always called her "limb" was broken—and though it had been properly set it had stiffened in some way, so that she could not walk without help. It was her nature, I suppose, which made her choose for support the back of a chair rather than the arm of either husband or son: at all events, bidding us all precede her, she walked from the drawing-room to the dining-room, leaning upon a chair which moved easily on castors as she pushed it before her, and evidently carrying out an established custom. Edward was repelled by the old lady's sharp, decisive manner, and could not like her thoroughly. At dinner, if anything her son said, though not addressed to herself, did not reach her ear, she demanded to have it repeated, and from her end of the table came a clear thread of voice, "John, John Ruskin, what was that you said?" When the sharply questioning sound at last penetrated to him he never failed with the utmost respect to repeat his words for her.

I cannot be sure whether it was on this occasion or afterwards that I first saw Robert Browning, but I know that it was at Denmark Hill. I remember too that some talk went on about the rate at which the pulse of different people beat, and that he suddenly leaned towards me saying, "Do me the honour to feel my pulse,"—but I could find none to feel. That was what he meant us to know, for he told us afterwards that it was never perceptible to touch, which seemed strange in so powerful an organization as his. Whether his bloodless complexion was a symptom connected with this peculiarity, I do not know.

At first after he came back from Italy Edward was very hard upon all that he had done till then, and felt disposed to rail at himself unreasonably; saying that he took good subjects only to spoil them, and there was nothing so base and mean as for a man to take a good subject and spoil it. His knowledge of what he aimed at was far too clear for him to be deceived into complacency about failure, and I began to know something of the difficulties with which he wrestled when I saw the misery that he passed through at one stage or other of almost every fresh picture. Usually the worst time was when it was half finished; then something seemed to go wrong, and he would work on without light or hope, but only because he would not give up what was begun; when suddenly, even he could not say how, the change came, the cloud lifted and he knew where he was and what to do. This I noticed at intervals all through his life, and the following description in his own hand of such a time, during the painting of "King Cophetua," shows how dark the cloud could be while it lasted.

"I work daily at Cophetua and his Maid. I torment myself every day—I never learn a bit how to paint. No former work ever helps me—every new picture is a new puzzle and I lose myself and am bewildered—and it 's all as it was at the beginning years ago. But I will kill myself or else Cophetua shall look like a King and the beggar like a Queen, such as Kings and Queens ought to be."

Later still he said in his own vehement way, "It takes an artist fifty years to learn to do anything, and fifty years to learn what not to do—and fifty years to sift and find what he simply desires to do—and three hundred years to do it, and when it is done neither heaven nor earth much needs it nor heeds it. Well, I'll peg away; I can do nothing else, and wouldn't if I could."

And as to finishing pictures, he says, "When is a picture finished? Never, I think—and is a symbol of life itself in that way: so when I say it is finished I mean it is cut off, and must go away." He used to say that it was only the van coming to take it away that finished a picture for him.

There was no exaggeration when he wrote from Venice that he could have done a dozen fresh designs whilst he was making one sketch from an old picture, and already even in these early days he was looking eagerly round for some channel besides painting into which he might pour the stream of his ceaseless imagination. Wood-engraving in England was at its last gasp, but the designs of Ludwig Richter and Alfred Rethel in Germany had given him fresh hope of what might yet be done.

"I am determined to labour in every direction to get good engraving again," he wrote to my sister, "and I shall need you beyond words—so work, my little darling, like anything.

"I see that for the engraving I want, the most perfect design and beautiful drawing is needed, more than in pictures even, for in them so many other qualities come in and have their say, and a picture may be great if it has only one quality pre-eminently grand. But in engraving every faculty is needed—simplicity, the hardest of all things to learn—restraint in leaving out every idea that is not wanted (and perhaps fifty come where five are wanted)—perfect outline, as correct as can be without effort, and, still more essentially, neat—and a due amount of quaintness. I really do not think anyone in England could have engraved the Rethels. Rossetti, in despair, gave a very careful block to Faulkner the other day, and that ingenious man's first attempt is a regular triumph—it is an illustration to Miss Rossetti's poems, coming out in February, so you will see it.

"By absolutely perfect wood-engraving, I mean such work as all the sixteenth-century engravings and such as those quite perfect examples in Rethel's Dance of Death and the Friend and Avenger. I don't believe that any attempt to express more than they do could possibly be successful.

"As to scribbly work, it enrages one beyond endurance. Nearly all book and periodical illustration is full of it—drawings, you know the kind, that have wild work in all the corners, stupid, senseless rot that takes an artist half a minute to sketch and an engraver half a week to engrave, for scribble is fearful labour to render. My dear, look at most things in 'Once a Week'—the wasted time of poor engravers in rendering all that scrawl, if rightly used, might fill England with beautiful work."

In the same letter he says he is positive that the only way to engrave on wood is "very simply, with little or no cross-hatching, and no useless cleverness, and no attempt whatever to do anything that copper or steel would do a thousand times better." His own desire is to publish "100,000 wood-cuts as big as Death the Friend or bigger," and he ends with a postscript containing advice which he himself never ceased practising.

"Keep up drawing the whole time through, say at the least half the day, and let it be from nature—faces, best of all, because hardest. Practise at anything that will reveal its mistakes most glaringly; not at foliage, because a hundred errors may be concealed in the general confusion, nor even drapery, but bare arms, necks, noses, tops of heads, &c. wherein one faltering step turns everything to ridicule."

To continue his comparison between painted pictures and designs in black and white, may be quoted here what he said in later life, when speaking of an artist who had ceased painting and did nothing but illustrations for books: "It is a pity to give up painting altogether—when any one does nothing but designing he unravels himself too quickly." I know that in his own case he valued the breathing-time given by the mechanical work of a picture.

The designs of Ludwig Richter that excited his admiration are described with unchanged enthusiasm twenty years later to a friend who had heard of them and wanted to know what they were like.

"The Richter you ask about is a veritable angel. There are many books of his, he made heavenly little pictures always, drawing everything that makes happy and never anything vile. He drew pictures to Bechstein—a sort of collection like Grimm, of Household Tales,—and he made pictures to everything that could be that was soft and nice and had cosy little family life in it and peasant life in the mountains; children, babies, puppies, birds, cats, cabbages, village taverns, smithies, every mortal pleasant thing that happens in the mountains—and nobody ever lived who imagined more sweetly. And there are thousands of designs—and now he is eighty and quite blind these three years past—and it is just twenty years since I made up my mind to send him a message to say how much I cared about him. I vowed a vow that another day should not end before I sent my message, and still it is unsent. There have been I know published at Williams & Norgate's, Covent Garden, two volumes called Richter Album, with selections from his vast world of invention. You would love him. It is good to be called Richter."

With his own world of invention ever urging him to give it shape, he could not be long unhappy about his work, nor was he, and in my letters to Mr. Ruskin there is constant mention of his finishing old pictures and beginning new ones.

"He has begun a water-colour, which he does not mean to make more than a sketch, of Bluebeard's wife putting the key in the closet door. It is a tall, narrow picture, only containing Mrs. Bluebeard with a long passage behind her down which she has come—and the door, of course. Edward is sitting by, and has just looked up to charge me not to tell you about Bluebeard's wife, because you will think that the skeletons are the principal features. I reply that his warning comes too late, for I have told you, but that you will think nothing of the kind, and know as well as I do that it is only the picture of Fatima."

Again, "Bluebeard's wife has grown apace since I gave notice of her beginning, and is almost all that her friends could wish her—at least they are polite enough to say so, and now Ned has begun a smaller water-colour of Love flinging open a lady's window in the early morning on St. Valentine's Day and greeting her. Love bears her a little letter in his hand."

And next, "Ned has begun another water-colour, a figure of Love quite blind, crowned with flowers, groping his way through the street of a city in the early morning, seeking the house he shall enter." This design Edward always meant to carry out on a larger scale in oils; indeed he began it, and the wreath of roses is painted on Love's head.

To an introduction of Mr. Ruskin's we owed our friendship with Mr. Simon, afterwards Sir John Simon, K.C.B., and his wife. At first we saw little of them, but liking never fell back in absence and we came to know each other very closely. Lady Simon's warm Irish nature was concealed from strangers by a singularly impassive manner, but, that once penetrated, her fine qualities revealed themselves: amongst them were constancy in friendship and a rare courage and magnanimity in times of trial. Sir John's more brilliant presence belonged perhaps to his French descent; at any rate he was a fascinating man of science, to whom Edward had no hesitation in offering his own imaginative version of newly acquired knowledge, while Sir John enjoyed seeing the hard-won jewel of truth shine in its new setting, and they laughed together like boys. I remember one of Edward's freshly assimilated scientific facts being dispensed to me, after a Sunday morning's visit from Sir John when conversation had fallen upon the subject of molecular formation: "Georgie, Mr. Simon has been here, and he has told me that we are made of millions of little bits, and it's only of my shoulder's own mercy that it doesn't march off to Hampstead Heath this afternoon."

One evening towards the end of this year Mr. Ruskin came after dinner and carried us off by appointment to Chelsea, to see the Carlyles, for he wished that his old friend and his young friend should meet. It was no use though; instinct told Edward that Carlyle could not care for the work he was busy about, and he would have protested against Mr. Ruskin's taking with him the water-colour of "Theseus and Ariadne," but that it would have made too much of the matter and of his own feeling. The evening passed off safely on its human merits—for it was the living voice of

Carlyle that we heard saying "the newspapers were shrill" about something, and with the hand that wrote The French Revolution we saw him carefully reach the kettle from the fire for his wife when she made tea. As for her, she was very kind, taking me into her own room to remove my wraps and helping me to put them on again afterwards with motherly tenderness. There were two other people there, Sir Walter and Lady Trevelyan, and all was friendly. A faint impression remains of Carlyle coming down to the door with pleasant words of parting, and then we went home to the Carlyle of the bookshelves whom we knew so much better than this one.

CHAPTER XIV

JOY AND SORROW TO SHARE
1863-1864

THE time that passed between our return to England and the autumn of 1864 seems in my memory like one long year, full of brightness and vitality, but so much of the same character that it would be difficult to preserve the exact sequence of its minor scenes and facts; the important ones are more easily placed.

Edward had never become reconciled to the absence of his friend Cormell Price, and was troubled also by an impression that, though he sent us no details, the circumstances of his life in Russia were difficult. The letter given below refers to this.

"Come back to us, Crom, I am sure you are not happy over there—throw it up and come back. You shall live with me till you find something—do come. All the best years of your poor little life are going over there and we are wanting you so much all the time. Come and stay with us—we are beautifully situated opposite the Museum, with a clear view of the trees in Russell Square out of the top windows, and an easy walk from Tottenham Court Road and Holborn. My studio is the jolliest room except for dirt; how I should love to see you smoking a pipe this night, what toddy I would make for you, what coffee Georgie would make for you."

But in spite of these entreaties Cormell struggled on for another year.

Younger men now began to frequent the studio, some of them students of the Royal Academy, whose interest and curiosity had been aroused by Edward's work at the Exhibition of the Hogarth Club: they were brought in the first instance, I believe, by Simeon Solomon, for whose gifts Edward had a sincere admiration. I remember his telling me before we were married about a book filled with Solomon's designs, which he said were as imaginative as anything he had ever seen—here was the rising genius—to which I listened with a jealous pang! This artist afterwards became a friend of mine as well as Edward's, and the tragedy of his broken career is one before which I am dumb; but all the more do I cling to recollections of hope and promise surely not false, though unfulfilled in this world.

Our friendship with William De Morgan, son of Professor Augustus De Morgan, began in Great Russell Street, when his rare wit attracted us before we knew his other loveable qualities. He remembers asking Edward one day about a fresh canvas he saw in the studio—was it for a new picture? "Yes," said Edward, quoting the stereotyped newspaper criticism of Pre-Raphaelite work; "I am going to cover that canvas with flagrant violations of perspective and drawing and crude inharmonious colour"; but later in the evening he said to De Morgan, "You know that was all gammon I was talking about perspective and drawing—I only do things badly because I don't know how to do them well; I do want to do them well." And another time: "Why should people attack pictures as they do? Artists mean no harm—at least I don't; I only want to make a beautiful thing, that will remain beautiful after I'm a bogey, and give people pleasure when they look at it."

Whilst Mr. Ruskin was abroad early in 1863, his father bought the water-colour of "Fair Rosamond" on which Edward was at work. The transaction was a pretty one, for his son knew nothing of it, but writing to us shortly afterwards the old gentleman says, "I keep nothing long from John. He was glad I had got the picture because he liked it very much himself"; and when Mr. Ruskin heard what had happened he wrote, "I'm pleased more than you are that my father likes Rosamond."

I have always treasured the few notes and letters received

from Mr. John James Ruskin, and find amongst them one that came after this picture was finished and sent to Denmark Hill.

"The picture came home last evening. I was charmed—excited—exalted by it, and I doubly thank Mr. Jones for getting me a frame in such fine taste. Would he kindly tell the frame-maker to bring his account to No. 7, Billiter Street, City, for payment.

"I have Rosamond now before me. I spent part of the morning at Mr. Bicknell's, whose pictures you will see on 25th and 29th April will bring many Thousands, and after my eye had dwelt on the canvases and paper of the first names of the Century I am happy to say my evening Contemplation of Rosamond yields me the greater satisfaction. I rejoice that I can truly say this because I believe my son would have it so, if he could."

All that we saw of the relations between this father and son interested us deeply, and helped us afterwards to appreciate the genius for truth which marks that wonderful piece of autobiography, Praeterita, where the very forms of the Ruskin family walk alive.

About the "Rosamond" time Mrs. Ruskin asked to see her son's godchild, and was evidently distressed when on inquiry she found that no visible sign of the spiritual relationship between him and his godfather existed. In vain I urged that we had stipulated for no christening present; she was determined to remedy what she considered neglect, and presently we received from her a kind parcel containing the orthodox knife, fork and spoon.

During a visit to our friend Spencer Stanhope at his house near Cobham, where our host's cheery companionship indoors did him as much good as the fresh country air outside, Edward painted on the water-colour "Annunciation" in which the Virgin kneels by her bed while the Angel appears amongst blossoming apple-trees. He also made studies in the woods for the background of "The Merciful Knight," but the town-garden of Russell Square furnished the marigolds that fill the space in the foreground beneath the wayside shrine. This picture of "The Merciful Knight" seems to me to sum up and seal the ten years that had passed since Edward first went to Oxford.

The world of models is closely connected with artistic life, and those who sat to Edward were, like any other class of people, some interesting and some not. I remember a splendid Italian one, Ciamelli by name, whose head with its bush of blue-black hair may be seen in the triptych "Adoration" as one of the Kings. He ground an organ in the streets and sang to it very finely out of his southern heart when he was not sitting, and sometimes brought it with him when he came to sit. His name is always associated in my mind with a ludicrous scene that happened one day when he was left to wait in the studio and it occurred to him to beguile the time with music. Edward was in the next room hastening over breakfast, but even through a wall the noise of the organ became so intolerable that he jumped up to stop it, as he thought, with a word: a harsh braying gust of tune, however, simply buffeted his ears as he opened the door and drove the words back into his throat, while Ciamelli, seated on the floor with his back against the wall and wrapped in a whirlwind of sound through which nothing could penetrate, ground on, unconscious of offence.

There was a very handsome German woman, too, from whom Edward sometimes drew, and who was known to us by the name of Norma. I think, looking back, that she must have been entangled in a kind of life that she hated and wished to get out of, and the door which it occurred to us in our simplicity to open that she might do so was that of our nursery. It touches me now to remember how much she seemed to like the idea of coming to take care of our baby. At first the arrangement appeared quite easy to make, but afterwards difficulties arose, and I do believe that Norma withdrew from it for our sakes and not because she did not wish to come.

Knowing the mischievous effect on work of letting his models get dull or cross, Edward always took pains to amuse them and often was amused in return: some, of course, he reckoned as friends. Italian ones he said were the best sitters and the most conscientious in keeping engagements; amongst the English there was no tradition of art, and the women with few exceptions seemed unable to understand that an artist's work was serious or that it could matter if they failed him at the last moment.

In the beginning of August, 1863, we paid a visit to Miss Bell and her school at Winnington Hall, Cheshire. This was the school referred to by Mr. Ruskin in his preface to the Ethics of the Dust, and his visits to it were a source of the greatest delight to everybody there and of much pleasure to himself. He had brought Miss Bell to Great Russell Street one day in the summer, when she warmly invited us to accompany him on his next visit to Winnington, and as we would have gone anywhere with him if he had urged it—and he did urge it in this case—Edward put everything on one side and went. We travelled down with him, and I remember how the train drew up to wait outside Crewe Station exactly in time for us to prevent some children near the line from eating berries of deadly nightshade which they were busily gathering.

Miss Bell was an extremely clever woman of a powerful and masterful turn of mind, evidently understanding that Ruskin was the greatest man she had ever seen, and that she must make the utmost use of the intimacy he accorded her and the interest he took in her school. At dinner the first evening she talked as much as if it were her last opportunity of speech, and as one listened to her it seemed that no subject could be too high and no difficulty too great for her to deal with. She accepted Edward at first as from Ruskin's hand and afterwards for his own sake. I do not think he had known any one of her type before, and he thoroughly enjoyed her brilliance. Then, this stimulating hour over, we were introduced to a large room where the school was assembled to welcome Mr. Ruskin. There was no doubt that his personality was felt through the whole house. The pupils looked a delightful set of girls, and Miss Bell brought some few chosen ones of them afterwards into the drawing-room, where we saw them more closely and found them still more pleasing. Her staff of teachers, too, was an unusual one, formed of most different materials, and yet at that time united as if it had but one mind and heart. Absolute submission to their Principal was expected and given, and in return life was made so vigorous and so many interests were presented to them that it was long before the bond of obedience felt irksome. This must have been one of the first schools—I do not know if it was literally the first—where girls were taught to play cricket. To dancing also Miss Bell gave an important place, and a pretty sight it was to see the long schoolroom or the gallery filled with white-frocked, light-hearted girls dancing together. Mr. Ruskin paid his tribute of admiration both in words and by taking his place occasionally in a quadrille or country dance. He looked very thin, scarcely more than a black line, as he moved about amongst the white girls in his evening dress.

A case of infectious illness, which developed at our own house directly we had left it, recalled us suddenly to London, but after due quarantine we accepted Miss Bell's invitation to return to Winnington, and as Mr. Ruskin, who had been paying visits in the North, came back also, we still had a happy week there together. He dismayed us, however, by speaking of a plan that had taken shape in his mind for building a house near Bonneville and going to live there—he had even begun negotiations for a piece of land on the mountain-side, and we saw before us a grievous prospect of separation. From a letter of Mr. J. J. Ruskin's, dated September 4th, it is evident I had written off hot-pen to tell him our trouble, and the sweet dignity and wisdom of the old gentleman's answer remains unchanged by time.

"I am happy," he begins, "to think of my Son possessing so much of your and Mr. Jones' regard and to hear of so many excellent people desiring to keep him at home: my own earnest wishes are, and since his visits to Winnington, to Thirsk, and to Wallington my hopes are, that my Son may ultimately settle in England; but these hopes would not be strengthened by his too suddenly changing his mind, throwing up his Engagements, breaking his Appointments or at all acting on the whim of the moment. He has so far proceeded towards a settlement in Savoy as to have begun treating with a Commune about a purchase of Land. His duty is therefore to go to Savoy and honourably withdraw from the Affair by paying for all Trouble occasioned, and I fully expect the Savoyards will afford him some grounds for declining a purchase by the exorbitant price they will ask for their Land. As for the ground he has bought at Chamouni, it will be a pleasure to him to keep it though he saw it not once in seven years. It is the Building Plan near Bonneville that I should rejoice to see resigned—but not suddenly abandoned for a momentary Indulgence among the Delights of Winnington, but deliberately and after some goings and comings and Comparisons between Weeks spent abroad and Weeks spent at home. He has made a short engagement to go to Switzerland with the Rev. Osborne Gordon which I hope he will keep, and I shall endeavour to hope that his Engagements abroad may in future be confined to a Tour with a friend and that Home Influences may in the end prevail. Tell Mr. Jones I think I know enough of him not to be jealous of any Influence he may have with my Son—I cannot be jealous of the Influence of Anyone on this Subject because I do not attempt to exercise any—I want my Son to find out for himself where he is likely to be most happy and am ready to acquiesce in any plan Swiss or English that shall most thoroughly secure this end.

"My Son's fellow Traveller now is the best he could possibly go with.—Being rather cynical in his views generally and not over enthusiastic upon Alps, he is not likely to much approve of the middle heights of the Brezon for a Building Site."

It was natural that the son should spare his father any expression of the melancholy that drove him about seeking rest and finding none, but from those whom it would pain less it was not concealed. The following letter was in answer to one from Edward suggesting a scheme by which, instead of seeking solitude abroad, Mr. Ruskin might find it at some place in England where he could either be quite alone or easily rejoin the world when he wished. For this imagined house a centre was to be made in the shape of a room, for which Edward intended to design a set of hangings covered with figures from Chaucer's Legend of Good Women, all to be embroidered by Winnington girls, with me as the captain of their industry. He had already begun a series of small figures from the Morte d'Arthur, of which I had finished Merlin and Morgan le Fay and begun Arthur and Lancelot, so that it seemed easy with so many willing hands to carry out a bigger scheme. Mr. Ruskin's reply was written from Denmark Hill on the morning of the day he went abroad: we were still at Winnington, whence a kind of round-robin on the subject had been sent to him.

"I am very deeply moved and comforted by all your letters—as who would not be, unless he were himself rock—instead of merely wishing to live among rocks. You would make me entirely happy with your loves if I felt strong and as if I should have life and time to stay with you—but I have a great feeling of its being too late. But do with me and for me as you will—that will be best for me. All that I mean to do, at the worst, is to buy this bit of rock land as I would a picture; you may like, some day some of you, to climb to it, with children's feet among Alpine Roses. And I've another notion of a thing the great cliff above may be useful for, some day—or night: but, for this time, have your own way. I daresay love is very nice when it doesn't always mean leaving people, as it always does with me, somehow: and if you can find this dream of yours with its walled garden, I don't think I should want to leave it, when I got in. And for the tapestry, please begin that directly—*that* at least I can live with—and let it be as you say, Chaucer's Legend. I should like that better than any—any—anything; and it is very beautiful and kind and lovely of the 12 damosels to work it for me; and I would not have had any others if I had chosen.

And it will be very wonderful and helpful and holy to me.

"I hope it will make you very happy to be there [at Winnington] as far as any outward thing can make you and Georgie happier than you always are, but I like so much to think of you there, and I can't bear to think of you in London. It is the only quite pleasant thing I have to think of in all the world. So stay as long as you can, that I may have it to think of."

Edward's answer to this was found after Mr. Ruskin's death put away by itself in a cabinet.

"I have not written to you since that sad letter you sent just before starting. I want to comment on every line of it at great length, but how can I now? for I write in the midst of damozels. It is such a comfort to begin the tapestry—already I have schemed it all out, assigned the figures and ordered the embroidery frames (*i.e.* Miss Bell ordered them) and the holland for working upon and the wools for working with, and now Winnington is full of excitement about it, and you are to have the sweetest and costliest room in all the world. But, dear, please never again say that about the little mountain spot you may want some day or night.

"Oh, don't despair about health, or ever think it is too late; you must and shall grow strong, and do lots of work, and when you are very old you shall sleep somewhere where we can kiss every stone or blade of grass that covers you. I sometimes think of that sad time when my light will go out when you are withdrawn, but when that comes I must spend my love about the place, and paint the place and make it pretty, and that shall be years to come when I am old myself, and worthy of doing it. So never any more mention that mountain top please, dear.

"And now about health and life—yesterday afternoon your cheery letter came and made us happy.

"We have found in very scientific maps that between Ross and Hereford on the Wye there are nearly fifty fine days in the year more than in London, sixty more than in

Manchester, and seventy more than in some other place, and the tourist books speak of abrupt precipices and jagged somethings and steep something elses—and the country is full of orchards and has mountains and mountains (some smaller peaks whereof Georgie says might be whitewashed to remind you of perpetual snow). We had a long hunt for a moral map to find out what kind of people live there, but the map wouldn't be found—only you see, if they are good so much the better, and if they are bad so much the better, you can set them right. I know all that country, and it is very lovely, and as warm as Devonshire. Also I believe Old Red Sandstone prevails there, which I am told is full of fascination for you: and a thousand advantages which you are to hear at full length. Are you so fixed to try —— There, now for the twentieth time I have left off writing to listen, and don't know what I was going to write.

"May we begin to advertise now for a suitable house, to be ready by next Lady Day? and if so will you let us know how many rooms you would want and any other requirements you might have—then we will do everything else, advertising, examining the place, building up the tapestry room, and so on. As far as I can calculate it will take nearly a year to get all the figures ready. They are about fourteen or fifteen in number, but are only half the work, for scrolls, roses, daisies and birds will more than double it. The design I think you will like.

"I have had to give much explanation about the subject, for damozels such as these at Winnington can't see how Cleopatra and Medea can be good women—but now they are persuaded. We are all so happy about it; all pictures seem small matters till I can get the designs finished: we will fill the room with everything you delight in, and make it a Joyous Gard for you, if it is possible for us. How sweet it is of you to promise to give way to us—but it is worth trying.

"I think you may have as much quiet as possible there, in Ross or some place near, and only see those you want, and only them when you want; we only bargain to be asked to tea one night in the tapestried room. Let me describe that tapestry.

"The ground thereof will be green cloth or serge, and a fence of roses will run all along behind the figures, about half way up them, these roses to be cabbage and dog, red and white. All the ground will be powdered with daisies —only where Dido, Hypsipyle, and Medea and Ariadne come there will be sea instead of grass, and shells instead of daisies. First will come Chaucer, looking very frightened according to the poem, and inditing the poem with a thrush upon his shoulder — then comes Love, a little angry, bringing Alcestis: Chaucer in black, Love in red and white, and Alcestis in green. Then a tree, and a vision of ladies begins, all to have scrolls with their name and life and death written, above their heads. The ladies are to be in uniforms of blue and white, and red and white, alternately, and at the end of all—to come by your fireplace—will be Edward the Third and Philippa sitting and looking on. So on one side of your fireplace will be Chaucer beginning the subject, and on the other side of it the king and queen.

"Shall you like it, dear, and will it ever make a little amends for sorrow? I know it won't, only you will pretend it will. I suppose nothing can ever make amends for your troubles—I think and think about it—it is so detestable for me to be happy and you not—I can't bear that sometimes.

"By this time I almost fit into Winnington like a brick that was meant for it—after much chipping and smoothing. I can look six in the face at one time, I can play at cricket, and read aloud, and even paint with three or four looking on, and I am deeply in love with several at a time, and don't want to leave a bit: and am altogether feeling well and peaceful and happy. I tell you this because I know you wanted it to be so. I am not as much good to them as they are to me at present—but that will come; meantime I am establishing enduring friendships with my six sisters to whom I am vowed henceforth to be loyal and obedient and to think of them a great deal."

As far as I know, the mention in this letter of our friend's sorrow had no reference to special trouble, but only to an excess of general sadness which we felt to be beyond anything personal.

Another letter from Mr. Ruskin, senior, reports: "My Son left us on Tuesday at 12 o'clock and this afternoon I have a telegram from Geneva, he and Mr. Gordon having arrived there quite well. His Letter received this morning is only from Boulogne but written in a fine Spirit. That short visit to the North was wonderfully effective: He never came home looking so well and he never left home with apparently so much of a feeling that he would be glad to come back again. I am pleased that he goes again to Savoy. He may waste a little money but he will gain some experience. He may perhaps buy the Ground and not build at all. I have, since I last saw him, a growing belief that my Son will be more at home for the future than he has been for these thirty years, for he was a young Traveller and we have all been abroad a great part of every year. His old guide Joseph Coutêt dissuades him from Bonneville but only to get him to his own Valley, and if he must be abroad he gives many reasons for choosing the Spot selected. I am somewhat appalled by the drawbacks of the Bonneville quarter. The Desolation that breaks in upon the beauty—the turbid and unruly River that knows no bounds and the sight of those crawling tottering Cretins looking so yellow, dropsical and idiotic, spoils the whole Scene, but higher up where John means to be are a fine peasantry and clear Streams, and some sheltered Nooks. We would have preferred the vicinity of Chamouni, but there is too much Glacier temperature and too much Snow for the Eyes: but why mind what there is—He comes back to us please God in Novr: for the Winter, and I find that every time he goes abroad his stay is shorter, and without thwarting him or making him uncomfortable I trust we may have him more and more at home, and perhaps we should rather be pleased that he chuses a spot when building abroad that is not habitable half the year."

An impression of almost passionate tenderness for his son, breaking through the measured wisdom of these words, was deepened in our minds by old Mr. Ruskin's manner one evening when, after our return to London, we dined alone with him and his wife at Denmark Hill. Of course we talked chiefly about the absent one, and just before we left "John's" father fetched a copy ot Poems by J. R. and gave them to us, charging us, however, not to tell his son, who did not like to have them mentioned. The old gentleman seemed to be far away in the past as he stood turning over the leaves of the book which contained so many references to a lost love, and tears coursed down his face while he told us how he should never forget the day when he and his son took "Adèle" to the ship that was to carry her from England, or the agony that the separation caused the youth. The old lady also sat brooding over bygone years, but she was dry-eyed, and only said thoughtfully, "Yes, any trouble that has happened to him since then was nothing compared to that." Apart from its own weight this scene is stamped on my memory because it was the last time we ever saw Mr. John James Ruskin.

It was during our stay at Winnington, I believe, that Edward shewed his copy of Omar Khayyám to Mr. Ruskin; certainly I remember that he was so delighted with it that before going abroad he wrote a letter of thanks addressed simply "To the Translator of Omar Khayyám" and gave it into our care, charging us to deliver it to the author if ever we learned his name.

After his return from Switzerland Mr. Ruskin wrote eagerly to Edward of a scheme in which he needed his help: "I want you to do me a set of simple line illustrations of mythology and figurative creatures, to be engraved and to make a lovely book of my four Political Economy papers in Fraser, with a bit I'm just adding. I want to print it beautifully and make it a book everybody *must* have. And I want a Ceres for it, and a Proserpine, and a Plutus, and a Pluto, and a Circe, and an Helen, and a Tisiphone, and an 'Ανάγκη, and a Prudentia, and a Sapientia, and a

Temperantia, and a Fortitudo, and a JUSTITIA, and a CHARITAS, and a FIDES, and a Charybdis and a Scylla and a Leucothea and a Portia, and a Miranda, and an Ἀρητή, and an Ophelia, and a Lady Poverty, and ever so many people more, and I'll have them all engraved so beautifully, you can't think—and then I'll cut up my text into little bits and put it all about them, so that people must swallow all at once, and it will do them so much good. Please think of it directly."

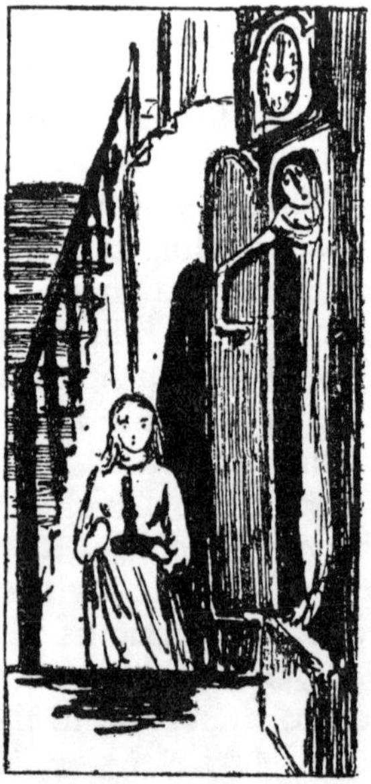

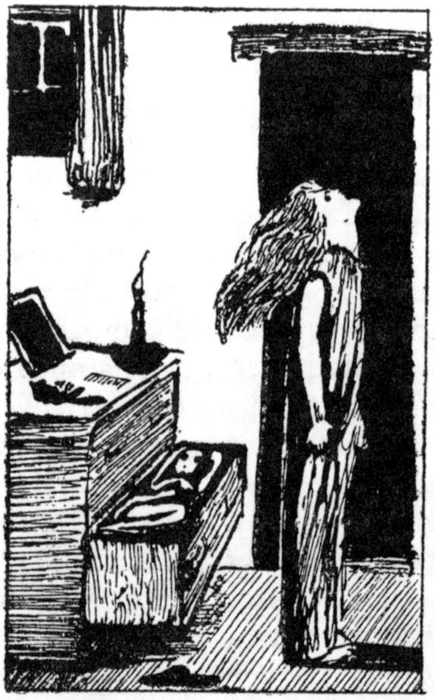

I do not know exactly where to place a class of drawings for which Edward was famous in our closest circle. We called them "Bogey drawings," and they dealt fearlessly with the fearful subject. We shuddered and laughed as we saw the old fears of our childhood embodied in the march of a Bogey up the floor of a bedroom towards two children who have leapt out of bed and cling together yelling into each others' faces with fright—whilst terrors which it was not yet too late to learn were suggested to us by a ghost who pushes open with his thin arm the door of an old clock-case on a dark landing, and leans forward to startle a girl who comes slowly and unconsciously upstairs, candle in hand. A third subject dealt with the new and terrible idea of "a Bogey come home from the wash," who lies neatly folded up in a drawer which another girl, alone in her chamber at night, has just drawn out, and turns from with a shriek that one all but hears. The imperturbable Charles Faulkner had a collection of these.

In February and March, 1864, we were at Winnington again, by ourselves this time, Edward hard at work on the cartoons for Chaucer's Good Women, one of which (Hypsipyle) was actually begun whilst we were there. Morris had not yet thought of weaving tapestry, but he had studied the kind of needlework that goes by the name, and had taught his wife and me what stitches to use and how to place them: my own experience was that his instructions could not be improved upon and that disaster followed their neglect. After the girls should have been fairly started at their work we had a half-formed plan of going with Mr. Ruskin to Florence this spring. He had proposed it long ago, and no one need be told how great was the temptation, but Edward dreaded breaking away again from his work, and only personal affection made him discuss the idea. A second visit to Florence, which he had already seen in 1859, was a luxury that he felt he had not yet earned. The thing was settled for us, however, very suddenly, by the death of Mr. Ruskin's father a week after we reached Winnington. The last words we received from him were of congratulation upon Edward's election as an associate of the Old Water Colour Society on February 8th.

"John did care," he wrote, "and we all cared very much, and I was myself really anxious about the Election, and I rejoice at Mr. Jones' success, for latterly there appears to be very great difficulty in obtaining admission into this Society. It has done nothing for years more likely to strengthen its hold on the public to whose enjoyment and admiration it has always contributed more largely than larger exhibitions, and if it has a weakness it is just where Mr. Jones will prove a host of power and strength to it." Then the kind voice was silenced.

Edward received the following letter from Mr. Ruskin two days after his father's death:

"I am at this moment more anxious about the effect upon *you* of this thing, than about anything else. My mother has behaved so wisely, as well as bravely, that my chief anxiety for her is passed. She slept a little last night, and this morning, when a woman who felt less would have insisted on staying beside the body, she let me take her away in five minutes: and has since been sitting quietly beside me, telling me directions of letters and talking just a little now and then, and I hope the deadliest of the shock is passed.

"But I'm very anxious about you and your fretting for me—not to speak of the disappointment about Florence.

"I must have you and Georgie go as *comfortably* as if I were with you: that 's the only thing you can do for me (that, and not drawing melancholy subjects, nor ill-made hands), so I mean to get you a courier who will insist on your doing things correctly.

"I'm used to live in pain, and this pain does not kill by withering as other sorts of pain do; I have no feeling of weakness nor of fever, and slept without dreaming last night—though the last forty hours were enough to make one dream, one should have thought. The *quite* wonderful thing to me is the way that it changes one's notion of the past character. I had often measured my feelings to my father, as I thought, but I never had any conception of the way I should have to mourn—not over what I lose, now, but over what I *have* lost, until now. I'll tell you more of this afterwards."

And Edward answered:

"What can I possibly write to you! I want to do everything you wish, and stay or go when you wish—but now I want to be in London even if I could only see you once or twice this Spring. It is so hard not to do anything for one I love as I do you. I am so, so grieved, for we loved your father and admired him, and shall never forget him in the least, or have anything but the sweetest remembrance of him.

"There is no disappointment about Florence, for Florence meant you, and everything is swallowed up now in such a grief that the journey becomes a trifle. Be kind and say no more about it, I should hate every day of the time, and every step of the journey: it may happen some better year. We will begin the design for the Political Economy all the sooner, and have colossal schemes for work. I think we are both happier when we get through a great deal of work. May we come back presently? Georgie would love to be hours and hours with your mother, and would never tire of reading to her; it would be kind to call us back for any use like that. And as the Spring goes on Winnington would be so nice and good for her, if you could bring her."

I do not know with whom the idea of bringing Mrs. Ruskin to Winnington originated, but it never came to anything—though in her zeal for the plan Miss Bell arranged which set of rooms on the ground floor should be devoted to the use of the possible visitor, and sent at once for a carpenter to cut and rehang the heavy mahogany doors of the passages leading to them, so that they should swing backwards and forwards noiselessly.

In another of Mr. Ruskin's letters at this time are words whose truth few people who have known the two sorrows will dispute: "I find a curious thing, that natural sorrow does not destroy strength, but gives it—while an irregular, out of the way, avoidable sorrow kills—according to its weight." And again, about the funeral: "No, there's no day worse than the first. You don't suppose that the dramatic performances of upholsterers trouble me, worse than a nightmare—and I'm the only person they *can* trouble." Then he turns to the needlework scheme: "The tapestry is just as much to me as it ever was, and far more likely to come into direct use now, than it was before—

not that I either have—or can form—any plans yet; my mother would live wherever I asked her to live, but I am not at all sure that I shall wish her to live elsewhere than here. Her old friends are useful to her—and I find that beautiful things don't make one happy (except only eyes and hair, and Turner drawings—but there are more of those in England than elsewhere) but only one's own quiet order and work and progress."

We stayed on at Winnington until Edward had finished many cartoons of "Good Women," but the joint embroidery scheme proved impracticable, and the drawings alone remained as a symbol of loving intentions.

On St. Patrick's Day the girls had a dance in the evening, and a very charming Irish girl made Edward dance with her and then declare himself an Irishman—a fact that he never forgot; and often has he called me to witness that he was indeed a sworn "Paddy."

"The Merciful Knight" was exhibited this year at the Old Water Colour Society, where it was regarded with great disfavour by some of the members. Of this the new associate, who was not personally known to them, was made clearly aware when he entered the gallery on "touching-up day." His friendship, however, with Sir Frederick (then Mr.) Burton was strengthened by this connexion with the Society.

Garibaldi's brief visit to England in April is fixed in my memory by his coming one day to see his friend Panizzi at the British Museum, when from our windows we saw him arrive, followed and surrounded by a great cheering crowd that surged through the gates and up to the house. There he stopped before entering, and as he turned on the top step and stood bareheaded for a moment, his red-shirted figure shewed clear above the dark mass of people below.

According to the book kept between Edward and the Firm their weekly meetings in Red Lion Square were quite regular until the end of the March quarter of 1864, when Faulkner went back to Oxford and resumed his place as resident Fellow and Tutor of his own college. The post of book-keeper and business manager to the firm was not one to be held permanently by him, and he would gladly have found more congenial work in London, but could not.

After three years of daily travelling between Upton and London it was no wonder Morris began to feel the journey a waste of time and strength. There was land to be had near Red House where workshops might be built, and if only Edward came to live there also, how much more could be got through together than separately. The idea was timely so far as we were concerned, for our rooms in Great Russell Street were now too small for our needs and we had thought of removing elsewhere; Edward says in the Notes: "A lovely plan was made, too happy ever to come about. It was that Morris should add to his house, making it a full quadrangle, and Webb made a design for it so beautiful that life seemed to have no more in it to desire —but when the estimates came out it was clear that enthusiasm had outrun our wisdom and modifications had sadly to be made."

The two sets of plans lie before me now, clean and unused, and it is curious to think how differently all our lives would have gone if this scheme had been carried out. We were not to have actually shared the house with the Morrises; there were separate entrances and rooms for the two families; but all was to have been under one roof with the garden in common. We looked forward to building in the spring of 1865, and meanwhile, in order to lose no chance of being together, it was arranged that the Morrises, the Faulkners and we should all meet for our autumn-holiday at Littlehampton, on the Sussex coast.

One day in August Mrs. Ruskin asked me to bring my child out to Denmark Hill, and the effort of kindness this involved was betrayed by her nervous anxiety for his safety as he ran about her sitting-room. She was no longer the same woman who had said, some five and forty years before, when her own child stretched out his little hand to the hot, shining tea-urn, "Let him touch it, nurse," as the shortest lesson *not* to touch. It was the first time I had seen her since the death of her husband and I noticed that she wore no widow's cap. Afterwards I learned that this was from love of her son, for, knowing how much he disliked that conventional sign of mourning, she never put one on, but had instead a soft, closely-fitting cap of another shape, with delicate net quillings round the face and narrow white satin strings. These were pinned with a fine diamond and emerald brooch, and later on she told me with tender remorse why she always wore this bright fastening upon her mourning dress. She said it had been given to her by her husband not very long before he died, and that she had received it with the remark that it was a pity he had chosen a coloured stone for the centre, as, if it had been all diamonds, she could have worn it when she was in mourning. So now she pinned her cap-strings with the green and white jewel for his sake. She talked to me once also about her youth; how she had gone as an orphan to live with her aunt, who was her husband's mother, and how her love for him had grown. The vain effort at self-reproach that she made, when she told of a night of passionate grief and tears spent upon the floor of her bedroom after he had first left home and gone away to business in London, was a clue to her nature that I never let go.

Sitting opposite to Mrs. Ruskin in her yellow drawing-room at Denmark Hill on the day in August that I have mentioned was a young girl, Joanna Ruskin Agnew, whose fresh, sweet presence made itself felt at once through a film of Scotch reserve and youthful modesty, but no one could have dreamed then of the strength that was to come forth from that sweetness. Her name will be known as long as Praeterita is read.

The Littlehampton plan was carried out, and three most happy September weeks we spent there. The presence of Faulkner's mother and sisters was an addition to our pleasure, and Kate's gentle nature, sympathetic understanding and keen sense of humour were especially attractive to Edward. Time passed lightly for Janey and me, with all responsibility of housekeeping taken from us by kind Mrs. Faulkner, and the evenings were always merry with Red House jokes revived and amplified: laughs with so little cause, and yet the cause remembered still! For instance; the broken spectacles hurled from the window one night by Morris, in momentary rage at their failure and in firm belief that he had another pair to replace them—then his discovery that spectacles number two were not at hand, his wretchedness at having cast away number one, and his search for them before breakfast next morning, bareheaded, painfully examining every step of the road in front of the house on the chance of finding and humbly taking them to be mended. This sight was made the subject of some words for his good which neither Faulkner nor Edward ever grudged him, especially when they had a satisfactory audience in the background. Details of the scene have faded, but if it passed through the usual stages it is likely that Morris first answered with heat and then burst into laughter, while the sermon upon hasty temper was continued in a monotonous voice by the two other men.

One day when Morris had to go up to London on business they devised an elaborate trick in his absence, and Faulkner spent hours in its preparation. The three friends used sometimes to play whist with a dummy, which Morris took, and into the heads of the two others entered the idea of a game so arranged that it should seem at first sight that dummy had a splendid hand and must win gloriously; but not so really, for the enemy always held higher cards, and destruction must gradually close round Morris. Janey and I went to bed early, and the game began as soon as the men were alone. Morris sniffed with joy when he had looked over his own hand and cast an eye on dummy's—and Edward and Faulkner bore up like those who saw that fate was against them. But presently it was impossible for Morris not to see that, however beautiful the balance between himself and dummy, the confederate partners were always lucky enough to be able to trump it. First came irritation and astonishment, then, as the well-laid scheme revealed itself, shoutings and fury—and finally laughter such as few could equal; while we smiled in our beds at the sound of the distant explosion.

Occasionally also Edward would take some trifle as text and preach us a sermon in exact imitation of the style of different preachers; convulsing us one evening, I remember, as he turned with solemn pomposity to the two girls, Lucy and Kate Faulkner, saying, "And now I address myself more particularly to the younger female portion of my congregation."

But the thought of his father alone in Birmingham with the sad anniversaries of this month underlay all merriment, and Edward was not content until he had persuaded him to come and join us. The old gentleman and his little grandson were very happy together on the acres of brown-sugar sands which then spread up to meet the edge of a green common as yet unruled by an esplanade; and Edward would go down to them and build sandbanks and throw stones into the sea, and was as near idle as I ever saw him.

The old church at Climping had not yet been restored, and when we found it in one of our walks it was neglected enough to give the excuse for which the restorer was waiting; worm-eaten pews were hung with spiders' webs and the floor was green with damp. Amongst its many smooth-worn gravestones there was a tiny sandwich of one to the memory of a child who had died a hundred and twenty years before, and with no sense of foreboding we read and sighed over its inscription:

> This little lamb that was so small
> Did taste of death when Christ did call.

Edward made one unsuccessful attempt to work out of doors, but he said that first of all flies came and settled on his drawing, and then rain came and glued them on, so not much resulted. Indeed, after painting "Green Summer" in the studio of Red House as he had done this year, there seemed little reason for him to torment himself by a struggle with the outer world, and as a rule he painted his backgrounds from notes of nature made here, there, and everywhere, and then dealt with by memory and imagination.

We wrote to Mr. Ruskin at Denmark Hill telling him, amongst other things, about Climping, and how while we were there a passing flock of sheep had played follow-my-leader into the churchyard and been fetched out again by the sheep-dog in a masterly way. Our tale evidently fitted in with some train of his own thoughts, for he answered at once, "I wish with all my heart that all churches were damp and full of spiders, and that churchyards were full of nothing but sheep. The canine St. Peter coming round the corner must have been delightful."

The holiday went by very quickly, and little did any of us think that this would be our last time of careless happiness all together or that illness and death were to be the next experience of the happy party. The report we sent of ourselves on the day we left Littlehampton was "We are all looking robust, especially Phil," but the next thing that happened after we were settled at home was that the child had scarlet fever, which was the beginning of much trouble. Considering the way in which we treated this most infectious disease, the wonder is that we failed to spread it right and left; for as it was a mild case we took no serious precautions. Our friend Miss Catherwood—"ye Ladye Annie" of Addington Place—used to come constantly to sit with and amuse the small patient, and with incredible rashness we sent for dame Wheeler, whose presence we had expected in December, to come and nurse him; whilst, as soon as he was well enough to be left, Edward and I actually went down, by the invitation of our friends, to Red House, where there were now two little children.

When Gabriel heard that Mrs. Wheeler was in Great Russell Street, he wrote asking me to tell her that she would soon receive from him a photograph of his wife which he had long intended her to have. Naturally I enquired at once what photograph he meant, for I did not know there were any and was eager to have one; but he answered, "The photographs of Lizzie are only from two of my sketches. On several occasions when attempts were made to photograph her from life, they were all so bad that none have been retained." He said also that he would send them both for me to see and choose whichever I preferred. The one I kept was from a drawing made shortly after their marriage, when Lizzie was ill, but it is extremely like her and gives the peculiar lustre of her downcast eyes.

Immediately after our return from Red House, where, thank God, we left no mischief behind us, I developed the fever. Together with it came the premature birth of a second son, who struggled against the disease through all the time that I was delirious and unable to notice him, but died just as we were hoping he would be spared for us to cherish. And because he had borne so heavy a weight as he crossed through the troubled waters of his short life, his father named him Christopher. In all this evil time Edward was surrounded by the love and sympathy of friends, though some were absent in the body, for Morris himself had fallen ill of rheumatic fever, Cormell Price was now a master at Haileybury, and Gabriel was in Paris. Those who might come without risk for others were constantly at the house, and I remember gratefully the sympathetic kindness of Mr. Poynter, Mr. Burton, and Mr. De Morgan, who sat up with Edward through the long hours of one intolerable night. Ruskin watched over us with the most thoughtful and practical kindness: it was he who had the street laid as deep as a riding-school with tan that kept the horses' feet from my brain; and Swinburne, prevented by the fears of a delicate mother and sisters from entering the house, wrote, "I would rather have undertaken to keep out of *their* way, if I could have hoped to be much with you or of any use or help to you." His unfeigned love for children also made him realize the death of our little Christopher in a way that few did. "You know how sorry I am," he wrote, "and how much more than I can say. The news has struck half my pleasure in anything away for the present—I had been quite counting on the life of your poor little child and wondering when I might see it."

Rossetti wrote to Edward from Paris, at a time when he believed things were better with us than they really were —and after some sympathetic and hopeful words, his letter turns to speak in a weary tone of himself: "I have done no work at all here for three weeks, and am sorely wanting to get home, but I stick in the mud everywhere and day after day I fail to get away." However, if he had done no work himself he been looking at that of others. "Really," he says, "Gerome is not a painter, though a stunner of a sort. There is a man named Millet who is the best going by far. Old Ingres is done for. Delacroix is worth the journey with all his faults, and I have looked a great deal at his collected works which are to close at the end of this month." A postscript adds, "To-day I went to the Zool: Gardens and scratched a wombat, who liked it."

If only on this visit to Paris Gabriel had met the "man named Millet," it would have been happy for them both. Millet was bound for Paris just then, we learn from his biographer Mrs. Ady, to see the Delacroix exhibition for the second time, but illness prevented the journey—otherwise one feels as if he and Rossetti must have recognized each other somewhere, in gallery or street, and taken and given fresh courage. A letter of Millet's to M. Sensier, written on the same day as Rossetti's to Edward, asks about some reproductions of Giotto's work which he heard were "superb and touching." "Where are the originals?" he asks. "How many subjects are there, and by whom are they published?" How Gabriel would have told him all!

Meanwhile anxiety about health was over at our house, and as soon as we could travel we went down to Hastings, but first Edward had to write to Morris and tell him that he feared our scheme for building and living together at Upton was at an end, as he could undertake no fresh expense of any kind. This letter has not been preserved, but the answer to it shows that it must have been sad and dispirited enough. Morris dates from "Bed, Red House," and the handwriting is feeble, but he was already recovering, and as he lay there with time to think over everything, both his friend's and his own trouble seemed to him no more than a temporary obstruction to their settled plans.

"As to our palace of Art," he writes, "I confess your letter was a blow to me at first, though hardly an unexpected one—in short I cried; but I have got over it now. As to our being a miserable lot, old chap, speaking for myself I don't know, I refuse to make myself really unhappy for anything short of the loss of friends one can't do without. Suppose in all these troubles you had given us the slip what the devil should I have done? I am sure I couldn't have had the heart to have gone on with the firm: all our jolly subjects would have gone to pot—it frightens me to think of, Ned. But now I am only 30 years old, I shan't always have the rheumatism, and we shall have a lot of jolly years of invention and lustre plates together I hope. I need hardly tell you how I suffered for you in the worst of your troubles; on the Saturday I had begun a letter to you but it read so dismal (as indeed I felt little hope) that I burnt it.

"I have been resting and thinking of what you are to do: I really think you must take some sort of house in London —unless indeed you might think of living a little way out and having a studio in town: Stanhope and I might join you in this you know. I don't see how you can do with chambers, and it would be too like the old way of living— but all this you have probably thought of yourself. There is only one other thing I can think of, which is when you come back from Hastings come and stay with me for a month or two, there is plenty of room for everybody and everything: you can do your work quietly and uninterruptedly; I shall have a good horse by then and Georgie and J. will be able to drive about with the kids jollily, meantime you need not be hurried in taking your new crib. Janey is exceedingly anxious that you should come and it is in her opinion the best thing you could do. I would give £5 to see you, old chap; wouldn't it be safe for you to come down here one day before you go?"

This was not possible, however, nor could the kind suggestion of a longer visit be thought of; for, worn as he was with fatigue and care, the only thing Edward saw before him was to find some place where he could settle and begin work again directly. "For these two months," he wrote to Allingham, "I have done no work, but lived most anxiously from day to day. The whole period has been so horrible and dismal that I try to forget it and will write no more about it."

My own memory of those sad days is fragmentary, and distorted by the delirium which made even the room where I had lain ill such an incarnate terror that Edward never let me enter it again, but, after Hastings, sent me home to my parents for Christmas, and with incredible quickness removed during my absence into a fresh house. His friend Cormell came to him and they managed it together.

A story from Hastings comes through De Morgan, who was there with his family and remembers walking by the sea with Edward and his little boy one day when a man was shooting gulls, and that Edward, turning to the child, said deliberately, "That man is a fool." Then, after a pause, "Now what 's that man?" And the answer coming correctly, he went on, "Now mind you never forget when you see a man with a thing like that, that he 's a fool." Which sounds to me quite typically true, for I know what Edward thought about wanton destruction of life. "Teach children to draw animals," he said, "and they won't wish to kill them."

CHAPTER XV

1865-1867

Alas, that spring should vanish with the rose,
That youth's sweet-scented manuscript should close.

THE house where we began life afresh was in Kensington Square, and we thought, when we took possession of it and closed the door behind us, that we should go on from where we left off in Great Russell Street. "Home is very nice again," wrote Edward; "last night I had the old songs over again." But when we turned to look around us something was gone, something had been left behind—and it was our first youth.

I have heard Edward say that his memory of the time spent in this house was dim, especially as to his intercourse with Morris, although he knew that they used to meet every week. But it was a self-absorbed time and one of restlessness and transition for all the friends: Edward setting himself hard to make up for lack of earlier training; Morris, beside his work as head of the firm, brooding over the gigantic scheme of The Earthly Paradise; Madox Brown engrossed by the exhibition of his collected work and all that came of it; and Swinburne awaking suddenly to fame on the appearance of his Atalanta. The apostolical succession of our friends was broken; new ones were made and new views of life were opening. So much for the inner history of our two years and ten months in Kensington Square.

The place itself was not strange to us, for once, when seeking rooms, we had gone as far as Kensington and seen its old square lying back undisturbed by the world, with nothing except gardens between it and the narrow High Street. The turnpike through which Edward took me to Little Holland House the first time we went there together had been removed, but the parish church was not yet rebuilt and the whole neighbourhood was quiet and self-contained in comparison with that of Holborn. Our house, No. 41, was on the north side of the square, a great drawback, because the south light was bad for painting and the only rooms with a north aspect were very small; Edward, however, was so eager to begin work that he put up with these difficulties. His friends did not find the distance too far to follow him, and he was soon surrounded by them again. At the end of January he writes to Allingham:

"We are settling fast, even looking a bit comfortable—Topsy has given us a Persian prayer-carpet which amply furnishes one room. I have a little crib which I call a library because there I keep my tobacco and my borrowed books—this room shall be yours for quiet when you come. We have a garden, ever so long—how shall our garden grow? I am the veriest cockney and know no times or seasons of planting, but I want a quiet summer at the back here to pay me for all my bothers—there I will pitch a little pavilion on warm days and lie in the shade of it—I must have a pavilion. And this luck has happened to me, of all lucks the best that could have happened, Ruskin has given me the four great engravings of Albert Durer—the Knight, Melancholy, St. Hubert, and Adam and Eve—all perfect impressions; also many woodcuts of the same and the great designs of the Apocalypse, glorious to behold."

Gabriel was well, the letter adds, and seriously thinking of buying a lion which he learned could be got quite a bargain somewhere in Ratcliffe Highway. The reason current among Gabriel's friends for his not finally buying the lion was, I remember, that he found he would have had to heat the garden with hot-water pipes for him in the winter. There was another story about Rossetti's wishing to have a young elephant, and the answer he gave to Browning, who, with momentary dearth of imagination enquired: "What on earth do you mean to do with him when you have him?" "I mean him," said Gabriel, "to clean the windows; and then, when some one passes by the house, they will see the elephant cleaning the windows, and will say, 'Who lives in that house?' And people will tell them, 'Oh, that 's a painter called Rossetti.' And they will say, 'I think I should like to buy one of that man's pictures'—and so they will ring, and come in and buy my pictures."

Our Bohemian days were over now, and De Morgan sighed for the old Great Russell Street evenings, when our little Yorkshire maid came in and asked, "'As any of you gentlemen seen the key of the beer-barrel?" The oak dining-table and painted sideboard soon made themselves at home in the new house, and the sideboard was varnished so that its colour showed up finely, while the firm supplied any fresh furniture that we needed. Some letters written home by my sister Agnes, who was with us this spring, form a diary that supplements and confirms my own memory. She speaks of sitting with Edward while he worked, and talking, "after their old custom in the studio, about all things in the world," and most people who came to the house are named day by day. Morris, now perfectly recovered from his illness, is described as seeming to her "so nice and kind, pleasanter than ever he was," and on the first evening he came, she says, "Mr. Poynter and Mr. Burton were here also, so we were a goodly company." This mention of Mr. Burton reminds me that in those days we thought he much resembled Garibaldi in appearance. Gabriel, too, dropped in one night, bringing with him "a Frenchman of great celebrity named Legros," and another time Morris arrived with "a glorious haul of picture-books—black letter and old engravings—a History of the Cross, a Biblia Pauperum, and a Looking Glass of Human Salvation."

Indeed it was so unusual a thing for no one to come in the evening that when that happened it was described as an event. "We had an evening entirely to ourselves yesterday, which was jolly. Ned was drawing, Georgie making a new and brilliant watch-pocket, while I read aloud a most delightful Arabian Night story, the Story of Joodar." The brilliant watch-pocket here mentioned belonged to a still more brilliant watch, entirely covered with chrysolites, which Edward had bought for me in Wardour Street a couple of years before, with almost the last eight pounds we possessed, but with such a certainty of its unusual beauty that he never hesitated. In the same way I remember his giving nearly all that he had for a set of photographs of Memling's "St. Ursula and her eleven thousand Virgins" which made the glory of our sitting-room in Great Russell Street.

This old home of ours was now occupied by our friend E. J. Poynter, and one evening whilst my sister was in town we went with her to revisit the familiar place. In spite of all the changes made, none of us could quite realize at first what had happened, and the freedom with which Poynter comported himself in "our rooms" was a subject of open comment on the part of his guests. The last joke was that after saying good night, Edward ostentatiously proceeded *upstairs*, with the tramp of a tired man in his own house.

Our Kensington garden was just large enough for a game of bowls, and many a game was played there. It was a pretty spot in springtime, when together with its neighbour-gardens it made a mass of fruit-blossom surrounded by red roofs. Edward Poynter began a water-colour drawing of it, which was never finished, but remains a faithful document so far as it goes. "American bowls" too was a game that Edward, Morris, Webb and Faulkner often played in town; dining together at some "pot-house" afterwards and never tired of each other's company.

My father was now living in Wolverhampton, and this year would have brought with it yet another removal for him, but his health and strength had been failing for some time, and we had the grief of seeing him sink into the condition of a perpetual invalid, instead of continuing the active round of his life. Some irritation of the spine was supposed to be the cause of his illness, but the diagnosis was not very clear, and in those days many people were still content to say "the doctors do not know what it is," and to seek more earnestly for patience under suffering than for its removal. It was understood, however, that all unnecessary excitement was bad for him, and so in March the marriage of my sister Alice with Mr. John Lockwood Kipling before he went out to India took place very quietly from our house. The death of Wilfred Heeley's wife in India had been a shock to us all, and our parents trembled at sending a daughter into the same risk, but the appointment was to Bombay, with its sea-breezes, was terminable at pleasure after three years, and seemed so exactly suited to John Kipling's talents and taste, that they refused to take the responsibility of urging him to remain in England. Cold was the March morning when we stood by our bride and bridegroom at the altar of St. Mary Abbott's Church, but no one doubted the good choice they had made of each other, and we were cheerful, if not merry. Our brother Frederick, through whom they had first known each other, had been ordained as a Wesleyan Methodist minister some little time now, and he came to give away his sister to his friend. Madox Brown, to our great joy, when speaking of the marriage, alluded to the bridegroom as "John Gilpin."

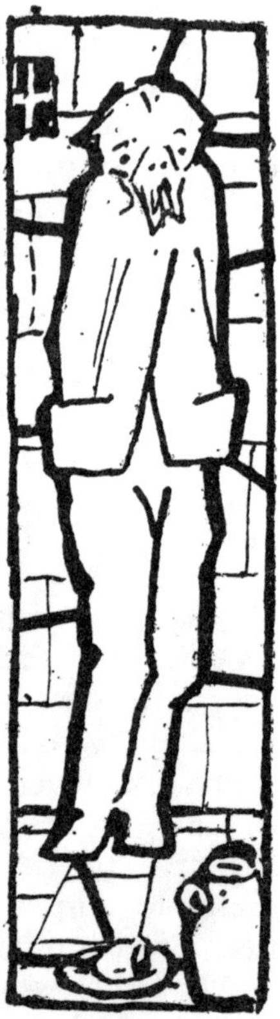

With the early days of Kensington Square is associated the memory of Warrington Taylor. We had known him first in Great Russell Street, but I cannot remember how he came amongst us: a tall, thin man with a very large Roman nose and an excitable and enthusiastic way of speaking. He had been at Eton, in the same division with Swinburne, and afterwards had become a Catholic, and entered the army, was married and had one child, but had not yet found his place in life. He knew and cared a great deal about the arts. At the time we first made his acquaintance his fortunes were low and his actual position was that of check-taker at Her Majesty's Theatre—then an Opera House. His strong individuality was not affected by circumstances, however, and was so well understood by Morris and others that as the work of the firm increased they began to consider the question of making him its business-manager. It was no easy thing to find any one capable of filling the place, but this strange, wild-looking Warrington Taylor proved to have the qualities wanted. Within a few weeks of his appointment the rumour spread amongst us that he was keeping the accounts of the firm like a dragon, attending to the orders of customers, and actually getting Morris to work at one thing at a time. He must have been happier in some ways during the five years of life that remained to him than he had ever been, for he loved the men he was associated with and the work he had to do.

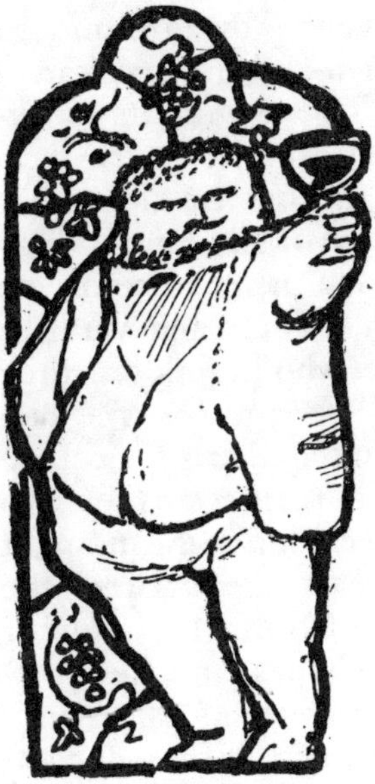

Two small parchment-bound volumes of accounts between Edward and the firm, covering the years 1861-1898, are excellent reading: on his side torrents of fun and on the other bald statements and figures. There are drawings also, in the form of sketches for stained-glass windows, in one of which Morris is represented plump and prosperous against a background of the vine, holding a brimming beaker in his outstretched hand, while opposite to him stands Edward, a thin and starving prisoner.

The exact date of a party given by Rossetti in April is fixed as the 12th by its being the day that the Lockwood Kiplings, who were to have been amongst the guests, left

England: it had been put off because Gabriel could not get the workmen out of the house who were doing something to his dining-room. Originally the invitations had been to dinner, but, with the frankness that reigned amongst us, as time went on Gabriel announced that he had asked too many people for that—he could not afford it—and it must be an evening party instead. No Thames Embankment had reached Chelsea then, and only a narrow road lay between the tall iron gates of the forecourt of 16, Cheyne Walk, and the wide river which was lit up that evening by a full moon. Gabriel had hung Lizzie's beautiful pen-and-ink and water-colour designs in the long drawing-room with its seven windows looking south, where if ever a ghost returned to earth hers must have come to seek him: but we did not sit in that room, the studio was the centre of the house. For the sake of those vanishing days let me name some of the people present that evening. William Rossetti and William Bell Scott were there; and Swinburne, who I think was then sharing the house with Gabriel; Morris and his wife had dined with us first, and we all came on together. Of course there were the Madox Browns, and with them were their two daughters—nothing further from expectation at the moment than a marriage that took place nine years later between the elder of these and William Rossetti. Munro the sculptor and his wife, Mr. and Mrs. Arthur Hughes, and the Warrington Taylors came, as well as Legros with his pale, handsome English wife: Christina Rossetti and Mrs. Bell Scott would have been there, we were told, but that it was Passion Week. I remember noticing that night a sign that we were mortal in the fact of Madox Brown's beautifully-thick thatch of hair having turned very grey, at which his wife when the men were not in the room expressed great vexation. He was not changed otherwise though, and made us happy with a long, characteristic description of the way by which he had brought his wife and daughters from Kentish Town in order to save cab-fare. First of all they had taken train for Kew, because he thought it must be near Chelsea. At Kew they were advised to wait half an hour and then go on to Clapham

Junction, where they would catch a train for Chelsea: this they exactly missed, and found there was no other for three-quarters of an hour. Finally, on reaching Chelsea Station, it proved to be so far from Cheyne Walk that they then took a cab, and arrived smiling and unruffled at Gabriel's door after two hours and a half by road and rail. I wish I could recall more details of the evening, which is still present to me as a scene, but nothing else of interest detaches itself from the background of house and studio.

Before the chronicle closes, however, one more delightful evening must be named; it is the last that I remember at the Madox Browns' house in Kentish Town. Many of the same people were there, but I think it may have been Legros' first formal visit to the Browns, for our host placed him next to himself at supper and, oblivious of everything else, spent the time in giving him an outline of the story of Sidonia in French. A slender vision of Swinburne in evening dress is presented to my mind, but I cannot be sure whether the custom of dressing was only his own or if the cloven foot of conformity to fashion had at this time shewn itself amongst us. And Whistler was there, looking ten times more like a Frenchman than Legros did, his face working with vivacity, his thick black hair curling down to his eyebrows, with an angry eye-glass fixed beneath it. But his rather alarming appearance was balanced by rumours of his tenderness to a widowed mother; how he took her to church on weekday mornings and otherwise comforted her. Gabriel was there in a magnificent mood—no other word describes it when he passed through a room bringing pleasure to great and small by his beautiful urbanity, a prince amongst men. With Morris and his wife came Miss Burden, Janey's sister, then and for some years afterwards living with them; Warrington Taylor also I remember, and Christina Rossetti, gently caustic of tongue. The little ten-year-old Nolly sat up all evening and clung most of the time to kind Charles Faulkner, demanding amusing stories from him, and yet finding time to ask Rossetti "what he thought Pompeii must have looked like." He had not quite lost his baby face, but it had grown thinner and longer. And on this day of the union and reunion of friends there was one who had come amongst us in friend's clothing, but inwardly he was a stranger to all that our life meant. This was Mr. Howell.

One of the happiest chapters of our life was closed this year by the sale of Red House. But it had to go, for Morris, having decided in his unflinching way that he must come up and live at his business in London, could not bear to play landlord to the house he loved so well—it must be sold outright and he would never see it again. Nor did he; but some of us saw it in our dreams for years afterwards as one does a house known in childhood.

The last visit we paid to Upton was in September, 1865, when on a lovely afternoon Morris and Janey, and Edward and I, took a farewell drive through some of the beautiful little out-of-the-way places that were still to be found in the neighbourhood. Indoors the talk of the men was much about The Earthly Paradise, which was to be illustrated by two or three hundred woodcuts, many of them already designed and some even drawn on the block.

About this plan my sister Louie was of course eager, for she was to help in the engraving, on which she dreamed of spending quiet, busy years. But she was mistaken in her reckoning, for love and marriage claimed her instead, and as her sister-friend had led the way upon this new path by becoming engaged to Mr. Poynter in the early summer, we had to look forward to the loss of both our playmates. The news of her engagement to Mr. Alfred Baldwin drew the following note from Edward to the younger of the two "wenches," as he called them amongst a score of other pet names:

"I am unchangeable in my love for you, don't doubt it: nothing will ever divide us—no chance nor circumstance will bring that about—but a little gloomy sulkiness is excusable in me. I only had two wenches, and they are both gone, and I am very much past thirty and growing selfish as Georgie will tell you. Tell the other wench she's another's and doesn't care for me."

In the figures of the two girls at a frozen fountain in the foreground of "Theophilus and the Angel" there is a reminiscence of these sisters.

But if this year threatened the loss of some of his companions, it also brought back to Edward a very welcome one in the shape of his friend Spencer Stanhope. A capricious asthma, on account of which he had first gone to live in the country, had now driven him away again, and he was trying whether it would be appeased if he wintered abroad and lived on Campden Hill when in England. He arrived fresh from his first winter in Florence in the highest spirits, though houseless at the time—but most things at which other people grumbled made him laugh. The picture he had painted during the winter, "Beauty and the Beast," was on view for a couple of days at Edward's studio before "sending in," and amongst those who came there to see it was Millais, very friendly and kind in manner.

The exhibition of his own pictures at the gallery of the Old Water Colour Society this summer gained Edward new believers. Two men especially, Mr. William Graham, M.P. for Glasgow, and Mr. F. R. Leyland of Liverpool, seemed to make up their minds firmly about his work: to them for some years went the most important things Edward did, and each of these shrewd business men became his real friend. He also received a commission from Mr. Birket Foster, to paint the story of St. George and the Dragon in seven pictures for the decoration of his house in Surrey. It was not the first time that Edward's pictures had been wanted by brother artists, and that they cared to possess them gave him the purest pleasure. Both Watts and Leighton, besides Mr. Boyce and Mr. and Mrs. Henry Wells, already had some of his earlier work.

When first Mr. Graham came to the studio he was a man of about forty-eight and Edward was some fifteen years younger. Their friendship lasted for nearly twenty years without a cloud, and then was only ended by Graham's death. Keen man of business though he was, simplicity and devotion of soul were as evident in him as in a cloistered monk. His face was that of a saint, and at times like one transfigured. He had an inborn perception about painting, and an instinct for old pictures that was marvellous. His eye was so keen that Edward said he knew good work even when it was upside down. Once this faculty helped him to see at a glance from the top of an omnibus that in the front room of a little house he was passing there was a picture worth looking at; so he got down at once, knocked at the door, found the picture good enough to buy and carried it home. His library at Grosvenor Place was filled with treasures he had gathered for himself. He liked to come and look on while Edward painted, appearing and disappearing very swiftly, but bringing no sense of disturbance with him. I believe Edward cared for his sympathy about his pictures next to that of Gabriel and missed it almost as much when it was gone. Morris's sympathy was another matter; that was a part of himself.

In a letter after Graham's death Edward says: "I am making my Sleeping Queen; I want her to be finished by Christmas and to look exceedingly splendid. But he who would most have liked it wouldn't stoop to see such a poor thing now—and my loss is perpetual." It was Graham who did a thing that surely no other man ever did, for Edward said that once when he shewed him a picture, "it had a part of it painted so much to his mind that he went up to it and kissed the panel."

When Mr. Birket Foster many years afterwards left the house for which the "St. George" series was painted, the pictures were sent to Christie's, and on going there to see them again before the sale I was surprised by their dramatic character, especially in the scenes where the King looks at the blood-stained clothes of the girls who have been devoured by the Dragon, and where the poor mothers crowd into the Temple while the Princess draws the lot. I spoke of this to Edward afterwards, asking him whether he had not purposely suppressed the dramatic element in his later work, and he said yes, that was so—for no one can get every quality into a picture, and there were others that he desired more than the dramatic. It was seldom that his own family asked him any questions about his work as he did it, for we saw how little he liked to talk of a thing before it was done, and realized what would be the irksomeness to him of anything like a running commentary on it.

When it was finished, too, he wanted every one to see in it what they could for themselves. He was often amused by the anxiety people had to be told what they ought to think about his pictures as well as by their determination to find a deep meaning in every line he drew. A rumour once reached him that there was a mystic intention in the number of beads that are threaded on a string held by *bambini* in the background of "Fides": and many were the letters he received from different parts of the world, asking for an "explanation" of "The Golden Stairs." It was to this that he refers in a letter written in one of his wearied hours. "If you had to paint pictures now, what would you do? Should you feel as bewildered as I do, who sit and stare at them and wonder why I began them and what I meant? I feel inclined to write to Mr. Burne-Jones and apologize for troubling him, but should be so grateful if he would tell me the hidden meaning of these pictures." Morris, on the other hand, always talked freely beforehand of plans and purposes of work, besides bringing every poem of The Earthly Paradise to read to us as soon as it was written. I remember, with shame, often falling asleep to the steady rhythm of the reading voice, or biting my fingers and stabbing myself with pins in order to keep awake. But no one ever reproached me.

Seventy designs for "Cupid and Psyche" were made this year; and we had the joy of giving them to Mr. Ruskin in fulfilment of the wish that Edward had expressed in one of his letters from Venice three years before. It was a busy household altogether now, and some of the duties that fell to my share were illustrated by Edward in various little family sketches that still exist. The sewing-machine in one of the drawings was a gift from Mr. Watts, whose kind imagination realized how many stitches had to be set, and was described by Edward as "a most clever little thing that makes dresses and buys the stuff and almost pays for it." This same year he very narrowly escaped losing his life in Spencer Stanhope's garden, by the fall of a great elm-tree which was blown down suddenly across his path.

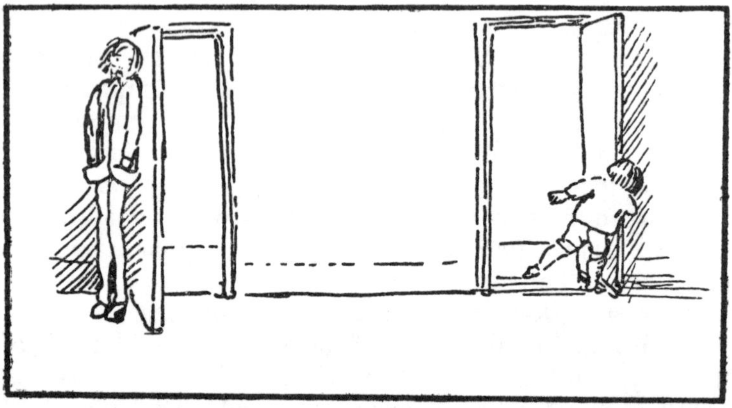

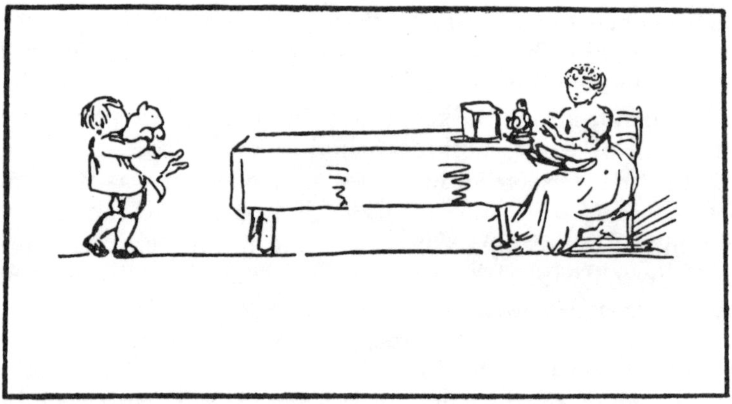

In November the Morrises made their removal to London. A house in Queen Square, Bloomsbury, had been found, large enough for them to live in the upper part, while the ground floor and outbuildings were used as showroom and workshops. In this particular spot the dinginess of the neighbourhood was conquered, and it had been made to shine with whitewash and white paint, a background that shewed better than any other the beautiful fabrics with which the house was furnished. Yet nothing ever made it a home like the one they had left, nor did they really take root anywhere else, until six years later they found Kelmscott Manor on the upper Thames.

A pleasant custom soon began of our dining in Queen Square once a week to meet other members of the Firm, and in these evenings the merriment of our youth was revived for a time, but Janey was now so much out of health that I fear her share of the entertainments was more fatigue than pleasure, and gradually they came to an end. The men never ceased to meet regularly, though, at one house or the other.

News came to us from Bombay at the beginning of 1866 that the Lockwood Kiplings had a son, and the youngest of the "wenches" was asked to be his godmother. She chose for him the name of Rudyard, the place where his parents had first seen each other.

We now saw a good deal of Mr. Ruskin again, and one April afternoon I remember his carrying us off to a performance of the Christy Minstrels, where he was received as an honoured patron, and something (I forget what) was added to the programme at his request. At this time he wished Edward to paint his portrait, and there were drawings made for it, but as these were not preserved I suppose they were unsatisfactory and the plan was never carried out. Truth to tell, portrait-painting was distasteful to Edward, who always said so on occasion, but special reasons overcame the feeling from time to time. He once wrote: "I do not easily get portraiture, and the perpetual hunt to find in a face what I like, and leave out what mislikes me, is a bad school for it." In one of Mr. Ruskin's notes of appointment for sittings there is a portrait in words (under the name Proserpine) of the fair-haired girl to whom as she grew up he gave his heart, with the tragic result that she could love no one else but him, yet not him completely. "I'll come on Monday and then be steady I hope to every other day—Proserpine permitting. Did you see the gleam of sunshine yesterday afternoon? If you had only seen her in it, bareheaded, between *my* laurels and *my* primrose bank!"

He used still to fetch or send for us to Denmark Hill to dine with him and his mother, whose demands upon his patience he met with indescribable gentleness. Her instinct for contradiction was revealed to me soon after we first knew her. I was sitting with her alone very happily, when she suddenly said, "Do you love God?" Overwhelmed with shyness at such a question, but feeling it would be a lie to say "No," I tried to appease the inquisition by the simplest form of what I meant, and humbly answered "Yes." On this reply she pounced, with the unlooked-for exclamation "I don't!" and, while I shrank within myself, discoursed to me upon the arrogance of any creature daring to say such a thing about the Creator, so great and so far above us all. But I believe it was sheer love of contradiction that led her on. I remember, too, an evening spent with her and her son, when Edward read aloud, from Lane's Arabian Nights, the Story of the Barber, in which there is scarce a a paragraph without some mention of God, the High, the Great, and at its conclusion Ruskin expressed great admiration for it. "God forgive you, my child," said a pitying voice from the fireside; and as we waited in silent astonishment for some explanation, she continued, "for taking His name in vain." Her son listened with perfect patience and dignity, and then, almost as if thinking aloud, answered with a solemn and simple refutation of the charge and a noble definition of what taking the name of God in vain really was. Would that I could remember his words! His mother seemed quite unmoved.

Old Anne, nurse for two generations in the house, was alive in those days; a white-haired, light-eyed, spare little figure, harsh and unattractive to our southern feeling. She had come as a bare-foot child into the service of the family, and was passionately devoted to her master and his son; but between her and her mistress relations were evidently strained, for I once heard Mrs. Ruskin address the aged dame in a tone such as one might use to a tiresome child, whilst Anne retorted with a want of deference that was certainly not the growth of the moment. But the best image to keep of the old nurse is that of her, having thrust all others aside, being first to mount the ladder reared in alarm against her old master's window and to enter the locked room where he lay seized with mortal illness. Of her, in Fors Clavigera, her second nursling, when he had become a man of fifty-four, wrote that she was the one being whom, next to father and mother, he "practically and truly missed the most."

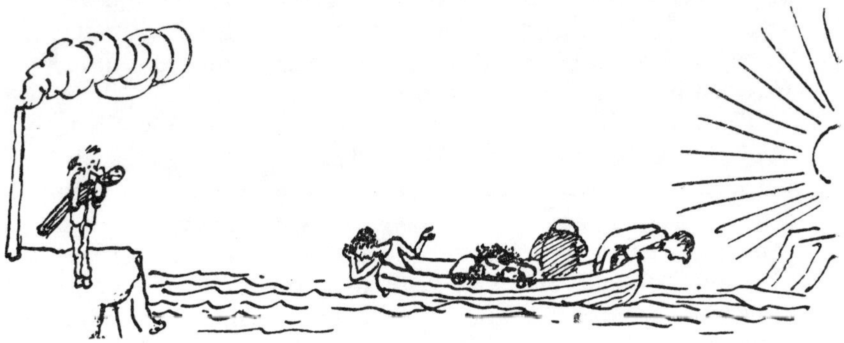

A letter from Edward in June tells his "dearest little wenches" of the birth of a daughter, whom he describes as "a maid some nine hours old," and adds: "So Phil's conjecture that it would be either a boy or a girl was not unfounded." But the arrival of this little girl prevented our carrying out a plan we had looked forward to, of going some time in the summer to North France with the Morrises, Philip Webb and Warrington Taylor, who now went without us. An expressive drawing at the end of a note of farewell to the travellers shews Edward standing desolate upon the English coast, with a long-clothed infant in his arms and a tall chimney smoking in the background, whilst the others, in an open boat, speed to the opposite shore where the sun shines brightly.

All this time the number of our general acquaintance was enlarging, while among our friends were some whose importance to us increased and that of others lessened. De Morgan used to come over to us from Haverstock Hill at least once a week; Henry Holiday and his wife were already much more than names to us, and there was Edward Clifford, one of a new group of Royal Academy students who had discovered and were enthusiastic about some pencil heads that Edward sent to a Winter Exhibition of the Old Water Colour Society. He came to ask from whom they were drawn, "for," says Mr. Clifford, "we did not fully realize that the drawings depended more on him than on the model." But he went away taking with him the address of Miss Augusta Jones, a noble-looking girl, who sat for "Astrologia" amongst many other things, and for whom Edward had much regard and respect.

The name of Mr. Henry Ellis Wooldridge, now Slade Professor at Oxford, is also connected with these days, but with him our chief bond was music. He introduced us to a new world of beauty in Italian songs of the seventeenth century—then almost entirely unknown—and his singing of Carissimi and Stradella gave us the keenest pleasure: Edward used to ask him for the same things over and over again. Most of these treasures Mr. Wooldridge had discovered for himself among manuscripts in the British Museum, and others he brought afterwards from the Bodleian and Christ Church Libraries and from Rome. I think the one that moved us all most deeply was a recitative and trio by Carissimi, which Mr. Hullah had cited in his course of lectures upon musical history. It was the cry of the lost souls who "walk ever in the darkness," saying, *Heu, heu, nos miseros*—with *Pereat nox* repeated like a passing bell, and at the last a whisper of despair breathed through the words *in qua concepti fuimus*, which seemed to drop into fathomless depths of silence as the lips of the singers closed.

The Madox Browns had now left Kentish Town and were settled in Fitzroy Square, which was nearer to us materially, but in the new house we never felt the same joy as in the old, and slowly—with no word to mark the change—as time went on we felt that our old friends had drifted apart from us. In later life we stretched out hands to each other again which touched but did not clasp, and it is by its early years that our friendship is reckoned in my mind.

I cannot remember when Mr. and Mrs. George Howard (now Lord and Lady Carlisle) first came to our house, but the image of them there, young, fresh, and eager about everything, is clear. Mr. Howard's gift as a painter of romantic landscape made him welcome in the studio at once, while the two wives drew more slowly, but quite steadily, together, and a friendship between our daughters perpetuates the one then begun. To Mr. Howard we owed a first knowledge of Mazzini's writings.

Another and very noticeable introduction of these days was to a part of what may be called the Greek colony in London. Before this we had had the pleasure of meeting the beautiful Miss Spartali and her sister, daughters of the Greek consul, but now, I forget in what way, we became acquainted with one or two other families of her nation.

Instead of going to Troyes with the Morrises in June, we went in August to Lymington, so as to be near Allingham, who had an appointment in the Customs there. One day the two men crossed over to the Isle of Wight and called on Tennyson, to whom Ruskin sent a message of thanks by Edward for the "noble sermon" contained in his poem of Aylmer's Field. We made an expedition also to Winchester, when Morris came down from London to meet us, and as we waited for him at the door of our hotel I remember his swinging towards us along the High Street with a look as if he had easily walked all the way. Then we went on together over the water meadows to St. Cross, and mourned over the "restoration" it was suffering. The whole time at Lymington increased our affection for Allingham, and made us wish that we lived nearer to each other. To bridge over the distance from his friends, he used often to run up to London at the week's end, and many were glad to welcome him. When he came to us, he and Edward generally took a walk on the Sunday afternoon if it was fit weather, and sometimes I was with them. On one of these walks we saw for the first time the house to which we were next to remove and where the rest of our life together was to be spent: I am glad to remember that it attracted our notice and indeed made a strong impression upon us as it stood there empty and waiting.

Meanwhile, whatever else happened, work never stopped. Illustrations for The Earthly Paradise went on steadily, and twenty subjects from the Hill of Venus were designed this year. Also, with help, the last four pictures of "St. George and the Dragon" were finished: the other three were already in place. This was the first time that Edward called in aid to carry out his designs, and in his assistant he was fortunate beyond expectation. Mr. Charles Fairfax Murray was then a mere youth, but one whose intellectual and artistic power was visible at first sight. He soon became a trusted friend, in whose work Edward took great interest.

June, 1867, found us still in Kensington Square, but the house had been sold during our tenancy, and as the new owner refused to extend our term, we were compelled for the third time in seven years to seek another home. Before this fresh upheaval we had one more holiday, which was our last with the Morrises; and the place and time chosen for it was Oxford in the Long Vacation. We, with our children, took some undergraduates' rooms in St. Giles', while the Morris family lodged in Beaumont Street: Faulkner was in college, but we met every evening, and then Morris read what he had written or the men played whist—without practical jokes now. I remember noticing how beautifully Faulkner shuffled the cards with his skilful fingers.

A small pocket-book of this time contains a note made by Edward from a canal-bridge in a poor quarter of the city, which nearly thirty years afterwards he developed into the background of his "Aurora." The main outlines of building and canal are preserved in the picture, and

Aurora with her cymbals comes lightly stepping along a waterside path from which in the original sketch a woman stoops to bathe her baby, but the canal has changed into an arm of a river and the houses have been welded into the long, low storage-places of a wharf, crowned by a great church lifted up against the sky. He enjoyed making up stories to himself about his backgrounds, as he painted them; and one day as he was working at "Aurora" he did a very unusual thing, for the humour seized him to think aloud, and he spun out a whole history of the place. "You see the city gets poorer as it gets towards the church," he said, "which makes it more interesting—the rich people have gone to live further off. It has had many epochs: first the Roman—you may see remains of that in the foundations: then was an oligarchic government, following on a time of anarchy and disaster, that put up many fine buildings, and some of them still remain. Then came an epoch of trade, capricious and varying in locality, that produced the strangest results on its architecture, one part of the town cutting out another by setting up nearer the sea further down the river, then being driven back again for reasons that can't be found out now—traces of prosperity and decay succeeding each other."

We kept Edward's birthday on the 28th of August, by all going down the river as far as Wallingford, and stayed on at Oxford till after St. Giles' Fair—a fine treat for the little ones, but Edward was restless to be back in his studio. "Tell me how your work prospers—mention Mantegna to me: I am doing nothing—can't in lodgings with the noise of children," he wrote to Mr. Murray. Indeed it always surprised me that a man of his nervous temperament was able to work as he did amongst the inevitable noises of a household; but they seldom seemed to fidget him, and any distraction they caused was less than he would have felt in going through the streets to a separate studio. Morning was the time when he arranged all his work, and he liked to rise quietly from the breakfast table, carrying his second cup of coffee with him straight to the painting-room.

It was our friend Robert Martineau, the artist, who first told us of the Grange, North End Lane, Fulham, being to let, and on going to see the house we found it to be the very one we had noticed in our walk with Allingham the year before. We were again strongly impressed by the place, and began to consider whether there would be any possibility of our taking it. The rent was a third more than we had yet paid, rates were high in Fulham, and the house was bigger than we needed, but there was a large room on the first floor with an east light, and that was temptation. We thought if some one shared it with us for a while we might perhaps venture, and then it occurred to us that Wilfred Heeley was in England for a year and seeking a home in London for himself and his second wife: our old friendship was unchanged, and as at first mention of the idea Wilfred wrote to say how well it would suit them to join us, the matter was settled.

On looking closely at the Grange we had found that what at first seemed like one house was in reality two, between which we could take our choice, as both were empty. Though belonging to different owners, they had been thrown together for the last tenant, and doors of communication were still open between them on different landings of the staircase. The whole building was some hundred and fifty years old, but the front of the northern part had been stuccoed in the beginning of the century and its many narrow windows replaced by two square ones, while a modern staircase had been introduced: the southern house still kept its original character. We went carefully over both, weighing their different advantages and finally deciding for the north because of its studio possibilities. But there was a room on the ground floor that perplexed Edward, for some one had covered its walls with pictures. They were apparently copies of various originals, and we never learned who did them, though rumour said they were recent creations. Their workmanship had no distinction and the scheme no connecting idea, varying in subject from a large Italian landscape to a study of the Farnese Hercules balanced by a chubby Cupid of equal size, while the shutter-boxes were painted in patches of separate raw colours. Still it had cost some fellow-creature both time and trouble, and Edward did not find in his heart to cover it up until the incongruity of the thing became so irksome that a veil of Morris paper and green paint was finally drawn over the whole.

The Grange had a beautiful garden of about three-quarters of an acre, with a fine old mulberry on its lawn, peaches against the walls, and apple-trees enough to justify us in calling part of it an orchard. The full charm of all this was not visible when first we took possession in November, but still we found late-blooming monthly roses and a hedge of lavender, whose sweet scent and soft pink and grey colour are inseparably connected in memory with the place and time.

A few days before leaving Kensington Square, Edward opened an account with a bank. Naturally he chose that of Morris, and was introduced by him to Messrs. Praeds of Fleet Street. I see that he placed with them on November 11th the sum of £127 10*s.* and in return they gave him a cheque-book which he did not know how to use, for I distinctly remember seeing Mr. Leyland shew him how to fill up the first cheque he drew—not without a protest from Edward at its being called "drawing." A legacy from Mr. Samuel Perry, his mother's half-brother, was of great help to us in the course of this winter, and enabled us for the first time to lay something by. I know now that Edward had more anxiety about money in those early days than I then realized; for it was not a subject he talked much about, and it never occurred to me that we should not have our wants supplied. Yet if his responsibilities weighed heavily upon him at times, it was not a very grievous burden that he bore, for his children were a joy to him from the first and grew dearer every year.

It might be said on reckoning the whole number of the years of his life that by this time Edward had passed through half of it, but the halves were not of the same kind. In the first must be reckoned forgotten infancy and sheltered childhood; it was now but twelve years since he had begun his special work, and much of this time had been passed lightly in the enjoyment of friendship and love and the exercise of new-found power. After this came the burden and heat of the day, in which as often as possible I shall let his own voice be heard or his work shall speak, for during it he passed, as does every man, through lonely places of which nothing can be known to his fellows except by a sign from himself.

Large schemes of work were always in his mind, "huge cloudy symbols of a high romance" that never failed him, though life failed before he could make a tithe of it visible to others. He had already begun a big picture of the Fates. They were seated aloft on a throne and below them were a man and a woman standing together, the woman's hand lightly resting on a sundial. For these figures he made numberless drawings, recognizable amongst his life-studies by their solemn and typical air. In 1872 he wrote down the names of four other subjects, saying: "These I desire to paint above all others." Nor was this an aspiration only, for at the time he wrote they were all begun in one form or other. They were:

"The Chariot of Love, to be painted life-size.

"The Vision of Britomart, also life-size.

"The Sirens, small life-size.

"And a picture of the beginning of the world, with Pan and Echo and sylvan gods, and a forest full of centaurs, and a wild background of woods, mountains, and rivers."

Before these he was at work upon a great triptych with predella pictures that was to tell the whole story of Troy; fragments of this scheme are known as "The Wheel of Fortune" and "The Feast of Peleus." A large "Fountain of Youth" was designed in 1873, and the great "Arthur in Avalon" in 1881. A still vaster scheme than any of these is suggested by some pencil notes made long afterwards, shewing a plan for a series of pictures which deal with the whole history of the world, for they were to represent its Four Ages. About the Golden Age his words, "Sin comes down to talk with men," are fearful in their simplicity of vision: I do not know if any drawing of it was made. His note for the Iron Age says: "Crime has the upper hand," and ends with "Scoundrel on a throne—soldiers—violence—injustice—folly—war."

Henceforth the number of people who surround the image of Edward in my mind is very great, and cannot be dealt with separately. I believe one thing that drew both men and women to him was that he never suspected them beforehand: to him each fresh acquaintance was new-born. Never in any sense did he become a man of the world, and up to a certain point it was always easy to take advantage of him: press that advantage too far, however, and he was gone like a bird from the snare. Two things had tremendous power over him—beauty and misfortune—and far would he go to serve either; indeed his impulse to comfort those in trouble was so strong that while the trouble lasted the sufferer took precedence of every one else. Beauty, so much rarer than misfortune, he was quick to recognize in spiritual form as well as physical. Some of the last words he uttered were about a plain woman who had done excellent work in the world. "What a beautiful soul that woman has," he exclaimed; "but," he added, with gentle humour, "I think I'd better not see her."

Our life at the Grange lasted thirty years, which were in themselves a second life, for there we finally put away childish things and had our share of sorrow; but I remember no more premonition when we entered the house than a wandering on the staircase and looking around with the thought, "What will happen to us here?"

END OF VOLUME I